REVELATION
Tribulation and Triumph

A DEVOTIONAL STUDY BY
PRACTICAL CHRISTIANITY FOUNDATION
L.L. SPEER, FOUNDER

GREEN KEY BOOKS

HOLIDAY, FLORIDA

REVELATION: TRIBULATION AND TRIUMPH
Published by Green Key Books

©2003 by the Practical Christianity Foundation.
All Rights Reserved.
International Standard Book Number: 0970599668

Cover Art: Mike Molinet

Printed in the United States of America

All scriptural references, unless otherwise noted, are quoted
from **The Holy Bible, New King James Version,** ©1982
by Thomas Nelson, Inc. Used by permission.

For information:
GREEN KEY BOOKS
2514 ALOHA PLACE
HOLIDAY, FLORIDA 34691

Library of Congress Cataloging-in-Publication Data available
upon request.

Table of Contents

Preface

From the conception of the Practical Christianity Foundation, it has been the goal of the organization to convey the truth in Scripture through verse-by-verse devotional studies such as this one. As part of that goal, we agree in an attempt neither to prove nor to disprove any traditional or alternative interpretations, beliefs, or doctrines but rather to allow the Holy Spirit to reveal the truth contained within the Scriptures. Any interpretations relating to ambiguous passages that are not directly and specifically verifiable by other scriptural references are simply presented in what we believe to be the most likely intention of the message based on those things that we are specifically told. In those instances, our conclusions are noted as interpretive, and such analyses should not be understood as doctrinal positions that we are attempting to champion.

This study is divided into sections, usually between six and eight verses, and each section concludes with a "Notes/Applications" passage, which draws practical insight from the related verses that can be applied to contemporary Christian living. The intent is that the reader will complete one section per day, will gain a greater understanding of the verses within that passage, and will daily be challenged toward a deeper commitment to our Lord and Savior Jesus Christ. Also included at certain points within the text are "Dig Deeper" boxes, which are intended to assist readers who desire to invest additional time to study topics that relate to the section in which these boxes appear. Our prayer is that this study will impact the lives of all believers, regardless of age, ethnicity, or education.

Each of PCF's original projects is a collaborative effort of many writers, content editors, grammatical editors, transcribers, researchers, readers, and other contributors, and as such, we present them only as products of the Practical Christianity Foundation as a whole. These works are not for the recognition or acclamation of any particular individual but are written simply as a means to uphold and fulfill the greater purpose of our Mission Statement, which is "to exalt the Holy Name of God Almighty by declaring the redemptive message of His Son, the Lord Jesus Christ, to the lost global community and equipping the greater Christian community through the communication of the Holy Word of God in its entirety through every appropriate means available."

Practical Christianity Foundation
Value Statements

1. We value the Holy Name of God and will strive to exalt Him through godly living, committed service, and effective communication. *"That you may fear the LORD your God, to keep all His statutes and His commandments which I command you, you and your son and your grandson, all the days of your life, and that your days may be prolonged." (Deuteronomy 6.2)*

2. We value the redemptive work of the Lord Jesus Christ for a lost world and will strive to communicate His redemptive message to the global community. *"And He said to them, 'Go into all the world and preach the gospel to every creature.'" (Mark 16.15)*

3. We value the Holy Word of God and will strive to communicate it in its entirety. *"16All Scripture is given by inspiration of God, and is profitable for doctrine, for reproof, for correction, for instruction in righteousness, 17that the man of God may be complete, thoroughly equipped for every good work. (2 Timothy 3.16–17)*

4. We value spiritual growth in God's people and will strive to enhance that process through the effective communication of God's Holy Word, encouraging them to be lovers of the truth. *"But grow in the grace and knowledge of our Lord and Savior Jesus Christ. To Him be the glory both now and forever." (2 Peter 3.18)*

5. We value the equipping ministry of the church of the Lord Jesus Christ and will strive to provide resources for that ministry by the communication of God's Holy Word through every appropriate means available. *"11And He Himself gave some to be apostles, some prophets, some evangelists, and some pastors and teachers, 12for the equipping of the saints for the work of ministry, for the edifying of the body of Christ." (Ephesians 4.11–12)*

Introduction

The word *Revelation* is derived from the Greek word *apoka-lypto*, which means to disclose, uncover, manifest, and reveal that which is hidden.[1] In the entire Bible, there is perhaps no other book that generates more conversation or controversy, none that is more studied yet less understood than this last one.

The problems of interpretation are generated from attempts to decipher each detail in such a way as to reflect the current world situation. However, as the world situation changes, so do the interpretations of this book. The first century church expected Jesus to return in a very short time. It is evident that Jesus' closest disciples began to rethink their position even before the apostolic period ended. Toward the end of his life (around AD 68), Simon Peter, the leader of Christ's apostles, wrote a second epistle which seemed to address such concerns. *"⁸But, beloved, do not forget this one thing, that with the Lord one day is as a thousand years, and a thousand years as one day. ⁹The Lord is not slack concerning His promise, as some count slackness, but is longsuffering toward us, not willing that any should perish but that all should come to repentance." (2 Peter 3.8–9)* Ever since that time, Christians have struggled to understand the Book of Revelation in the context of world history as they watch the slow progression of events that impact their lives. In times of terrible persecution, famines, wars, and human atrocities, Christians have concluded that the end was near, wondering when Jesus would return and right all wrongs.

Because of these multiple streams of Christian thought, today's Christians, no matter how sincere and passionate in their pursuit of biblical knowledge, find themselves at a juncture which challenges their best efforts at unraveling the mystery of this marvelous book. In the midst of this noble pursuit, they may discover that there is no other subject that will generate more heated debate than this one. Instead of discovering the glorious Christ of John's Revelation, they often find themselves embroiled in debates that appear to have no satisfactory solution.

For all of the debates, for all of the numerous theories and interpretive systems, and for all of the controversies that consume the energy of Christ's Church, there is perhaps no more exciting book in all of God's Word. It is the crowning jewel of God's unfailing plan to save for Himself a multitude that will live with Him and praise His holy name for all eternity. From the beginning of Genesis, one overriding, all-consuming theme comes to light in God's Word— *redemption*. Revelation is the consummation of that theme when Christ completely destroys all evil and invites His bride to the marriage feast of the Lamb. We view Christ as high and lifted up. Here we discover the glorious riches of His kingdom that He has prepared for those who have been invited to share in this feast. Now, at long last, the Lord Jesus Christ ascends His throne that has been preserved for Him from the foundation of the world, and every knee bows at the awesomeness of His unsurpassed majesty, power, dominion, and glory. On this theme—on this revelation—all Christians who love the Word of God will universally and enthusiastically agree.

Generally, there are four positions by which the Book of Revelation is traditionally interpreted: historicist, preterist, futurist, and idealist (sometimes called the spiritual or symbolic view). The historicist believes that the Book of Revelation is an outline of the history of the church between the first and second comings of Christ. A preterist believes that a majority of the prophecy in Revelation was fulfilled in the first century and that the main theme of the book points to the destruction of Jerusalem in AD 70. A futurist believes that Revelation contains end-times prophecies and, more specifically, prophecies pertaining to the tribulation and Second Coming of the Lord Jesus Christ. An idealist believes that Revelation is largely (in some cases exclusively) symbolic, that it should not be taken literally, and that it merely illustrates the greater cosmic struggle between good and evil.[2]

Obviously, these camps vary greatly in their viewpoints, and the impact and significance of this book depend upon whether one believes that the events depicted within have already occurred, are yet to occur, or have never and will never occur in a physical sense at all. Granted, these positions were created by men, defined by men, and defended by men. If any one of these positions could be shown to be true beyond question or doubt, all other positions would be rendered obsolete. Such is evidently not the case. Each position has certain arguments that seem valid and worthy of consideration, just as each position has certain areas of susceptibility and fallibility. Some verses of the book are more easily understood through the arguments of one position while other verses seem to make more sense as interpreted by an alternate position. This is both the frustration and fascination that surrounds the Book of the Revelation.

The dilemma is that as soon as one agrees with a certain interpretation on a specific point, he is quickly dismissed by an opposing view as an advocate for the position that most closely aligns itself with that interpretation. To avoid such labels, some have even adopted new labels, such as "partial preterists," but in doing so perhaps only further cloud the already murky waters.[3]

The point is this: each position has at least some merit or else it would not have gained credibility among the other viewpoints. There is no "safe" way to approach the interpretation of Revelation except to agree neither to fully adopt nor to fully reject any of these positions. Still, such an approach should not be misconstrued as indecisive or uncertain. Rather, it is only with a clear understanding of these and other viewpoints that one could even attempt to interpret the book accordingly. There is always a sense of mystery when attempting to explain the ways of God.

For instance, one can scarcely question that the seven churches addressed in chapters one through three were literal, historical churches that existed in Asia Minor, yet one would have great difficulty proving that all of the events depicted in later chapters of Revelation have already occurred. Therefore, one must conclude that the book contains both historical and prophetic elements. Similarly, both symbolic and physical elements coexist. Few can doubt that there is a great deal of symbolism in the book, yet to suggest that its contents in their entirety are merely symbolic illustrations of spiritual realms is to disregard the physical ramifications of its many conditional warnings, such as "repent...or else..." *(Revelation 2.5, 2.16, 2.22, 3.3, 3.19)* Indeed, the entire book is imbued with physical judgments, physical conditions, and physical consequences.

Furthermore, a variety of interpretations have been entertained regarding the authorship of Revelation. Most of the early church fathers agree that the book was written by John, the beloved apostle of Jesus. Some critics doubt the apostolic authorship of Revelation because of the inferior style and grammar of the Greek with which the book was written when compared to that of other Johannine writings.[4] However, Acts 4.13 refers to John as "uneducated and untrained," so the use of such unpolished Greek should not be surprising, especially considering the urgency and exhilaration with which he surely felt compelled to record the visions as they were occurring. Some commentators even suggest that John owed the more skillful Greek demonstrated in his gospel and epistles to an amanuensis (or secretary), who was, for obvious reasons, not accessible to the apostle during his banishment on the isle of Patmos.[5] For these and many other reasons, the acceptance of an apostolic authorship is favored.

Even more a subject of debate is the dating of the text. Most preterists insist on an authorship occurring between AD 54–68 during the reign of the notorious Roman emperor Nero, which assists an explanation that the events in the book depict the grueling cultural climate of the first-century church, culminating with the destruction of the temple and the city of Jerusalem in AD 70.[6] More popular and more convincing are the arguments that the writing occurred between AD 90–96 during the reign of the Roman emperor Domitian. The historical recordings of early church fathers such as Irenaeus, Clement of Alexandria, and Jerome substantiate a later dating of the book.[7] Furthermore, some scholars have suggested that chapters two and three reveal the prominence of certain cities that would only be historically consistent with their conditions in the late first century.[8]

An in-depth study of the varied interpretations regarding the countless symbols, numbers, events, judgments, sequences, and visions presented in Revelation is surely better reserved for those books which endeavor to present a thorough critique. In virtually every book ever written about Revelation, even the smallest details are credited with having monumental significance. Ultimately, there is far too much controversy over Revelation to be adequately presented in what is intended as a devotional study. As such, and with the preceding foundation laid, we approach this commentary on Revelation from the viewpoint that the prophecies within are perhaps telescopic (also called expanded or double-fulfillment prophecy). Whereas, not to dismiss altogether the possibility of an earlier date of authorship and a partial fulfillment of certain prophecies with the destruction of Jerusalem in AD 70, we uphold the tenet that the events described within Revelation pertain to the final judgment of Almighty God upon the reprobate inhabitants of the earth in the last days. Apart from such an interpretation, one might find little validity or usefulness to this book in the modern world.

Almighty God has yet to judge the entire sum of unrepentant inhabitants on the earth. *(Revelation 6.16–17 and 14.7)* He has yet to pour out the full measure of His wrath and indignation. *(Revelation 14.10)* The world has yet to experience the utter devastation that will come upon its environment. *(Revelation 16)* The Lord Jesus Christ has yet to return to the earth in triumphant glory *(Revelation 19.11–16)*, to wholly conquer the world's evil *(Revelation 19.19–21)*, to reign upon the earth for a thousand years *(Revelation 20.1–5)*, to finish the judgment of Satan and his followers *(Revelation 20.7–15)*, or to establish and reign in His eternal kingdom with His faithful believers *(Revelation 21 and 22)*.

Aside from the wrath and tribulation uniquely depicted in Revelation, no other book so fully illustrates the magnificent splendor of the everlasting kingdom that awaits those who have placed their faith and hope in Jesus Christ. Indeed, there is much to be gained by reading this book despite its tendency at times to seem frightening, overwhelming, and even puzzling.

So, what is the benefit in reading a book whose interpretation is so difficult to dogmatically endorse? God did not give us the Book of the Revelation to frustrate us but to strengthen us, not to confuse us but to encourage us.[9] Rather, we must take confidence both to persevere in the midst of tribulation and to anticipate the Lord Jesus Christ's glorious, ultimate triumph. Therefore, we approach this book with full cognizance of the debates with which the Christian community struggles, but with full devotion to the Savior Who has redeemed us, Who is redeeming us, and Who will one day redeem us when He ushers us into His eternal Kingdom. While we acknowledge that we "see in a mirror dimly, but then face to face" *(1 Corinthians 13.12)* and admit that our understanding will always be obscured by the boundaries of our human limitations, we can perhaps find the simplest benefit written in the first lines of the first chapter: "Blessed is he who reads and those who hear the words of this prophecy, and keep those things which are written in it; for the time is near." *(Revelation 1.3)*

Chapter One

Revelation 1.1–6

Verses 1, 2- ¹The Revelation of Jesus Christ, which God gave Him to show His servants—things which must shortly take place. And He sent and signified it by His angel to His servant John, ²who bore witness to the word of God, and to the testimony of Jesus Christ, to all things that he saw.

Almighty God revealed the events contained within this book to the apostle John through an angel who delivered the message declared and embodied by the Lord Jesus Christ. A main theme of the Book of Revelation is to establish Jesus as the Judge of all creation and the coming King of kings. The mysteries that the Lord unveiled to John further illuminate teachings revealed in other parts of God's Word. The truths of this book are meant as an encouragement to believers so that they will not be afraid or deceived about events that will take place in the last days and that they will find joy and hope in Christ as the final authority.

For nearly two thousand years, Christians have asked, "When will these events occur?" Only God knows for certain. In this verse, the word *shortly* connotes something happening quickly.[1] However, God's timetable is not our timetable because God is not constrained by time. He is not swayed by man's actions or desires, so He will fulfill these prophesies according to His divine plan. *(2 Peter 3.8)*

John introduces himself to his readers as a servant of the Lord. As one of the original twelve disciples of Jesus, John was qualified to bear witness to "the Word of God and to the testimony of Jesus Christ" from first-hand experience. In his gospel account, John acknowledged the identity of the Word as Christ Who became flesh:

> *¹In the beginning was the Word, and the Word was with God, and the Word was God. ²He was in the beginning with God. ³All things were made through Him, and without Him nothing was made that was made. ¹⁴And the Word became flesh and dwelt among us, and we beheld His glory, the glory as of the only begotten of the Father, full of grace and truth. (John 1.1–3, 14)*

John had walked with Jesus, had witnessed and experienced the Lord's ministry in a personal way, and had endured persecution for proclaiming the gospel of Jesus Christ. He undoubtedly believed the things he witnessed and recorded in this book.

Verse 3- Blessed is he who reads and those who hear the words of this prophecy, and keep those things which are written in it; for the time is near.

This verse does not simply mean that one who reads and hears this message will be blessed. Rather, the implication is that God bestows peace and happiness only to the one who absorbs the message and allows the truths to impact his life.[2]

John clearly stated that this book is prophetic. More specifically, we know from later verses that it regards prophecy of the last days. Although many of these events remain unfulfilled, they will certainly occur at a future time, so by studying this book, we will equip ourselves with biblical truths that should make us feel confident and secure about facing the future.

Verse 4- John, to the seven churches which are in Asia: Grace to you and peace from Him who is and who was and who is to come, and from the seven Spirits who are before His throne,

It is commonly accepted that John wrote to seven literal churches which existed in Western Asia.[3] However, there are also several interpretations regarding the universal symbolism of these churches. Among these, the most persuasive interpretation contends that these churches also represent a general variation found in spiritual conditions still prevalent throughout churches today.[4]

John opened his letter with a familiar salutation, "Grace to you and peace." This greeting was extended on behalf of Jesus Christ and "the seven spirits who are before His throne," which will be studied in greater detail in later verses.

Verse 5- and from Jesus Christ, the faithful witness, the firstborn from the dead, and the ruler over the kings of the earth. To Him who loved us and washed us from our sins in His own blood,

Peace and grace were also offered from the Lord and Savior Jesus Christ, the Son of God. While He was on earth, Christ was the faithful witness to the perfection of God the Father in that He lived the perfect and sinless life. Even now, He remains the faithful witness to the fulfillment of God's promise to send a Messiah Who would deliver people from their sins.

This verse also characterizes Jesus as "the firstborn from the dead." The Bible testifies of others who were raised from the dead through Jesus' power. *(Matthew 9.24-25; Luke 7.12-15; and John 11.11-44)* Their resurrections, however, were not eternal because they were raised only to eventually experience physical death again. Jesus alone was the firstborn to be resurrected into an eternal, glorified body over which death held no power.

Finally, John called Jesus "the ruler over the kings of the earth." Christ sovereignly appoints all earthly dominions. *"'In order that the living may know that the Most High rules in the kingdom of men, gives it to whomever He will, and sets over it the lowest of men.'" (Daniel 4.17b)* This title may also allude to Christ's position as King of kings and Lord of lords. Whichever is intended, He has the right to this power simply because He is God, motivated by His perfect love, absolute justness, utter holiness, and complete supremacy.

The last part of this verse reemphasizes the splendid gospel message: Jesus is the One Who loves us and washes us with His own blood from our otherwise condemning sins. He willingly laid down His life to redeem us from the consequence of sin, and we, too, will one day inherit our glorified bodies and dwell eternally with Him. *"Beloved, now we are children of God; and it has not yet been revealed what we shall be, but we know that when He is revealed, we shall be like Him, for we shall see Him as He is." (1 John 3.2)*

Verse 6- and has made us kings and priests to His God and Father, to Him be glory and dominion forever and ever. Amen.

Old Testament priests assisted the high priest in the tabernacle and in the temple. One had to be born into the tribe of Levi to serve as a priest. *(Numbers 3.6–9)* However, through the atonement of Jesus Christ, our High Priest, we are now able to stand with Him as a royal priesthood and as beneficiaries of His blessings. *"⁹But you are a chosen generation, a royal priesthood, a holy nation, His own special people, that you may proclaim the praises of Him who called you out of darkness into His marvelous light; ¹⁰who once were not a people but are now the people of God, who had not obtained mercy but now have obtained mercy." (1 Peter 2.9–10)*

John credited and lauded the Lord for His glory and dominion over the earth. Then, the apostle concluded with an *Amen,* which means "so be it," thereby affirming that these things that he said about Jesus Christ were eternally and unequivocally true.

Notes/Applications

Antique dealers consider a number of factors when determining the value of an artifact. The age of the piece and, more importantly, its physical condition greatly factor into the dealer's evaluation. If an antique dish is cracked or chipped, its value drastically diminishes despite its age or beautiful, artistic adornments.

Fortunately, that principle does not apply when considering our valued usefulness to God. Who among us does not have a cracked or even completely broken soul? If that were the criteria, even the apostle John would have been rendered unemployable. In fact, the opposite is true. Only when we are broken and bowed as a bondservant before God's supremacy are we most equipped to serve Him because God has chosen to use the base and weak elements of the world to build His kingdom:

²⁶For you see your calling, brethren, that not many wise according to the flesh, not many mighty, not many noble, are called. ²⁷But God has chosen the foolish things of the world to put to shame the wise, and God has chosen the weak things of the world to put to shame the things which are mighty; ²⁸and the base things of the world and the things which are despised God has chosen, and the things which are not, to bring to nothing the things that are, ²⁹that no flesh should glory in His presence. ³⁰But of Him you are in Christ Jesus, who became for us wisdom from God—and righteousness and sanctification and redemption—³¹that, as it is written, 'He who glories, let him glory in the LORD.' (1 Corinthians 1.26–31)

John considered himself a bondservant of the Lord Jesus Christ. It is God's will that all believers develop this attitude. When we become liberated from the slavery of sin and become bondservants to our Lord and Master Jesus Christ, we will experience the abundant life found only in Him. We will receive an inner freedom that cannot be destroyed by the bondage of outward circumstances. Have we personally surrendered ourselves to the Master Craftsman?

Revelation 1.7–11

Verse 7- Behold, He is coming with clouds, and every eye will see Him, even they who pierced Him. And all the tribes of the earth will mourn because of Him. Even so, Amen.

Jesus will return with the clouds, presumably in a manner similar to that by which He left the earth after His resurrection:

> *⁹Now when He had spoken these things, while they watched, He was taken up, and a cloud received Him out of their sight. ¹⁰And while they looked steadfastly toward heaven as He went up, behold, two men stood by them in white apparel, ¹¹who also said, 'Men of Galilee, why do you stand gazing up into heaven? This same Jesus, who was taken up from you into heaven, will so come in like manner as you saw Him go into heaven.' (Acts 1.9–11)*

When Jesus returns, He will come in unimaginable glory so extraordinary that every eye on earth will see Him, including those "who pierced him," which symbolically represents the sum of people who have rejected the Savior.[5] Though all unbelievers will grieve over Almighty God's coming judgment, Jews will also mourn specifically for their rejection of Christ as their Messiah.[6] *"And I will pour on the house of David and on the inhabitants of Jerusalem the Spirit of grace and supplication; then they will look on Me whom they pierced. Yes, they will mourn for Him as one mourns for his only son, and grieve for Him as one grieves for a firstborn.'" (Zechariah 12.10)* The "tribes of the earth" has similarly been described by many commentators as a reference to an all-encompassing body of unbelievers.[7]

Verse 8- "I am the Alpha and the Omega, the Beginning and the End," says the Lord, "who is and who was and who is to come, the Almighty."

Alpha and *Omega* are respectively the first and last letters of the Greek alphabet, so in using this imagery, the Lord Jesus Christ emphasized His lordship over the past, present, and future. *"'I am the Alpha and the Omega, the Beginning and the End, the First and the Last.'"* *(Revelation 22.13)* Jesus also described Himself as He "who is and who was and who is to come" and identified Himself as "the

Almighty," a term reserved for God alone. Jesus has always existed with God the Father and is responsible for the creation of the world. *(John 1.1–3)* Though He is not a created being, He manifested Himself in a temporal human existence to accomplish His divine purposes. He has otherwise never been bound, limited, restricted, or constrained by the time that He created. This appears to be the significance of His declaration. He is the Creator, we are His creation. We live and die within the boundaries which He has created and not the other way around.

DIG DEEPER: *ALPHA AND OMEGA*

Jesus refers to Himself in these terms four times in this book, indicating that He is the beginning and the end of all creation. Created in God's image, man struggles with the concept of God's eternality. *(Ecclesiastes 3.11)* Isaiah reminds us that God planned the world's end from its very beginning. *(Isaiah 46.9b–10)* The writer of Hebrews tells us that Jesus is also "the author and finisher of our faith, who for the joy that was set before Him, endured the cross, despising the shame, and has set down at the right hand of the throne of God." *(Hebrews 12.2)*

Verse 9- I, John, both your brother and companion in the tribulation and kingdom and patience of Jesus Christ, was on the island that is called Patmos for the word of God and for the testimony of Jesus Christ.

John referred to himself as a "brother and companion" in suffering hard times, one able to persevere in his earthly tribulation not with his own patience but by the patience given to him by the Lord Jesus. John could testify from personal experience that Christians will endure hardships, but they will never face trials alone because Jesus never forsakes His own. *"'These things I have spoken to you, that in Me you may have peace. In the world you will have tribulation; but be of good cheer, I have overcome the world.'" (John 16.33)* Even during the recording of this vision, the apostle endured isolation and persecution. The Romans had exiled him to the isle of Patmos, a small, rocky island located off the southwest coast of Asia Minor, commonly known today as Turkey. This barren island is approximately ten miles long and six miles wide.[8] John had been banished to this remote location as punishment for preaching "the word of God" and for His "testimony of Jesus Christ." Although no man would desire imprisonment, this was all in God's plan as a means to reveal to John these great visions of the end times. While in exile, John was alone and not distracted by the world. He was given time to commune with God and to record all that he witnessed. God purposed such isolation to complete His message to man and to write the last book of what is the inspired and inerrant Holy Word of Almighty God.

Verse 10- *I was in the Spirit on the Lord's Day, and I heard behind me a loud voice, as of a trumpet,*

The fact that John was aware that it was the Lord's Day indicates that the apostle retained full control of his senses even though he had been exiled to an isolated, deserted island.[9] He had not become disoriented or delusional. John was "in the Spirit," captured by the Holy Spirit of God by which he could enjoy a unique, unhindered fellowship with His Lord and, thereby, could be in a condition to receive divine revelation.[10]

As the vision began, he heard a great voice like that of a loud trumpet from behind him. It can be presumed that a comparison is made between this voice and a trumpet to describe an effort to seize John's fullest attention.

Verse 11- *saying, "I am the Alpha and the Omega, the First and the Last," and, "What you see, write in a book and send it to the seven churches which are in Asia: to Ephesus, to Smyrna, to Pergamos, to Thyatira, to Sardis, to Philadelphia, and to Laodicea."*

Obviously, the great voice belonged to Jesus Christ, Who again identified Himself as "the Alpha and Omega, the First and the Last." This is the second of three times in this chapter that this reference is made to the Lord's eternal existence.

The Lord then told John to record in a book the things he would be shown in the visions and to send this book to seven specific churches in Asia Minor. The word *church(es)* as used in this verse is translated from the Greek word εκκλησιαί (ekklesia), which means "a calling out."[11] These churches, therefore, were not buildings or temples of worship as we many times associate this word. The New Testament use of the word *church* signifies the entire core of believers throughout a particular city. Accordingly, Christ told John to deliver messages to the believers in seven specific cities: Ephesus, Smyrna, Pergamos, Thyatira, Sardis, Philadelphia, and Laodicea.

Notes/Applications

"O, Christ the heavens' eternal King,
Creator, unto Thee we sing,
With God the Father ever One,
Co-equal, co-eternal Son...
All praise be Thine, O risen Lord,
From death to endless life restored;
All praise to God the Father be
And Holy Ghost eternally."[12]

These words penned around the sixth century by an unknown author mirror Jesus' message when He proclaimed, "I am the Alpha and the Omega, the Beginning and the End, who is and who was and who is to come, the Almighty." Christ is the Almighty—the supreme One. He is the Alpha—no one came before Him, and He is the Omega—none will come after Him:

[15]He is the image of the invisible God, the firstborn over all creation. [16]For by Him all things were created that are in heaven and that are on earth, visible and invisible, whether thrones or dominions or principalities or powers. All things were created through Him and for Him. [17]And He is before all things, and in Him all things consist. [18]And He is the head of the body, the church, who is the beginning, the firstborn from the dead, that in all things He may have the preeminence. (Colossians 1.15–18)

How does this passage from Colossians impact our understanding of Who Jesus is and our acceptance of Him as the one, true, and eternal God? The Lord Jesus Christ transcends all, yet His supremacy does not negate the individual attention He bestows upon each of His children. He is eternally both a preeminent and personal God. Such supremacy is difficult for our limited minds to comprehend; nevertheless, the Holy Spirit convicts our hearts of its truth. Such a Savior is trustworthy. Such a Lord is worthy of our sole devotion. Only when we accept the loving Messiah as our personal Savior can we allow Him to be the Lord and Master over every facet of our lives.

Revelation 1.12–20

Verses 12, 13- ¹²Then I turned to see the voice that spoke with me. And having turned I saw seven golden lampstands, ¹³and in the midst of the seven lampstands One like the Son of Man, clothed with a garment down to the feet and girded about the chest with a golden band.

John turned to see the source of the voice that spoke to him, and he saw seven golden candlesticks. We are told in the interpretation offered at the end of this first chapter that these lampstands or tall candlesticks correspond to the aforementioned seven churches. It can be concluded, therefore, that the candlesticks themselves bore no light apart from the Light that shone in and through them. References to Jesus as the essence of light are used many times by this same author in his gospel account. *"⁶There was a man sent from God, whose name was John. ⁷This man came for a witness, to bear witness of the Light, that all through him might believe." (John 1.6–7) "Then Jesus spoke to them again, saying, 'I am the light of the world. He who follows Me shall not walk in darkness, but have the light of life.'" (John 8.12)*

Jesus Christ stood in the midst of the seven golden candlesticks. His appearance made it obvious to John that He was the Son of Man, the true Light of the world. John had seen Jesus in His earthly, human form, and he had also seen Him in a glorified form during Christ's transfiguration. *"¹Now after six days Jesus took Peter, James, and John his brother, led them up on a high mountain by themselves; ²and He was transfigured before them. His face shone like the sun, and His clothes became as white as the light." (Matthew 17.1–2)* The garment in which He was now clothed was virtually identical to that of the vision of Christ that appeared to the prophet Daniel in the Old Testament. *"⁵I lifted my eyes and looked, and behold, a certain man clothed in linen, whose waist was girded with gold of Uphaz! ⁶His body was like beryl, his face like the appearance of lightning, his eyes like torches of fire, his arms and feet like burnished bronze in color, and the sound of his words like the voice of a multitude." (Daniel 10.5–6)*

Outstanding similarities aside, there can be no doubt concerning the identity of this Being that now stood before John, for He had already identified Himself twice as the Alpha and Omega, a claim that could have been made only by the eternal, almighty Lord and Savior.

Verse 14- His head and hair were white like wool, as white as snow, and His eyes like a flame of fire;

In this vision, Jesus' white crown of hair did not depict aging, but it instead symbolized His righteousness, purity, and infinite wisdom.[13] In addition, Jesus' eyes blazed with a purifying, refining fire, perhaps signifying His ability to see not only what is on the surface but also what is in the heart of man.[14]

Verse 15- His feet were like fine brass, as if refined in a furnace, and His voice as the sound of many waters;

Most biblical expositors agree that John's efforts to describe the nearly indescribable appearance of Christ often inherit symbolic importance. Interpretations vary widely regarding the significance of Christ's feet appearing as fine brass, but such imagery is more likely used to convey the magnificence of Jesus' glory as He stood before John.[15]

Furthermore, the Lord's voice resembled the sound of many waters. This depiction parallels descriptions of God's voice in other biblical accounts. *"When they went, I heard the noise of their wings, like the noise of many waters, like the voice of the Almighty, a tumult like the noise of an army; and when they stood still, they let down their wings."* (Ezekiel 1.24) *"And behold, the glory of the God of Israel came from the way of the east. His voice was like the sound of many waters; and the earth shone with His glory."* (Ezekiel 43.2) By this verse and others, we may ascertain that the Lord's voice can be heard both near and far when He speaks.

Verse 16- He had in His right hand seven stars, out of His mouth went a sharp two-edged sword, and His countenance was like the sun shining in its strength.

We are told in the interpretation that concludes this chapter that these stars represent angels or messengers. Therefore, we need not explore too deeply the significance of this comparison, yet we should conclude that the stars were under the full control and direction of Jesus Christ, Who held them in His right hand. Their ministry to the seven churches was appointed and empowered by Him Who sent them.

Christ radiated with the light of His glory, and a two-edged sword emerged from His mouth. In other biblical passages, the Word of God is described as a sword. *"For the word of God is living and powerful, and sharper than any two-edged sword, piercing even to the division of soul and spirit, and of joints and marrow, and is a discerner of the thoughts and intents of the heart." (Hebrews 4.12) "And take the helmet of salvation, and the sword of the Spirit, which is the word of God." (Ephesians 6.17)* John compared the Word of God that came from Christ's mouth with a sharp, double-edged sword because God's truth precisely and justly divides soul and spirit, good and evil, truth and lie, thought and motive. *"But with righteousness He shall judge the poor, and decide with equity for the meek of the earth; He shall strike the earth with the rod of His mouth, and with the breath of His lips He shall slay the wicked." (Isaiah 11.4)*

Verse 17- And when I saw Him, I fell at His feet as dead. But He laid His right hand on me, saying to me, "Do not be afraid; I am the First and the Last.

When John saw the Son of Man, his reaction resembled the responses of Daniel *(Daniel 10.8–9)*, Ezekiel *(Ezekiel 1.28)*, and Manoah *(Judges 13.22)* when manifestations of God appeared unto them. John fell at Christ's feet in paralyzed fright.

John was the Lord's beloved disciple during His earthly sojourn. John had also been present when the Lord was transfigured on the mountaintop and held counsel with Moses and Elijah. *(Mark 9.4–5)* Yet this same John, when he encountered the presence of His Lord in the full revelation of His glory and holiness, experienced overwhelming terror. His response was no voluntary gesture of esteemed regard but a reaction of fear so intense that He was driven "as dead" to the ground. However, Christ touched him and commanded him not to be afraid. Then, as if to validate this command, the Lord repeated a third time that He is the First and the Last, reminding John of their previous moments together and identifying Himself as the same Lord.

Verse 18- "I am He who lives, and was dead, and behold, I am alive forevermore. Amen. And I have the keys of Hades and of Death.

Jesus further identified Himself as the One Who lived, died, and conquered death forevermore by rising from the grave. It seems almost as if God desired to encourage John by saying in a sense: *John, you know me. I am the same One Who walked with you, Who taught you. I am the One you witnessed on the cross and then watched ascend into Heaven.*

The Lord's statement, "I have the keys of Hades and of Death," confirmed His supreme authority over life and death in both a physical and spiritual sense. Christ displayed this power when He raised people from the dead during His earthly ministry as well as when He Himself defeated sin and death for the redemption of mankind. When Jesus appeared to John on Patmos, He had already conquered death at Calvary, finished the atonement, and thereby secured "the keys of Hades and of Death."

Verse 19- "Write the things which you have seen, and the things which are, and the things which will take place after this.

Imagine how exciting this must have been for John! As a disciple, John had known the Christ that walked on earth and had witnessed His transfiguration. Now, Jesus stood before him as the living, eternal God. Even though the sight before John and the visions that would be revealed to him seemed unbelievable, they were, are, and always will be true and certain. Therefore, John was instructed to document all that was about to be revealed to him.

Verse 20- "The mystery of the seven stars which you saw in My right hand, and the seven golden lampstands: The seven stars are the angels of the seven churches, and the seven lampstands which you saw are the seven churches.

Jesus interpreted this first vision for John and, indirectly, for us as well. The seven stars mentioned in verse sixteen represent seven angels or messengers, and the seven candlesticks represent the seven aforementioned churches in Asia Minor. As we study these seven churches, we will see that some of them shone the light of Jesus more brightly than others did.

Notes/Applications

As we will study in the upcoming chapters, the fundamental message that Christ issued to these seven churches challenged them to repent and to examine the motives behind their acts of service, but such a charge does not only apply to these believers. We, too, should prayerfully consider our motives in relation to our service to God. *"⁴⁰Let us search out and examine our ways, and turn back to the Lord; ⁴¹let us lift our hearts and hands to God in heaven."* *(Lamentations 3.40–41)* Periodically, we should get alone with God and seek His heart as we assess our spiritual relationship with Him. By asking ourselves some basic yet revealing questions, we can apply the lessons imparted upon the seven churches.

1) Have we totally committed our hearts to Jesus Christ, the Light of the world? *"Examine yourselves as to whether you are in the faith. Test yourselves. Do you not know yourselves, that Jesus Christ is in you?"* *(2 Corinthians 13.5a)*

2) Have the cares of this world—money, success, family, friends, and recognition—distracted us from serving the Lord? Have we allowed the pursuit of these temporal things to overshadow our pursuit of eternal treasures? *"¹⁹'Do not lay up for yourselves treasures on earth, where moth and rust destroy and where thieves break in and steal; ²⁰but lay up for yourselves treasures in heaven, where neither moth nor rust destroys and where thieves do not break in and steal. ²¹For where your treasure is, there your heart will be also.'"* *(Matthew 6.19-21)*

3) We may say that our relationship with Christ is the most important thing to us, but according to our speech and actions, what would others say we treasure the most? *"⁵'I am the vine, you are the branches. He who abides in Me, and I in him, bears much fruit; for without Me you can do nothing. ⁶If anyone does not abide in Me, he is cast out as a branch and is withered; and they gather them and throw them into the fire, and they are burned. ⁷If you abide in Me, and My words abide in you, you will ask what you desire, and it shall be done*

for you. ⁸By this My Father is glorified, that you bear much fruit; so you will be My disciples.'" (John 15.5–8)

4) What motivates our obedience to Christ? Obligation? Tradition? Fear? Recognition? Love? *"But that the world may know that I love the Father, and as the Father gave Me commandment, so I do.'" (John 14.31a)*

5) Are we willing to suffer persecution or even death for the cause of Christ? *"For to me, to live is Christ, and to die is gain." (Philippians 1.21)*

6) What are some of the principles that God has taught us as a result of suffering? What might He be teaching us in the midst of current struggles? Are we willing to thank God for the struggles that refine our faith in Him? *"²My brethren, count it all joy when you fall into various trials, ³knowing that the testing of your faith produces patience. ⁴But let patience have its perfect work, that you may be perfect and complete, lacking nothing." (James 1.2–4)*

7) How is our lifestyle separate from the ways of the world? How do we respond when faced with worldly temptations? *"⁷Therefore submit to God. Resist the devil and he will flee from you. ⁸Draw near to God and He will draw near to you. Cleanse your hands, you sinners; and purify your hearts, you double-minded. ⁹Lament and mourn and weep! Let your laughter be turned to mourning and your joy to gloom. ¹⁰Humble yourselves in the sight of the Lord, and He will lift you up." (James 4.7–10)*

8) What false, carnal teachings pervade our thinking? Do we diligently search God's Word for truth, or do we readily accept the world's propaganda? What impact has false teaching had upon our view of God and upon our lives in general? *"And do not be conformed to this world, but be transformed by the renewing of your mind, that you may prove what is that good and acceptable and perfect will of God." (Romans 12.2)*

The purpose of completing a spiritual inventory is to assess our commitment to the Lord Jesus Christ and the motivation behind that service, whether religion, ritual, or personal relationship. By His grace, may He find each of us to be completely His. *"Examine me, O Lord, and prove me; try my mind and my heart." (Psalm 26.2)*

The Seven Churches in Asia Minor
Chapters 1–3

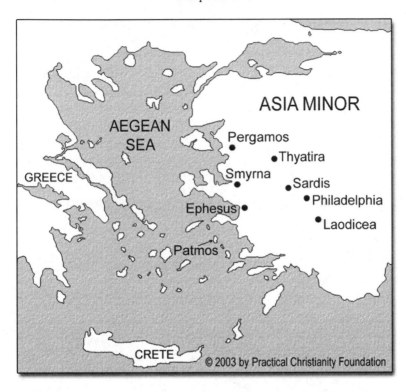

Chapter Two

Revelation 2.1–7

Verse 1- "To the angel of the church of Ephesus write, 'These things says He who holds the seven stars in His right hand, who walks in the midst of the seven golden lampstands:

The first church addressed was in the city of Ephesus, whose name means "full purposed."[1] Ephesus, located on the west coast of what is now Turkey, was the largest city in Asia Minor. It was situated at the junction of many natural trade routes and was on the main road from Rome to the East, so the city's economy was chiefly built around commerce and trade.[2] It was also a very religious city, boasting great temples to gods and goddesses. The temple of Artemis (Diana) was one of the seven wonders of the ancient world.[3] The gospel message may have been introduced to Ephesus through Aquila and Priscilla, though their efforts were surely advanced with the return of Paul, who lived there for two years.[4] *(Acts 18.18–19)* It is perhaps the apostle John who should be credited most with the discipleship of those Christians in Ephesus since he had committed much of his life to the church there. This may be the reason that this city is listed first among the seven churches.

John was instructed to write this message and to identify the sender of the message as He Who holds the seven stars and walks among the seven candlesticks. *"And in the midst of the seven lamp-stands One like the Son of Man, clothed with a garment down to the feet and girded about the chest with a golden band." (Revelation 1.13)* No one could rightfully claim this authority and position except for God's Son, the Lord Jesus Christ. Therefore, this claim gave John's words the authority of Heaven.

Verse 2- "I know your works, your labor, your patience, and that you cannot bear those who are evil. And you have tested those who say they are apostles and are not, and have found them liars;

Jesus acknowledged the fruits of their labors. Their works and patience were outward displays of Christ's presence in their lives. They did not tolerate those who falsely claimed to be fellow believers. God had given them the ability to discern between true disciples and religious imposters. They were not easily deceived.

Verse 3- "and you have persevered and have patience, and have labored for My name's sake and have not become weary.

The church of Ephesus had patiently endured in Jesus' name. Jesus not only lauded them for their works but also recognized that these acts had been done in Christ's name. These believers had endured against the ungodliness that was so prevalent in their environment. Amid hardship and hostility, they remained true to the Lord and persevered in their labors. Although Jesus commended the Ephesians for their faithfulness, He knew their hearts intimately and would admonish them accordingly.

Verse 4- "Nevertheless I have this against you, that you have left your first love.

Jesus admonished this group of believers by stating that they had left their first love. Evidently, the Ephesians' love for Christ that at one time consumed their lives, their works, and their actions had waned over time. They still loved God and expressed their commitment to Him through their faithful works, but the Lord recognized that their passion and enthusiasm needed restoration. They remained obedient to God and labored in His name, but it appears their works were motivated more by their Christian responsibility than their intimacy with Christ. *(Deuteronomy 30.20; Titus 3.8, 14; and 2 Timothy 3.17, 5.25)*

Verse 5- *"Remember therefore from where you have fallen; repent and do the first works, or else I will come to you quickly and remove your lampstand from its place—unless you repent.*

Christ told them to recall the time when they most closely communed with the Lord. They were to repent by redirecting their hearts, refocusing their priorities, and moving forward once again in their love for Almighty God. If they did not repent, God would judge them by removing their lampstand, Christ's presence, from among them.[5]

The word translated as *repent* comes from the Greek word μετανοέω (metanoeo) which means "to change the mind."[6] When an individual repents, he must align his direction and way of thinking with God's will instead of his own. Conviction over sin and confession of sin are important components of repentance, but sincere repentance is best expressed through reform. Although the Ephesians were liable to stumble again, they were to avoid the actions that initially distracted them from their intimate fellowship with God.

Verse 6- *"But this you have, that you hate the deeds of the Nicolaitans, which I also hate.*

Jesus again commended the Ephesian church on another point. They agreed with the Lord in their hatred of the Nicolaitans' deeds. Not much is known about the Nicolaitans, but evidently, they were disciples of a false doctrine that was prevalent during that time. They were a Gnostic cult that practiced a heresy which taught that a person could do anything in the physical realm without reaping spiritual consequences.[7] Jesus declared that He did not hate the Nicolaitans, but He despised their irreverent practices.

Verse 7- *"He who has an ear, let him hear what the Spirit says to the churches. To him who overcomes I will give to eat from the tree of life, which is in the midst of the Paradise of God."'*

Jesus no longer cautioned only the believers of this church but *all* who have spiritual ears and can listen earnestly to the Holy Spirit's instructions. Whereas the message was directed to a specific church, its significance and implications address countless recipients still today. The admonitions addressed to each of the churches were and are intended for all believers that fall into each of the indicated spiritual conditions. This message, though differing slightly in its expression, was given as a final admonition to each of the churches: those that *overcome*—that is, those who remain true to their calling in the Lord Jesus Christ and who do not succumb to false prophets and perversions of truth—will receive eternal life in Heaven.[8] This promise of eternal life is expressed as an entitlement to "eat from the tree of life." *(Revelation 22.14)*

Notes/Applications

Maltbie D. Babcock, a nineteenth century pastor and hymnist, once said, "The Christian life that is joyless is a discredit to God and a disgrace to itself."[9] It appears that the believers at Ephesus had lost heart in the spiritual dogfight. They still performed notable acts of service but not with the die-hard passion they had once possessed. When these believers lost their zeal for their mission, they also lost their vision. Christ corrected the Ephesians by commanding them to recall the time when they cherished their relationship with Him more than anything else, when they marched closely at His side savoring His presence, and when their desire to glorify Him motivated their good works. *"No one engaged in warfare entangles himself with the affairs of this life, that he may please him who enlisted him as a soldier." (2 Timothy 2.4) "Repent therefore and be converted, that your sins may be blotted out, so that times of refreshing may come from the presence of the Lord." (Acts 3.19)*

Can we identify with these believers? Has our joy diminished? Are we simply performing acts of Christian service out of routine? Renowned twentieth century evangelist W.A. ("Billy") Sunday observed: "If you have no joy in your religion, there's a leak in your Christianity somewhere."[10] It is so easy to become consumed in serving the Lord that we lose focus of the Lord Himself. When this happens, we are easily shot down by the enemy's regime, becoming prime targets for the devil's advances in areas where we never considered ourselves vulnerable. *"That they may come to their senses and escape the snare of the devil, having been taken captive by him to do his will." (2 Timothy 2.26)* The principle is simple: we must not withdraw from the presence of our Holy Commander. May we strive to maintain a fiery passion for our calling in Christ, Who has rescued us from life's foxholes and empowered us to serve in His kingdom. *"That the man of God may be complete, thoroughly equipped for every good work." (2 Timothy 3.17)*

Revelation 2.8–11

Verse 8- "And to the angel of the church in Smyrna write, 'These things says the First and the Last, who was dead, and came to life:

John was then told by the sender of this message, Who this time identified Himself as "the First and the Last" and as He Who "was dead, and came to life," to write to the church of Smyrna. *"¹⁷And when I saw Him, I fell at His feet as dead. But He laid His right hand on me, saying to me, 'Do not be afraid; I am the First and the Last. ¹⁸I am He who lives, and was dead, and behold, I am alive forevermore. Amen.'" (Revelation 1.17–18a)* Clearly this church, like the first one, would know that the message was given directly from the Lord Jesus Christ.

The city of Smyrna was located on the western coast of Asia Minor about forty miles north of Ephesus at the mouth of the Hermus River. Smyrna, too, was a populous and prosperous city, second only to Ephesus in trade and commerce.[11] Culture thrived in this city that featured the largest public theatre in all of Asia. It is also believed by many to be the birthplace of Homer, author of the great epics *The Odyssey* and *The Illiad*.[12] Smyrna gained her notoriety, however, from the bloody campaign that the Roman emperors had waged against the Christians there. It was in this city that Polycarp, John's closest disciple, was appointed bishop of the early church by the apostles and was later martyred and buried.[13] Interestingly, the name *Smyrna* means "myrrh," which was one of the ingredients used as an embalming ointment by the ancients.[14] Therefore, it can be said that the name *Smyrna* carries connotations of death.

Verse 9- "I know your works, tribulation, and poverty (but you are rich); and I know the blasphemy of those who say they are Jews and are not, but are a synagogue of Satan.

As with the previous church, Jesus told the people of the church of Smyrna that He knew their works. He also acknowledged their many tribulations and persecutions. The Lord Jesus esteemed the suffering of this church because He, too, suffered greatly. The believers at Smyrna were physically and economically poor as a result of their persecution, but Jesus turned their focus upon the eternal wealth and riches prepared for them in Heaven. *"Listen, my beloved brethren: Has God not chosen the poor of this world to be rich in faith and heirs of the kingdom which He promised to those who love Him?"* *(James 2.5)* It is important to note that this church's persecution apparently did not result as judgment from God because of some wrongdoing but, rather, for their faithfulness to Almighty God.

The believers in this church were viciously attacked by the Jews, who earnestly bolstered the Romans' efforts to kill the Christians.[15] Jesus called these Jews "a synagogue of Satan" because they rejected Jesus as the Messiah and violently opposed any who followed His teachings. It is important to note that not all Jews were included in Christ's harsh rebuke simply because of their ethnicity. Unquestionably, a vast percentage of Jesus' followers at that time were Jews, and it was obviously not these to whom the Lord referred. Rather, this "synagogue of Satan" was comprised of those blasphemers who "say they are Jews and are not." *"[28]For he is not a Jew who is one outwardly, nor is circumcision that which is outward in the flesh; [29]but he is a Jew who is one inwardly; and circumcision is that of the heart, in the Spirit, not in the letter; whose praise is not from men but from God." (Romans 2.28–29)*

Verse 10- "Do not fear any of those things which you are about to suffer. Indeed, the devil is about to throw some of you into prison, that you may be tested, and you will have tribulation ten days. Be faithful until death, and I will give you the crown of life.

The Lord explained the trials awaiting the faithful believers at Smyrna. Specifically, some of them would be imprisoned for their faith. The direct cause of this suffering, as Jesus clearly revealed, was the devil. Some believers might even be required to give up their physical lives for the cause of Christ.

This tribulation, however, would not be without purpose or without end. There are varied explanations that define this period of "ten days." This could, of course, refer to a literal ten-day duration. Some scholars believe these ten days are a reference to ten periods of intense persecution under ten pre-Constantine emperors while others believe this refers to the ten years of persecution at the hands of Diocletian.[16] Whatever the case, God reassured the believers in Smyrna that their suffering would last only for the appointed period of time He had ordained.

Because God had preplanned it, He had also prepared to give these faithful ones the strength and power to endure it. Those found faithful to the very end would be given the "crown of life." Though much has been speculated about the significance of such a crown, specifically in relation to the city of Smyrna, it can be said with reasonable certainty that the "crown of life," at the very least, signifies the unmerited reward of eternal life that these believers would receive.[17]

Verse 11- "He who has an ear, let him hear what the Spirit says to the churches. He who overcomes shall not be hurt by the second death."'

Again, we are advised to listen to the message of the Holy Spirit. The promise of eternal life is again promised to the overcomers (all who have placed their faith in Christ Jesus) and is expressed to this church as exemption from the second death, which will occur after the final judgment when all unbelievers will be cast into the lake of fire. *"14Then Death and Hades were cast into the lake of fire. This is the second death. 15And anyone not found written in the Book of Life was cast into the lake of fire." (Revelation 20.14–15)*

Notes/Applications

The encouragement directed to the church of Smyrna, and ultimately to all believers, was to endure in the midst of suffering. Sometimes, tribulations occur as an act of judgment, but they may also transpire to refine our faith, to strengthen the testimony of our witness, or to correct us. The rains of suffering fell upon our Lord Jesus during His time on earth, and they will surely fall upon us as His disciples. However, when we feel trampled by hardships, we need to remind ourselves of the inheritance that we have in Christ. *"4But God, who is rich in mercy, because of His great love with which He loved us, 5even when we were dead in trespasses, made us alive together with Christ (by grace you have been saved), 6and raised us up together, and made us sit together in the heavenly places in Christ Jesus, [7]that in the ages to come He might show the exceeding riches of His grace in His kindness toward us in Christ Jesus." (Ephesians 2.4–7)*

Many Christians count Heaven as their glorious treasure—their blessed hope. Certainly, assurance of an eternal, heavenly home in the Father's presence is a fundamental doctrine of our faith that should move us to grateful anticipation. However, we do not have to wait until then to enjoy our wealth in Christ—the precious Treasure beyond appraisal. In knowing Him, we can experience abundant life even now. We may incur financial, physical, and emotional challenges, but we have acquired indescribable security by the miraculous grace of Christ, our present and future "hope of glory":

> [24]*I now rejoice in my sufferings for you, and fill up in my flesh what is lacking in the afflictions of Christ, for the sake of His body, which is the church, [25]of which I became a minister according to the stewardship from God which was given to me for you, to fulfill the word of God, [26]the mystery which has been hidden from ages and from generations, but now has been revealed to His saints. [27]To them God willed to make known what are the riches of the glory of this mystery among the Gentiles: which is Christ in you, the hope of glory. (Colossians 1.24–27)*

Revelation 2.12–17

Verse 12- "And to the angel of the church in Pergamos write, 'These things says He who has the sharp two-edged sword:

This message was addressed to the third church, *Pergamos* (also called *Pergamum*), whose name means "much marriage."[18] This message to Pergamos, like the others, was given directly from the Lord Jesus Christ, referred to as "He who has the sharp two-edged sword." *"He had in His right hand seven stars, out of His mouth went a sharp two-edged sword, and His countenance was like the sun shining in its strength." (Revelation 1.16)* The two-edged sword depicts the word of judgment against this church, and "He who has" it is the One who will dispense this judgment.[19]

Pergamos lay inland from the coast of the Aegean Sea about sixty-five miles north of Smyrna and was the provincial capital of Roman Asia.[20] The city boasted many grand Hellenic and Roman temples and was also home to an impressive library second only to the one in Alexandria.[21] Persecution of Christians was rampant in Pergamos, but as with the church of Smyrna, the persecution did not destroy the faith of most Christians there.

Verse 13- "I know your works, and where you dwell, where Satan's throne is. And you hold fast to My name, and did not deny My faith even in the days in which Antipas was My faithful martyr, who was killed among you, where Satan dwells.

As with the previous churches, the Lord told this church that He knew her works. He further acknowledged that these works were accomplished in the midst of the most dire and challenging of circumstances. Though the Lord commended the overall commitment of this church, there was a minority of believers who had yielded to the sway of false teaching, so Jesus not only rebuked the minority who adhered to the false doctrine but also the majority who tolerated the rebelliousness of a few.[22]

The Lord called Pergamos the home of Satan's throne, indicating that the church was situated in the heart of rampant wickedness and spiritual perversion.[23] Pergamos was a center of heathen worship and practices, and the ungodly influences so prevalent within the city had infiltrated the church. However, even in the midst of Satan's strongest temptations, many were able to "hold fast to [His] name" and remain faithful to the Lord. As a result of their faithfulness, these believers were persecuted, and several were martyred. One of them, as mentioned in this verse, was Antipas, who the Lord called the "faithful martyr." In fact, some scholars credit Antipas as being the pastor of the first church in the city.[24] Regardless, this reference to Antipas verifies that these were actual letters to specific churches and not merely an illustration of distinct periods of the Church throughout history.[25]

Verse 14- "But I have a few things against you, because you have there those who hold the doctrine of Balaam, who taught Balak to put a stumbling block before the children of Israel, to eat things sacrificed to idols, and to commit sexual immorality.

The Lord admonished the church at Pergamos for several sins that He held against them. One of these sins was that many in the church adhered to the "doctrine of Balaam."

In the Old Testament account, the Moabite king asked Balaam to curse Israel, but Balaam could not do this because he was God's servant. Since God forbade Balaam to speak against the Israelites, Balaam then deviously encouraged the Israelites to ally themselves with the Moabites through intermarriage. Balaam's plan was indeed corrupt, but the Israelite people were also at fault for blindly following his suggestions to intermarry with this pagan nation and to eat its defiled foods. *"They have forsaken the right way and gone astray, following the way of Balaam the son of Beor, who loved the wages of unrighteousness." (2 Peter 2.15)* In essence, a stumbling block was cast, and the people faltered because their spiritual eyes were closed. *"Look, these women caused the children of Israel, through the counsel of Balaam, to trespass against the LORD in the incident of Peor, and there was a plague among the congregation of the LORD." (Numbers 31.16)* Had their spiritual eyes been opened, they would have better resisted the worldly enticements offered to them through this alliance with the Moabites.

The doctrine of Balaam, therefore, describes the seduction of fornication and idolatry. Many in Pergamos who claimed the name of Christ tolerated the pagan teachings that embraced worldliness and rejected the absolutes of godly truth.[26] They had succumbed to the temptation that they could simultaneously serve the Lord and remain a part of this world.

Interestingly, these are the very same issues addressed nearly forty years earlier at the Jerusalem Counsel, the first official meeting of Christians regarding the foundational doctrines being determined for the establishment of the early churches. *(Acts 15)*

Verse 15- *"Thus you also have those who hold the doctrine of the Nicolaitans, which thing I hate.*

Unlike the church of Ephesus that hated the doctrine of the Nicolaitans as the Lord did, some in Pergamos adopted this philosophy. As we studied before, not much is known about the specific practices of the Nicolaitans except they believed that their physical actions bore no spiritual consequences. We do know that God hated their heretical teachings, which appear to be very similar to the doctrine of Balaam. Several scholars, in fact, consider these two doctrines essentially one and the same.[27] The meanings of their names are virtually identical.[28]

Verse 16- *"Repent, or else I will come to you quickly and will fight against them with the sword of My mouth.*

The Lord instructed the church in Pergamos to repent. It can be reasonably assumed that He was addressing those who had adhered to this false doctrine as well as those members who had not indulged themselves in such practices but were tolerant of those who had. If they would not repent, there would be swift judgment as indicated by the term *quickly,* which signifies something that is done without delay. The Lord would judge them with the sword of His mouth according to His perfect justness.

Verse 17- *"He who has an ear, let him hear what the Spirit says to the churches. To him who overcomes I will give some of the hidden manna to eat. And I will give him a white stone, and on*

*the stone a new name written which no one knows except him
who receives it.'"*

The Lord once again repeated the admonishment to all those
willing to open their spiritual ears to hear "what the Spirit says to
the churches." As with the previous churches, the overcomers were
promised eternal life, expressed to this church as two things: hidden
manna and a white stone. When the Israelites wandered in the
wilderness, they obtained nourishment from physical manna that
descended from Heaven. In like manner, those believers that refuse
to compromise and are able to withstand the temptations of the
world will similarly be nourished with a spiritual manna. *"⁴⁸'I am the
bread of life. ⁴⁹Your fathers ate the manna in the wilderness, and are dead.
⁵⁰This is the bread which comes down from heaven, that one may eat of it
and not die. ⁵¹I am the living bread which came down from heaven. If anyone eats of this bread, he will live forever; and the bread that I shall give is
My flesh, which I shall give for the life of the world.'" (John 6.48–51)*

Overcomers would also receive a white stone. There are many
interpretations regarding the significance of the white stone, though
none can be convincingly proven to be anything more than speculation. The specification of a *white* stone may in some manner symbolize triumph, righteousness, or atonement. Whatever the case may
be, the significance of the stone is in the "new name written" on it.[29]
In some manner, this new name bears the mark of the unique and
personal relationship between Almighty God and those who belong
to Him.

Notes/Applications

The message proclaimed to the church of Pergamos and to the
believers represented by this church's attributes was to remain faithful even in the midst of ungodly influence. *"²⁶That He might sanctify
and cleanse her with the washing of water by the word, ²⁷that He might
present her to Himself a glorious church, not having spot or wrinkle or any
such thing, but that she should be holy and without blemish." (Ephesians
5.26–27)* Christ desires for His followers, no matter the hour in history, to penetrate the darkness pressing upon them with the light of
absolute truth. *"¹⁵'I do not pray that You should take them out of the world,*

but that You should keep them from the evil one... *[17]Sanctify them by Your truth. Your word is truth.* *[18]As You sent Me into the world, I also have sent them into the world." (John 17.15, 17–18)*

But why remain faithful when we are perplexed under extreme pressures loading us down? Our faithfulness expresses our fidelity to the One Who was first faithful to us. The words of fourteenth century priest Thomas A. Kempis remind us of our calling:

It is a great honor, a great glory to serve You and to despise all things for Your sake. They who give themselves gladly to Your most holy service will possess great grace. They who cast aside all carnal delights for Your love will find the most sweet consolation of the Holy Ghost. They who enter upon the narrow way for Your name and cast aside all worldly care will attain great freedom of mind. O sweet and joyful service of God, which makes man truly free and holy! O sacred state of religious bondage which makes man...worthy of the commendation of all the faithful![30]

Are we faithfully persevering, or are we tolerating evil? Perseverance requires a daily resolve to guard our hearts and minds from influences leading us to sin. May we as His followers be washed by His Word, be set apart by His truth, and be found faithful until His return. *"[22]Abstain from every form of evil. [23]Now may the God of peace Himself sanctify you completely; and may your whole spirit, soul, and body be preserved blameless at the coming of our Lord Jesus Christ. [24]He who calls you is faithful, who also will do it." (1 Thessalonians 5.22–24)*

Revelation 2.18–29

Verse 18- *"And to the angel of the church in Thyatira write, 'These things says the Son of God, who has eyes like a flame of fire, and His feet like fine brass:***

The fourth message was issued to the church of Thyatira, whose name means "odor of affliction," and came directly from the Son of God, whose eyes appeared as flames of fire and whose feet resembled refined brass.[31] *"[14]His head and hair were white like wool, as white as snow, and His eyes like a flame of fire; [15]His feet were like fine brass, as if refined in a furnace, and His voice as the sound of many waters." (Revelation 1.14–15)*

Of the seven churches mentioned in the Book of Revelation, the longest letter was addressed to the church in Thyatira. However, less is known about this city than any of the other six cities. Thyatira was located inland about forty miles east of Pergamos.[32] Seleucus I founded the city as a military strategy to guard one of his empire's main routes against Lysimachus.[33] After the death of Alexander the Great, Lysimachus was appointed to govern Asia Minor.[34] Thyatira was perhaps best known for its thriving trade guilds, which included bronze smiths, potters, bakers, tanners, and various garment workers.[35] Lydia, mentioned in the Bible as a seller of purple-dyed garments, was a Jewish citizen of Thyatira. *(Acts 16.14)*

Verse 19- *"I know your works, love, service, faith, and your patience; and as for your works, the last are more than the first.***

The works of the faithful believers in Thyatira seemed very praiseworthy. It appears that their love for God and their service to Him were properly motivated since He commended them. With much patience, they remained faithful to Almighty God despite the ungodliness that surrounded them. Furthermore, the mention of their later works being greater than their earlier works indicates that their acts of service progressed in both quantity and quality.[36]

Verse 20- *"Nevertheless I have a few things against you, because you allow that woman Jezebel, who calls herself a prophetess, to***

***teach and seduce My servants to commit sexual immorality and
eat things sacrificed to idols.***

Most scholars agree that the description of "that woman
Jezebel" is an allusion to the Old Testament character by that name.
Jezebel was a wicked queen who promoted the worship of Baal,
the storm god that the Canaanites believed was responsible for rain
and fertility.[37] So strong was Jezebel's hatred toward Almighty God
that she commanded the execution of His prophets throughout the
land and promoted the idolatrous, sensual rituals associated with
her pagan religion. *(1 Kings 17 & 18)*

In His address to the church in Thyatira, the Lord made this allusion to expose an individual whose heretical teachings had apparently been allowed to continue within the church without rebuke.
Considering the gender reference, it seems likely that this teacher
was a woman because other allusions could have been made if
such was not the case. Furthermore, this woman must have attained
some status within the church, perhaps due to her claim of being a
prophetess, since some within the church were eager to follow her
teachings.[38] Nevertheless, according to verse twenty-four, there were
clearly several who saw through her apostasy.

Some commentators actually attempt to specifically identify
this person.[39] However, solid evidence does not exist to corroborate
such claims, so we must instead pay attention to the reason this person was singled out, the reason being that she taught and seduced
God's servants "to commit sexual immorality and eat things sacrificed to idols."

DIG DEEPER: *FALSE TEACHERS*

It is a detestable thing when believers are led astray by false teachers.
We need to continually and prayerfully examine those who teach us
by making sure that the teachings are biblically sound. We must not
allow ourselves to be led astray from the truth in God's Holy Word.
(Colossians 2.8; 1 Timothy 4.3-5; and Titus Chapters 1 and 2)

Verse 21- "And I gave her time to repent of her sexual immorality, and she did not repent.

The Lord afforded this woman generous opportunities to repent of her fornication, but she refused. Therefore, because of her lack of repentance, she would reap the consequences of her wicked, stubborn ways.

Verse 22- "Indeed I will cast her into a sickbed, and those who commit adultery with her into great tribulation, unless they repent of their deeds.

The judgments explained in this verse refer to the physical consequences that could be expected by this woman and all who followed her teachings. The "sickbed" seems to be a metaphor that alludes to the place where she committed many of her acts of fornication and expresses the intense suffering and ailment that would befall her.[40] In addition, her followers could expect similar "tribulation" of physical torment.

Verse 23- "I will kill her children with death, and all the churches shall know that I am He who searches the minds and hearts. And I will give to each one of you according to your works.

This verse specifically expresses the spiritual consequences awaiting those who indulged themselves in this fornication. Some commentators contend that the phrase "her children" refers to this false teacher's followers.[41] Although this may be the case, the phrase may also allude once again to the Old Testament Queen Jezebel and the violent death that she and her descendants suffered due to the gravity of her transgressions. *(2 Kings 9.8–10)* Furthermore, some scholars argue that the phrase "killed…with death" refers to the second death spoken of in Revelation chapter twenty.[42] However, as indicated by the common Hebraic use of the phrase, which means "to slay utterly," perhaps it describes an unusually brutal death by which others would know that God directed this judgment.[43]

Christ alone possesses the power to search the minds and hearts of every individual and to know the motive behind every deed. Whereas the Lord addressed the entire church in Thyatira, He also offered assurance that every believer within that church would not be condemned for the exploits of a few but would be judged on an individual basis:

> *⁵But in accordance with your hardness and your impenitent heart you are treasuring up for yourself wrath in the day of wrath and revelation of the righteous judgment of God, ⁶who 'will render to each one according to his deeds': ⁷eternal life to those who by patient continuance in doing good seek for glory, honor, and immortality; ⁸but to those who are self-seeking and do not obey the truth, but obey unrighteousness—indignation and wrath, ⁹tribulation and anguish, on every soul of man who does evil, of the Jew first and also of the Greek. (Romans 2.5–9)*

Verses 24, 25- "²⁴Now to you I say, and to the rest in Thyatira, as many as do not have this doctrine, who have not known the depths of Satan, as they say, I will put on you no other burden. ²⁵But hold fast what you have till I come.

The Son of God spoke more gently to those in Thyatira who had not accepted the doctrine of Jezebel. He promised these believers that they would not encounter any additional burden. This did not mean that they would never experience other struggles or tribulations but that they would not share in the consequences of those who embraced this heretical teaching. The Lord Jesus Christ encouraged those believers who had "not known the depths of Satan" to persevere until His return. The meaning of "the depths of Satan" is ambiguous, and its interpretation varies widely, but in the very least, it denotes the difficulty of escaping the snares of Satan's deceiving ways. A particular encouragement to this church is not only to those who overcome but also to those who remain faithful in the midst of the struggle. The Lord encouraged these believers to persist or "hold fast" with their present efforts looking forward to the glorious return of the Lord. (1 John 3.2–3)

Verses 26–28- "²⁶And he who overcomes, and keeps My works until the end, to him I will give power over the nations—²⁷'He shall rule them with a rod of iron; They shall be dashed to pieces

like the potter's vessels'—as I also have received from My Father; *²⁸and I will give him the morning star.*

The configuration of this letter to the church of Thyatira changes to a style present also in the letters to the remaining churches. In the letter to the first three churches, the conclusion began with the command, "He who has an ear, let him hear what the Spirit says to the churches," and was then followed by various promises of eternal life to those who overcome. Beginning with this letter, however, the order of these two elements is reversed. Though the change is obvious, the reason for it is not. Furthermore, this is the only letter in which a condition, "he who…keeps My works until the end," accompanies the promise. Despite the distinction, we should not presume that this is an additional stipulation but rather a necessary criterion for being an "overcomer."

These verses are a direct reference to a psalm that proclaims the Messiah's authority. *"⁸'Ask of Me, and I will give You the nations for Your inheritance, and the ends of the earth for Your possession. ⁹You shall break them with a rod of iron; You shall dash them to pieces like a potter's vessel.'"* *(Psalm 2.8–9)* Though this promise is believed to refer to Christ's first advent, it is also traditionally interpreted to refer to His victorious second coming.[44] It seems that the overcomers will be given some level of authority to rule with Christ.

The concluding promise of "the morning star" has also received varied explanation. The most defensible interpretation of this phrase contends that it refers to Jesus Christ Himself.[45] *"'I, Jesus, have sent My angel to testify to you these things in the churches. I am the Root and the Offspring of David, the Bright and Morning Star.'"* *(Revelation 22.16)* Using this explanation, this promise parallels the promises to the other churches in which Christ assured the overcomer of everlasting life in His presence in Heaven.

Verse 29- "He who has an ear, let him hear what the Spirit says to the churches.'"

Once again, the Lord Jesus exhorted all believers, all those possessing spiritual ears, to listen to the message of this letter and to heed the warnings given therein.

Notes/Applications

The message to the church of Thyatira encouraged believers to persevere in the truth by rebuking teachings contrary to God's Word. Even within the realm of Christendom, religious figures may pervert Scripture to propel their own agendas or to excuse moral or spiritual compromise. *"For the wrath of God is revealed from heaven against all ungodliness and unrighteousness of men, who suppress the truth in unrighteousness."* *(Romans 1.18)* Such false teaching may be blatantly heretical, but most often, it is subtly disguised as philosophical opinions which place man's desired outcome at the forefront without sincerely seeking God's perfect will. When any form of errant interpretation of Scripture emerges among a body of believers or an individual life, it does more than just mislead. If left to fester, it will destroy lives. *"¹⁷Now I urge you, brethren, note those who cause divisions and offenses, contrary to the doctrine which you learned, and avoid them. ¹⁸For those who are such do not serve our Lord Jesus Christ, but their own belly, and by smooth words and flattering speech deceive the hearts of the simple."* *(Romans 16.17–18)*

To guard against heresy's infiltration, we must first know truth, and we must then become adept discerners of truth. *"²By this you know the Spirit of God: Every spirit that confesses that Jesus Christ has come in the flesh is of God, ³and every spirit that does not confess that Jesus Christ has come in the flesh is not of God. And this is the spirit of the Antichrist, which you have heard was coming, and is now already in the world."* *(1 John 4.2–3)* A person does not identify counterfeit money by studying it. One learns to recognize an imposter by studying the real thing, knowing its distinguishing marks and characteristics, the way it feels and the way it smells. Likewise, we learn to differentiate false teaching from truth by immersing our hearts and minds in God's Word until it becomes so ingrained in us that we can proficiently identify any perversion of it. *(2 Timothy 2.15; 1 John 5.19–20)*

Chapter Three

Revelation 3.1–6

Verse 1- "And to the angel of the church in Sardis write, 'These things says He who has the seven Spirits of God and the seven stars: "I know your works, that you have a name that you are alive, but you are dead.

The fifth message was addressed to the church in Sardis, whose name means "red ones."[1] The church would know that the message was given to them directly from the Lord Jesus Christ, the One described as "He who has the seven Spirits of God and the seven stars." *"He had in His right hand seven stars, out of His mouth went a sharp two-edged sword, and His countenance was like the sun shining in its strength." (Revelation 1.16)*

Sardis lay inland approximately thirty miles south of Thyatira and fifty miles northeast of Ephesus.[2] Early in its history the city was one of the most influential in the ancient world and served as the capital city of Lydia, a province of Asia Minor.[3] It was most noted for the Acropolis, a temple built to Artemis, the Greek name for the goddess Diana.[4] The vertical rock walls of the Acropolis rose nearly fifteen hundred feet above the lower valley, thereby providing the city with an excellent natural defense.[5] Despite numerous attacks on the city throughout history, its fortress was only captured twice, once in the sixth century BC and again in the fourth century BC.[6] In AD 17, a catastrophic earthquake destroyed the city. Though Sardis was eventually rebuilt, it never regained the prominence and affluence it once enjoyed, and by the time this letter was written, the city was a pitiful hub of moral debauchery.[7]

The Lord told the believers in Sardis that He knew their works, and despite their reputation for being a church that was alive, He knew that their works were no longer prompted by faithfulness and loyalty to Him. Within their community, and perhaps throughout surrounding regions, they had gained good reputation for their Christian works and vitality. Nevertheless, the Lord knew their hearts and recognized that their works were void of any true commitment to Christ, and as such, Jesus considered them not as merely sick but as utterly lifeless. *"27b'For you are like whitewashed tombs which indeed appear beautiful outwardly, but inside are full of dead men's bones and all uncleanness. 28Even so you also outwardly appear righteous to men, but inside you are full of hypocrisy and lawlessness.'" (Matthew 23.27b–28)*

Verse 2- *"Be watchful, and strengthen the things which remain, that are ready to die, for I have not found your works perfect before God.*

The church of Sardis was far from righteous in God's eyes. If they did not fortify and rebuild those few remaining qualities still deemed virtuous, even those things would be taken away. Most of their works were motivated by selfish ambition and not with any intention of glorifying God. Jesus' message seems to indicate that there was something worth holding on to, though what exactly is not identified. It may seem somewhat insignificant in light of the Lord's overall chastisement of these believers, yet they were warned that if they did not cling to that last shred of true life worthy of mention, even that would be removed from them. *"Watch and pray, lest you enter into temptation.'" (Matthew 26.41a)*

Verse 3- *"Remember therefore how you have received and heard; hold fast and repent. Therefore if you will not watch, I will come*

upon you as a thief, and you will not know what hour I will come upon you.

Jesus spoke to the believers and told them to hold fast to what they had been taught. If they did not repent of their spiritual indifference and did not cling to the few admirable qualities that they still possessed, the Lord would "come upon [them] as a thief" and remove those things. Some commentators insist upon an eschatological rendering of "come...as a thief" simply because this description resembles those found in "end-times" references, such as 1 Thessalonians 5.2 and 2 Peter 3.10. However, the phrase as used in this passage seems to express the sudden and unexpected manner with which the Lord will act.[8] Failure to repent would result in swift judgment, not in the hastening of the Lord's second coming before its appointed time.

Verse 4- "You have a few names even in Sardis who have not defiled their garments; and they shall walk with Me in white, for they are worthy.

This verse clearly reveals that the Lord deals with the body of Christ, the Church, as individuals. Jesus knows every person's heart and motivations and deals with them accordingly. Though He condemned most in Sardis, a few people in this church had not defiled themselves but had remained strong in their faith and lived obediently. The description "defiled their garments" does not mean that they were sinless but that they did not compromise their beliefs by succumbing to the lures of worldliness. These few had been found worthy in the eyes of the Lord, and He promised them that they would walk with Him "in white," which is explained in the next verse.

Verse 5- "He who overcomes shall be clothed in white garments, and I will not blot out his name from the Book of Life; but I will confess his name before My Father and before His angels.

As with the other churches, the true and faithful believers of this church were assured eternal life. In Heaven, these overcomers would be dressed in white garments, displaying the righteousness received only through the grace of the Lord Jesus Christ. *"And to her it was granted to be arrayed in fine linen, clean and bright, for the fine linen is the righteous acts of the saints." (Revelation 19.8)*

Those whose names are found written within the Book of Life are those who have been redeemed unto Almighty God, and those whose names are not found within the book are those who have been condemned unto eternal damnation because of their unrepentant hearts. *"And anyone not found written in the Book of Life was cast into the lake of fire." (Revelation 20.15) "But there shall by no means enter it anything that defiles, or causes an abomination or a lie, but only those who are written in the Lamb's Book of Life." (Revelation 21.27)* In addition, according to this verse, the Lord Jesus will vouch for each and every believer before God the Father and His angels. *"'Therefore whoever confesses Me before men, him I will also confess before My Father who is in heaven.'" (Matthew 10.32)*

Verse 6- "He who has an ear, let him hear what the Spirit says to the churches.'"

For a fifth time, we are told to listen, learn, and apply the Holy Spirit's message to the churches. Implied in this command is a call for obedience. We must listen to what Jesus said to these churches, apply these evaluations to our own lives, and obey them by making the necessary improvements as the Holy Spirit prompts.

Notes/Applications

Christ admonished the church of Sardis to repent of spiritual lifelessness. Why was this church dead? Was it their lack of passion for ministry, their worldliness, their attitudes, or their craving for self-glory? Any of these reasons would be detrimental to the growth of believers, but we are not told what specific area was amiss among this body. The passage simply states that the members of this church externally appeared to be spiritual, yet they were internally empty and used up like abandoned shells upon the seashore.

Even today, churches throughout the world have enjoyed commendable starts only to eventually lose their zeal, grow stale, and become ineffective in evangelizing new converts. The Lord instructs those believers that have lost fervor and vision for their calling to tear down the façade and to reexamine their position in Christ.

Is it time for a spiritual tune-up in our lives? God's Holy Word instructs us not to be indifferent people who dutifully complete the work of the church. He wants us to seek His empowerment so that our every endeavor reflects genuine joy and enthusiasm when serving Him because only then will our service impact others. *"¹⁰Create in me a clean heart, O God, and renew a steadfast spirit within me. ¹¹Do not cast me away from Your presence, and do not take Your Holy Spirit from me. ¹²Restore to me the joy of Your salvation, and uphold me by Your generous Spirit. ¹³Then I will teach transgressors Your ways, and sinners shall be converted to You." (Psalm 51.10–13)*

Revelation 3.7–13

Verse 7- "And to the angel of the church in Philadelphia write, 'These things says He who is holy, He who is true, "He who has the key of David, He who opens and no one shuts, and shuts and no one opens":

This is the message of the sixth angel to the church at Philadelphia, which means "brotherly love."[9] The Lord identified Himself to this church as "He who is holy, He who is true." He further confirmed His identity by distinguishing Himself as the fulfillment of messianic prophecy. *"The key of the house of David I will lay on his shoulder; so he shall open, and no one shall shut; and he shall shut, and no one shall open." (Isaiah 22.22)* Such phrases exemplify the absolute sovereignty of Almighty God.

Philadelphia was located about twenty-five miles southeast of Sardis. It was situated along a major thoroughfare, and as a result, it became a prominent city for both commercial and military purposes.[10] The same great earthquake that leveled Sardis in AD 17 also destroyed Philadelphia, which was prone to suffering the aftermath of earthquakes.[11]

Verse 8- "I know your works. See, I have set before you an open door, and no one can shut it; for you have a little strength, have kept My word, and have not denied My name.

The Lord prefaced the message to this church in the same manner as He had addressed all of the churches. Whatever varied admonitions followed, it was for this one common reason, "I know your works," that the Lord resolved to exhort these churches.

Although Philadelphia was among the smallest of the seven churches addressed in Revelation, it was only the second one (Smyrna being the first) that did not provoke any measure of condemnation from the Lord. These believers were not perfect, but they were true to the Word of God, and they did not deny Christ.

The meaning of the "open door" seems most likely to refer to Christ as the Doorkeeper of the Kingdom. Despite the Jews insistence that they alone would inherit the Kingdom of David, the Lord assured these believers that their participation lay in His hands.[12] Those to whom the Lord opens the door are guaranteed entrance, and such was the case with these Philadelphians who had kept His word and boldly proclaimed His name. In context, such an interpretation seems preferable to those which identify this open door as an opportunity to service, as is familiar imagery used in other biblical references.[13] *(1 Corinthians 16.9; Colossians 4.3)*

Verse 9- "Indeed I will make those of the synagogue of Satan, who say they are Jews and are not, but lie—indeed I will make them come and worship before your feet, and to know that I have loved you.

As with the church in Smyrna, the Christians in Philadelphia faced persecution from devout Jews that rejected Jesus as the Messiah. Christ again referred to these Jews as "the synagogue of Satan." In the Lord's eyes, there was a vast difference between the one who was a Jew by birthright yet rejected Jesus and the one who accepted Christ regardless of his ethnic heritage. *"[6b]For they are not all Israel who are of Israel, [7]nor are they all children because they are the seed of Abraham; but, 'In Isaac your seed shall be called.' [8]That is, those who are the children of the flesh, these are not the children of God; but the children of the promise are counted as the seed." (Romans 9.6b–8)* The Lord promised the faithful of this city that the liars who were of this "synagogue of Satan" would one day bow at the feet of the faithful believers as evidence of how much the Lord had loved them. The tables would be turned on those Jews who had persecuted God's faithful for challenging the believers' rightful inheritance into the Kingdom.[14]

Verse 10- "Because you have kept My command to persevere, I also will keep you from the hour of trial which shall come upon the whole world, to test those who dwell on the earth.

The interpretation of this verse is primarily dependent upon one's perception of "the hour of trial." Some scholars uphold this verse in defense of a pre-tribulation rapture while others dismiss a literal interpretation of "the whole world," thereby nullifying the message's universal impact. Whereas valid arguments can be made asserting that the message of this letter applies to more than just those in the church of Philadelphia at that time, it should never be presumed that the message was not initially intended for that church. Surely, it is easier to defend the certainty of the latter than it is to explain the ambiguity of the former. Though alternative and universal applications may be employed, it is safest to refrain from defining "the hour of trial" as any singular event.[15] Doing so negates this message's relevance to the first-century church in Philadelphia to whom this letter was addressed. Furthermore, the phrase "I will also keep you from," as rendered from the Greek, seems less to imply a physical removal from the world than to suggest that God will always uphold His faithful in the midst of their struggles.[16] *"I do not pray that You should take them out of the world, but that You should keep them from the evil one."* (John 17.15) As such, it is perhaps best to adhere to the conclusion of Matthew Henry, a renowned eighteenth-century biblical scholar, who stated: "Those who keep the gospel in a time of peace shall be kept by Christ in an hour of temptation. By keeping the gospel they are prepared for the trial; and the same divine grace that has made them fruitful in times of peace will make them faithful in times of persecution."[17]

What a marvelous promise this church was given. These believers had persevered through their sufferings based upon their faith in the Lord. In addition, this church had clung to its faith in hard times and had remained true to its stand for the Lord Jesus Christ. *"²My brethren, count it all joy when you fall into various trials, ³knowing that the testing of your faith produces patience. ⁴But let patience have its perfect work, that you may be perfect and complete, lacking nothing." (James 1.2–4)*

Verse 11- *"Behold, I am coming quickly! Hold fast what you have, that no one may take your crown.*

This should not be construed as a biblical error in which Christ promised that His return would occur shortly after He had addressed this church. The Lord was only promising that He would return and that His return would come upon man without delay according to His timing. He intended, it seems, to keep His followers expectant of His glorious return so that their perseverance would be strengthened by this promise being foremost in their minds.

There are several similarities between the churches in Philadelphia and Smyrna. Both received commendation without admonition, both contended against the "synagogue of Satan," and both persevered for a period of intense persecution and tribulation. Jesus further reminded the believers in Philadelphia to hold firmly to their faith so that nothing could steal their crowns, similar to the challenge He had given those in Smyrna. *"Be faithful until death, and I will give you the crown of life.'" (Revelation 2.10b)*

Verse 12- "He who overcomes, I will make him a pillar in the temple of My God, and he shall go out no more. And I will write on him the name of My God and the name of the city of My God, the New Jerusalem, which comes down out of heaven from My God. And I will write on him My new name.

The Lord repeated His promise of eternal life, which He expressed to this church as a two-fold reward to these overcomers. First, He would make them as a tall and unmovable pillar in the heavenly temple, an eternal home from which they would never have to depart. This would have received significant appreciation from a church that had remained strong despite being comparatively few in number by the standards of the other six churches. As already stated, Philadelphia had endured more than its fair share of catastrophic earthquakes, so the promise of being made a permanent pillar in God's temple would not have been received with somber indifference.

Second, the name of God would be written upon each believer thereby declaring the Lord's ownership. *"They shall see His face, and His name shall be on their foreheads." (Revelation 22.4)* The name of the holy city would also be written upon the believers, and this city, the New Jerusalem, would serve as their new eternal address. These names would be the physical marks by which their inclusion in the kingdom of Heaven was declared and authenticated. This promise provides a tremendous sense of security to those who have trusted Christ unto salvation.

Verse 13- "He who has an ear, let him hear what the Spirit says to the churches."'

Once again, Jesus Christ urged the believers to open their spiritual ears and to heed the Holy Spirit's message to these churches. We are to hear and obey.

Notes/Applications

Unlike His warnings to most of the other churches, Christ commended the believers at Philadelphia because they had patiently endured tribulation and temptation, had kept His Word, and had not denied His name. The Lord promised that He would reward them for their fidelity with eternal, pillar-like strength. They would be a monument inscribed with a testament to the One they served as Master (the name of God), the place of their ultimate dwelling (the name of the city of God), and the One they entrusted as their Redeemer (the new name). Sixteenth-century hymnist John Newton eloquently paraphrases the Lord's glorious intent for this church in the hymn "Thus Saith the Holy One, and True":

A pillar there, no more to move,
Inscribed with all my names of love;
A monument of mighty grace,
Thou shalt forever have a place.
Such is the conqueror's reward,
Prepared and promised by the Lord![18]

Are we living as monuments of the Lord's "mighty grace"? *"That the name of our Lord Jesus Christ may be glorified in you, and you in Him, according to the grace of our God and the Lord Jesus Christ." (2 Thessalonians 1.12)* What inscription appears on the tablets of our souls? We may be of "little strength," but when we faithfully live out our love for Him, Christ will give us His power to patiently endure and to uphold His name:

[14]For this reason I bow my knees to the Father of our Lord Jesus Christ, [15]from whom the whole family in heaven and earth is named, [16]that He would grant you, according to the riches of His glory, to be strengthened with might through His Spirit in the inner man, [17]that Christ may dwell in your hearts through faith; that you,

being rooted and grounded in love, [18]may be able to comprehend with all the saints what is the width and length and depth and height— [19]to know the love of Christ which passes knowledge; that you may be filled with all the fullness of God. (Ephesians 3.14–19)

Revelation 3.14–22

Verse 14- "And to the angel of the church of the Laodiceans write, 'These things says the Amen, the Faithful and True Witness, the Beginning of the creation of God:

This is the message to the seventh and final church, the church at Laodicea, which means "the people's rights."[19] As with each of the previous six churches, the believers in Laodicea would know that this message was sent directly from the Lord Jesus Christ, Who identified Himself as "the Amen, and the Faithful and True Witness." *"Jesus answered and said to them, 'Even if I bear witness of Myself, My witness is true, for I know where I came from and where I am going.'" (John 8.14a)* Jesus Christ, Son of God, is the fulfillment of all messianic promise. He is the Amen, the firm witness. *"For all the promises of God in Him are Yes, and in Him Amen, to the glory of God through us." (2 Corinthians 1.20)* Jesus also referred to Himself as "the Beginning of the creation of God." *"¹In the beginning was the Word, and the Word was with God, and the Word was God. ²He was in the beginning with God." (John 1.1–2)*

The city of Laodicea was located approximately forty-five miles southeast of Philadelphia.[20] It was founded by Antiochus II in the middle of the third-century BC and was named after his wife Laodice.[21] At the time of this letter, the city was among the wealthiest in the region. It was a renowned banking center and had made a name for itself in the production of black wool products.[22] The city was also recognized worldwide for its medical school, especially noted for its development of renowned ear ointment and eye salve.[23] Despite the difficulties posed by its lack of a convenient water source, Laodicea had become a city of great agricultural and commercial prosperity.[24]

Verse 15- "I know your works, that you are neither cold nor hot. I could wish you were cold or hot.

As with each of the other churches, the Lord told the church of Laodicea that He knew their works. This metaphor to the problematic Laodicean water supply seems evident. It appears that they lacked moral conviction. They had one foot in the church and one foot in the world and were, therefore, ineffective believers. If these people were hot, it would have shown in their passion for following Christ and their testimony of His Word. If they were cold, their spiritual deficiency would at least be unmistakable. The Lord told them that He would rather they be one or the other—be obvious in their affiliation—than to be spiritually indistinguishable.

Verse 16- "So then, because you are lukewarm, and neither cold nor hot, I will vomit you out of My mouth.

Christ would rather people be hot and zealous in their devotion to him or boldly oppose Him than to claim His name yet be ambiguous in their faith and ineffective in their service. Those who are lukewarm are complacent and fruitless, and to the naked eye, there may be no difference between a believer in this position and an unbeliever. The Lord compares this spiritual apathy to being lukewarm—somewhere between hot and cold. Unlike those who are hot or cold, those who are lukewarm are entirely useless to either side. God cannot use those who are lukewarm and as such, like the distastefulness of a tepid drink, Christ says He will spit them out of His mouth.

Verse 17- "Because you say, 'I am rich, have become wealthy, and have need of nothing'—and do not know that you are wretched, miserable, poor, blind, and naked—

The church of Laodicea was not burdened by a lack of material goods but by the abundance of them. Their excess of material provisions caused them to believe that they could confront any problem, resolve any conflict, and care for the needs of their people by themselves, so they no longer relied upon God to meet their needs. This church neglected the need to strive for spiritual riches in Christ Jesus. *"Your gold and silver are corroded, and their corrosion will be a witness against you and will eat your flesh like fire. You have heaped up treasure in the last days." (James 5.3)* Perhaps they assumed that their wealth was an indication of God's favor toward them and blessings upon them.[25]

The Lord further warned these people that their reliance upon their own physical riches had blinded them of their spiritual destitution, and as a result, they were unable to recognize their deplorable, apathetic condition. God exposed their spiritual condition to be exactly opposite of what they perceived it to be. Rather than prosperous, they were poor and naked; rather than content, they were wretched and miserable; and rather than enlightened, they were spiritually blind. Their earthly wealth gave them a false sense of security, but in the end, they would be left without direction and be found in desperate need.

Verse 18- "I counsel you to buy from Me gold refined in the fire, that you may be rich; and white garments, that you may be clothed, that the shame of your nakedness may not be revealed; and anoint your eyes with eye salve, that you may see.

Jesus Christ offered the Laodiceans the only remedy to their spiritual ambiguity: "to buy from [Him] gold refined in the fire." Refined gold is pure gold without blemish, and here, it signifies the righteousness of Christ.[26] This is not meant to suggest that we can "buy" salvation through any amount of works. The cost of salvation is the sacrificing of our own will to pursue the will of our Heavenly Father.[27] *(Romans 12.1–2)* The incentive to buy this refined gold from Christ is to obtain the true spiritual riches available only through Him.

In addition, Christ also admonished the Laodiceans to cover the shame of their spiritual nakedness by dressing in the beautiful white garments that He provided them, which again symbolizes the righteousness they received from Jesus Christ by His atoning sacrifice on the cross. *"He who overcomes shall be clothed in white garments, and I will not blot out his name from the Book of Life; but I will confess his name before My Father and before His angels."* (Revelation 3.5)

Finally, the Laodiceans were to seek healing from their spiritual blindness through Christ's anointing. The Lord used this illustration of blindness to show the people their spiritual condition, which fell far short of God's standards. The lies of the world had blinded many believers within this church, but Jesus promised that those who sought after Him would have their spiritual eyes opened, and His truths would be revealed to them. *(Matthew 6.33)*

Verse 19- "As many as I love, I rebuke and chasten. Therefore be zealous and repent.

Christ corrects and disciplines those He loves. Those that belong to Christ will be rebuked. *"¹¹My son, do not despise the chastening of the Lord, nor detest His correction; ¹²for whom the Lord loves He corrects, just as a father the son in whom he delights." (Proverbs 3.11–12)* The correction of the Lord can often be difficult, but we are children in need of much instruction. *"⁶'For whom the Lord loves He chastens, and scourges every son whom He receives.' ⁷If you endure chastening, God deals with you as with sons; for what son is there whom a father does not chasten? ⁸But if you are without chastening, of which all have become partakers, then you are illegitimate and not sons." (Hebrews 12.6–8)* Through His rebuke and correction, the Lord shapes His faithful into the people He wants them to become.

As with the previous churches, Christ urged the believers at Laodicea to be enthusiastic and passionate about their faith and to repent for their idleness. He wanted them to change their ways and do away with their indifference and apathy.

Verse 20- "Behold, I stand at the door and knock. If anyone hears My voice and opens the door, I will come in to him and dine with him, and he with Me.

Many pastors and teachers are quick to cite this verse as an open invitation to any and all unbelievers to come to Christ. We must remember, though, that Christ was still addressing the "lukewarm" people in the church of Laodicea who had grown apathetic toward their relationship with Christ within the complacence of self-sufficiency.[28] Though this verse well serves as a convenient tool for evangelism, for the purposes of commentary, we must remain true to its context and leave comment on its evangelistic appeal to other discussions.

Christ announced to the believers in Laodicea that He stood knocking outside the doors of their hearts. His presence, at one time, permeated throughout the church. Passion for Him motivated their good works, but now, He was excluded—He was standing outside the door. As is frequently used in the Bible to emphasize intimacy more so than eating, the Lord used the illustration of dining as a gentle reminder that He waited patiently for those who had neglected their relationship with God to again welcome Him in and to restore the warm and personal fellowship that was once shared.

Verse 21- "To him who overcomes I will grant to sit with Me on My throne, as I also overcame and sat down with My Father on His throne.

Similar promises of an eternal inheritance were offered at the conclusion of each of the messages given to the previous six churches. Eternal life is expressed in this verse with a comparison that is drawn between Christ and the overcomer. The victory *of* Christ has made possible our victory *through* Christ. What a blessed promise! We will sit with Him in Heaven just as He sits with His Father.

Verse 22- "He who has an ear, let him hear what the Spirit says to the churches.""

Again, the warning was sounded. This declaration at the end of each of the seven messages to the individual churches stresses its importance. In each instance, this command to hear suggests a response of obedience. Those who overcome—those faithful believers that respond to the prompting of the Holy Spirit and remain obedient to His will—are certain to receive the reward of fellowship with their Lord and Savior Jesus Christ in His presence forevermore.

Notes/Applications

The Lord Jesus Christ admonished the church of Laodicea for existing under the corrupt pretense that they could linger in the indistinguishable spirituality between zealous commitment to Christ and outright opposition to Him.

Eighteenth-century theologian Matthew Henry notes: "If religion is a real thing, it is the most excellent thing, and therefore we should be in good earnest in it; if it is not a real thing, it is the vilest imposture, and we should be earnest against it. If religion is worth any thing, it is worth every thing."[29]

Complacency, as tepid water incapable of quenching a thirst or soothing a throat, wastes the potential intimacy accessible through a relationship with the Savior, and Christ warned the Laodiceans that He would vomit the indifferent out of His mouth. We may consider this description appalling, but it appropriately portrays God's aversion to spiritual apathy—filthy and repulsive. Thankfully, we are reminded of God's mercy amid such vivid and piercing language. Those He loves will be rebuked, chastened, and offered a passageway to restoration.

How do we get to such a place of spiritual apathy? By way of deception, self-consumption, and conceitedness. *"And whoever does not bear his cross and come after Me cannot be My disciple."' (Luke 14.27)* More importantly, how do we leave this place to gain restoration in our relationship with the Savior? Again, Henry eloquently summarizes Christ's message: "Part with sin and self-sufficiency, and come to Christ with a sense of your poverty and emptiness, that you may be filled with his hidden treasure...a new and glorious scene would then open itself."[30]

Although the devil deceives many into thinking that they can remain status quo in their Christian walk, we cannot rightly claim genuine fellowship with the Lord if we harbor spiritual half-heartedness. *"[12]'And it shall come to pass at that time that I will search Jerusalem with lamps, and punish the men who are settled in complacency, who say in their heart, "The Lord will not do good, nor will He do evil." [13]Therefore their goods shall become booty, and their houses a desolation; they shall build houses, but not inhabit them; they shall plant vineyards, but not drink their wine."' (Zephaniah 1.12–13)* Therefore, may we earnestly seek the Lord every day "that we may not be left to flatter and deceive ourselves in the concerns of our souls."[31]

Chapter Four

Revelation 4.1–5

Verse 1- After these things I looked, and behold, a door standing open in heaven. And the first voice which I heard was like a trumpet speaking with me, saying, "Come up here, and I will show you things which must take place after this."

The purpose of this message, to show the "things which must take place after this," is of great significance. It transitions the text from the challenges given to the seven churches in chapters two and three to the apocalyptic portion of this book. A sense of ambiguity regarding the identity of the speaker exists, but on the basis of the description in this verse and Revelation 1.10, we may reasonably conclude that Jesus Christ issued these words as well. Another indication that there has been no alteration in the speaker's identity is that John does not notify readers of any change, and such disclosure seems to be his common practice when a shift occurs. *(Revelation 7.2, 8.3, 10.1, 14.6–18, and 18.1)* Though "red letter" Bible versions do not render these as Christ's words, this claim seems more feasible since another source has not been introduced to the reader, and many commentaries from both pre- and post-red letter Bible eras agree with this conclusion.[1]

After John had received the messages from the Lord Jesus Christ to the seven churches of Asia Minor, the apostle peered upward and saw a door open in Heaven. Then, a voice like the sound of a trumpet called for him to ascend into Heaven and to witness visions of future events. Jesus Christ stood at Heaven's door and invited John to enter in so that he could be shown the "things that must take place after this."

Many believers go to great lengths to explain this verse as a symbolic illustration of the rapture of God's elect.[2] Though they extract references from this verse with loose parallels from more traditional "rapture" passages, the effort seems, at best, supposition. Apart from distinguishing John as a symbol of the Church, for which there is no justifiable cause or purpose, there is little evidence to suggest anything other than what we are told.[3] If we symbolize John as the Church simply because he was called up to Heaven, then are we not required to also carry out the purpose of that calling and say that the raptured Church would only be taken up into Heaven to be shown the things that were yet to take place? Accordingly, any such interpretations as applied to this verse seem too speculative to be defended with biblical certainty.

Verse 2- Immediately I was in the Spirit; and behold, a throne set in heaven, and One sat on the throne.

God called John up into Heaven "in the Spirit." There are two main interpretations regarding the meaning of this experience. The first contends that John was physically transported via the Spirit from Patmos into Heaven to witness the things he was to be shown.[4] This condition is likely the same state that the apostle Paul once tried to describe. "*3And I know such a man whether in the body or out of the body I do not know, God knows— 4how he was caught up into Paradise and heard inexpressible words, which it is not lawful for a man to utter.*" (2 Corinthians 12.3–4) The second interpretation suggests that John merely witnessed the events which follow as a vision, whereby his consciousness was the only thing altered.[5] Either interpretation can be accepted as long as the interpretation of later verses is not based upon conclusions drawn from this verse.[6]

When John arrived in Heaven, he was welcomed with a beautiful sight of a Person sitting on a throne. This glorious Being is soon identified as Almighty God, the Father. *"God reigns over the nations; God sits on His holy throne." (Psalm 47.8)*

Verse 3- And He who sat there was like a jasper and a sardius stone in appearance; and there was a rainbow around the throne, in appearance like an emerald.

Though certainly God's magnificent presence is indefinable, John compared God's glorious appearance to the beauty of the precious gems jasper and sardius. Jasper is a type of brilliant, transparent quartz, and a sardius is a reddish gem similar to a ruby. The grandeur of this scene is further magnified by the description of "a rainbow around the throne," which is compared to an emerald. Surely, the magnificence of this spectacle surpassed any human comprehension, but nevertheless, John, limited to earthly physical comparisons and inadequate human words, attempted to illustrate verbally the indescribable by drawing comparisons to the most beautiful gems that he knew.

Verse 4- Around the throne were twenty-four thrones, and on the thrones I saw twenty-four elders sitting, clothed in white robes; and they had crowns of gold on their heads.

These twenty-four "elders" gathered around God's throne seem to have been granted some special authority or distinction from the other heavenly beings. Though some commentators have defined them as angels, they were singled out from the host of Heaven as having white robes and golden crowns, so they were evidently unique beings. *"Then I looked, and I heard the voice of many angels around the throne, the living creatures, and the elders; and the number of them was ten thousand times ten thousand, and thousands of thousands." (Revelation 5.11)* Scholars have speculated a variety of theories regarding their identity. Among a few of the more prevalent interpretations are these: 1) their number symbolizes the twelve tribes of Israel and the twelve apostles, and therefore, they represent the entire sum of God's redeemed, both of Old Testament and New

Testament saints[7]; 2) they are the heavenly model of the twenty-four priests who served in the earthly temple[8] *(1 Chronicles 24 and 25)*; and, 3) they represent only New Testament saints.[9] It cannot be defended with any certainty that these twenty-four elders seated on thrones of distinction have any symbolic implication at all. More important than who or what they might represent is what we are specifically told about them within these chapters—they serve the King's purposes and worship Him without ceasing.[10]

Verse 5- And from the throne proceeded lightnings, thunderings, and voices. Seven lamps of fire were burning before the throne, which are the seven Spirits of God.

Scholars differ in their theories regarding the significance of this description "lightnings, thunderings, and voices." Some claim that this is the voice of God forewarning judgment.[11] *"The voice of the Lord is powerful; the voice of the Lord is full of majesty." (Psalm 29.4)* Near the Father's throne were seven lamps representing "the seven Spirits of God." There are no corroborating biblical references outside of Revelation to suggest that this pictures seven individual Spirits of God. Rather, it seems more accurate to conclude that these "seven Spirits" depict the omnipresence and various operations of the Holy Spirit.[12] *"But one and the same Spirit works all these things, distributing to each one individually as He wills." (1 Corinthians 12.11) "Grace to you and peace from Him who is and who was and who is to come, and from the seven Spirits who are before His throne." (Revelation 1.4b)*

Notes/Applications

Submerged between two mountains in the state of Virginia, the Natural Bridge is one of North America's most spectacular natural wonders. Thomas Jefferson referred to the bridge as "undoubtedly one of the sublimest curiosities in nature."[13] Consider also the snow-capped peaks of the Swiss Alps, the lush foliage of the South American Rain Forests, and the crimson sands of the Kalahari Dessert. Like Jefferson when he studied this enormous rock formation of the Natural Bridge with its interesting jagged edges and striations of color, most of us have observed awe-inspiring scenes in nature, a spectacular sunset or dew-kissed butterfly's wing, and thought, *Amazing*. However, nothing we might see or dream could compare with John's experience of beholding the Creator situated upon His throne, filling Heaven's expanse. *"³²Sing to God, you kingdoms of the earth; Oh, sing praises to the Lord, ³³to Him who rides on the heaven of heavens, which were of old! Indeed, He sends out His voice, a mighty voice." (Psalm 68.32–33) "Out of Zion, the perfection of beauty, God will shine forth." (Psalm 50.2)*

We can only somewhat imagine the striking beauty of Almighty God arrayed in a spectrum of His heavenly glory, for we have yet to behold Him. *"⁹For we know in part and we prophesy in part. ¹⁰But when that which is perfect has come, then that which is in part will be done away. ¹²For now we see in a mirror, dimly, but then face to face. Now I know in part, but then I shall know just as I also am known." (1 Corinthians 13.9–10, 12)* Nevertheless, the day approaches when we, too, will behold the kaleidoscopic vision of Almighty God ruling in majestic beauty and strength. We will then bow before Him, overtaken by the light of His gloriousness as we eternally honor Him with multitudes upon multitudes of our brothers and sisters in Christ. *"But as it is written: 'Eye has not seen, nor ear heard, nor have entered into the heart of man the things which God has prepared for those who love Him.'" (1 Corinthians 2.9)*

Revelation 4.6–11

Verse 6- Before the throne there was a sea of glass, like crystal. And in the midst of the throne, and around the throne, were four living creatures full of eyes in front and in back.

The throne of God must have been the most beautiful sight in all of Heaven! The floor surrounding the throne appeared as a crystal sea, a transparent sheet that was as wide and deep as the eye could see. Evidently, it was completely void of darkness, shadows, and flaws.

Seated all around the throne were four creatures that had many eyes in front and in back. The Greek word for *creatures* here is ζῶα (zoa) which means "a living being."[14] These beings, therefore, probably did not appear to be abhorrent monsters but magnificent heavenly creatures. As with the aforementioned elders, much speculation has been made about a greater symbolic relevance of these creatures and their many eyes, but it seems difficult to reconcile dogmatically any of these interpretations with certainty. Surely, such an arrangement of eyes is unfamiliar to our human understanding and clearly depict some manner of heavenly uniqueness. There is no reason to conclude that the heavenly scene before John was intended to compel any comparisons to earthly things.

Verse 7- The first living creature was like a lion, the second living creature like a calf, the third living creature had a face like a man, and the fourth living creature was like a flying eagle.

John described in further detail these four creatures surrounding the throne. The first creature resembled a lion, the second a calf, the third a man, and the fourth an eagle. This description bears striking similarities to a vision described by the prophet Ezekiel. *"As for the likeness of their faces, each had the face of a man; each of the four had the face of a lion on the right side, each of the four had the face of an ox on the left side, and each of the four had the face of an eagle." (Ezekiel 1.10)* Comparisons have also been drawn between the characteristics of the animals described in this verse with the attributes of God.[15] Others have attempted to equate these four animals with the four gospels.[16] Any such efforts appear unnecessary since they lend no assistance in the interpretation of the Revelation. John merely observed four dynamic, complicated, magnificent beings that worshiped and attended Almighty God on His throne.

Verse 8- The four living creatures, each having six wings, were full of eyes around and within. And they do not rest day or night, saying: "Holy, holy, holy, Lord God Almighty, Who was and is and is to come!"

Each creature had six wings, which perhaps enabled the creatures to fly as well as to cover their form in the Lord's presence. Again, similarities are evident between the four beasts described here and the four beasts in Ezekiel's vision. *"And under the firmament their wings spread out straight, one toward another. Each one had two which covered one side, and each one had two which covered the other side of the body." (Ezekiel 1.23)* In addition, the creatures were "full of eyes around and within." The beings praised the eternal existence of God Almighty, Who is forever past, present, and future, and their worship of Him never ceased.

> ### DIG DEEPER: HEAVENLY CREATURES
>
> There are some similarities between this vision of God's throne and that which Ezekiel received during his Babylonian captivity. Ezekiel also saw four living creatures. *(Ezekiel 1.10)* In all of God's creation, there are no other creatures like these, and their sole purpose was to praise God continually.

Verses 9, 10- ⁹Whenever the living creatures give glory and honor and thanks to Him who sits on the throne, who lives forever and ever, ¹⁰the twenty-four elders fall down before Him who sits on the throne and worship Him who lives forever and ever, and cast their crowns before the throne, saying:

These unique heavenly beings evidently served one primary purpose: to offer their worship "to Him who sits on the throne." Whenever the four beasts gave glory to Almighty God—which, as explained by the previous verse, is unending—they were joined in praise by the twenty-four elders. Though speculation about a greater significance of the elders is perhaps best deferred, some good arguments have been made, specifically that these elders represent in some form redeemed man due to the white garments that the elders wore and the crowns that they cast before the throne.[17]

Verse 11- "You are worthy, O Lord, to receive glory and honor and power; for You created all things, and by Your will they exist and were created."

After the elders cast down their crowns before the Father, they cried aloud declaring that God alone was worthy to receive glory, honor, and power. The elders had acknowledged God as the Creator of all things. *"[16]For by Him all things were created that are in heaven and that are on earth, visible and invisible, whether thrones or dominions or principalities or powers. All things were created through Him and for Him. [17]And He is before all things, and in Him all things consist." (Colossians 1.16–17)*

It is evident that the worship of Almighty God will also be our primary if not sole activity in Heaven, and of the countless praiseworthy characteristics of God, we will focus our praise, like these beings, on the awesomeness of His role as Creator.

Notes/Applications

These four beings along with the twenty-four elders gathered around God's throne and continually proclaimed His worthiness as the powerful Creator and Sustainer of all life.

We easily forget our frailty—by God's will, we consist, and by His grace, we exist. With so many technological and medical advances that have been made in recent years, we may subconsciously rely upon man's ability to extend life. However, just as our Lord spoke creation into being with supreme utterance, He has determined our days with loving authority, and His word is perfect:

[2]Give unto the Lord the glory due to His name; worship the Lord in the beauty of holiness. [3]The voice of the Lord is over the waters; the God of glory thunders; the Lord is over many waters. [4]The voice of the Lord is powerful; the voice of the Lord is full of majesty. [5]The

voice of the Lord breaks the cedars, yes, the Lord splinters the cedars of Lebanon...[7]*The voice of the Lord divides the flames of fire.* [8]*The voice of the Lord shakes the wilderness...* [9]*The voice of the Lord makes the deer give birth, and strips the forests bare...* [10]*The Lord sat enthroned at the Flood, and the Lord sits as King forever. (Psalm 29.2–5, 7-8a, 9–10)*

Some may deny God's mastery as Creator and Sustainer of every facet of creation, but His character remains unchanged. He is complete; He does not need our adoration. Still, His Word tells us that He desires praise from devoted vessels. *"*[23]*'But the hour is coming, and now is, when the true worshipers will worship the Father in spirit and truth; for the Father is seeking such to worship Him.* [24]*God is Spirit, and those who worship Him must worship in spirit and truth.'" (John 4.23–24)* How our hearts and burdened souls would be dynamically transformed by such a glimpse of Heaven found when we worship Him in the beauty and wonder of His being. *(Psalm 29. 1–5)*

Chapter Five

Revelation 5.1–7

Verse 1- And I saw in the right hand of Him who sat on the throne a scroll written inside and on the back, sealed with seven seals.

This verse is a continuation of the vision of Heaven that began in the previous chapter. The Heavenly Father held in His right hand a sealed scroll with writing on both sides, likely an indication of the contents' length and gravity. Interpretations regarding the scroll range from it representing the redemptive history of mankind to the consequential destiny of the world.[1] Whatever the symbolism intended, it is safe to conclude by the evidence of the subsequent chapters that the scroll represents "the mystery of God's purpose for the world."[2]

Historically, it was not uncommon for a message to be bound with a clay or wax seal in order to bear the mark of the sender and to ensure the privacy of the letter.[3] This particular scroll, however, bore seven seals, and many commentators attribute this to the document's importance and to the guarantee of its secrecy.[4] Some Bible versions render the object in God's hand as a book, not in form but in length. This leads a few commentators to speculate that this book was actually comprised of seven scrolls, each affixed with a seal and each serving as a volume or portion of the sum of the contents.[5] Regardless, each individual seal bears unique consequence, and the judgments ensue after each seal is broken, as described in subsequent verses.

DIG DEEPER: SEAL

Seals were a vital component of the ancient Middle East. Artifacts have been found dating more than 3,500 years before the birth of Christ. The purpose of these seals varied depending upon the application, but they always provided evidence of ownership. Seals were never to be broken by anyone except those having the proper authority, either the owner or the person to whom the document was addressed. Seals were so important that they were often attached to a man's garment so that it could be used at any given moment when authenticity was required. In this case, Jesus alone had the authority to open the seals of this scroll, indicating His unique position as the Lamb of God and also the unchangeable decrees that were written within the document.

Verse 2- Then I saw a strong angel proclaiming with a loud voice, "Who is worthy to open the scroll and to loose its seals?"

Some expositors ascribe this powerful angel with asserting a public challenge to any who might come forth and attempt to unlock this scroll and disclose its contents.[6] However, it seems more appropriate to assume that this utterance was made more for the benefit of the human observer, both John at that moment and his readers thereafter. Surely, as evidenced by the lack of response in the verse that follows, all other created beings already knew that there was none among them able to reply satisfactorily. Therefore, this appears to be a rhetorical question, one made for the purpose of proclamation. Although this angel was mighty, he, too, was unable to break the seals because it was not a question of strength but of worthiness. The seals could only be broken by One worthy to do so—the Person for Whom the scroll was intended.

Verses 3, 4- ³*And no one in heaven or on the earth or under the earth was able to open the scroll, or to look at it.* ⁴*So I wept much, because no one was found worthy to open and read the scroll, or to look at it.*

No created being existed that was worthy to break the seals, so the contents of the scroll could not be read. John wept openly at this, though we can only speculate why he did so. Some have suggested that this disappointment was generated by unanswered questions.⁷ Perhaps, however, John feared that he might not be shown the "things that must take place after this" as promised.⁸

Verse 5- *But one of the elders said to me, "Do not weep. Behold, the Lion of the tribe of Judah, the Root of David, has prevailed to open the scroll and to loose its seven seals."*

One of the twenty-four elders comforted John by assuring him that there was indeed One Who was worthy to break the seven seals and to look at the contents of the scroll. He called this One the "Lion of the tribe of Judah," probably as an allusion to an Old Testament reference considered by most to be messianic prophecy:⁹

> ⁸*'Judah, you are he whom your brothers shall praise; your hand shall be on the neck of your enemies; your father's children shall bow down before you.* ⁹*Judah is a lion's whelp; from the prey, my son, you have gone up. He bows down, he lies down as a lion; and as a lion, who shall rouse him?* ¹⁰*The scepter shall not depart from Judah, nor a lawgiver from between his feet, until Shiloh comes; and to Him shall be the obedience of the people.'* (Genesis 49.8–10)

The line of kingship was given to Judah. As evidenced in the genealogy of Matthew chapter one, Christ is of that royal bloodline. Jesus fulfilled prophecy by being born in the line of David. *"²Which He promised before through His prophets in the Holy Scriptures, ³concerning His Son Jesus Christ our Lord, who was born of the seed of David according to the flesh." (Romans 1.2–3)* However, this Lion is also called the "Root of David," indicating that He was not only a descendent of David but also *preceded* David as the Root of that bloodline. *"Jesus said to them, 'Most assuredly, I say to you, before Abraham was, I AM.'" (John 8.58)*

That He was born of the line of David confirms His absolute human-ness, and that He is the Root of David verifies His absolute deity.

Verse 6- And I looked, and behold, in the midst of the throne and of the four living creatures, and in the midst of the elders, stood a Lamb as though it had been slain, having seven horns and seven eyes, which are the seven Spirits of God sent out into all the earth.

Ironically, this "Lion" (of the tribe of Judah), the Lord Jesus Christ, appeared in the midst of the throne as a lamb—the perfect Lamb sacrificed for the sins of all men. *"The next day John saw Jesus coming toward him, and said, 'Behold! The Lamb of God who takes away the sin of the world!'" (John 1.29)* Although the Lamb bore the marks of having been slain, He, nevertheless, stood in the midst of the throne. It was not required that Jesus remain in the grave for His atoning sacrifice to take effect; it was His shed blood that secured salvation for all who believe.[10]

The Lamb had seven horns and seven eyes, which some schol-ars suggest illustrates Christ's strength, dominion and omniscience.[11] Whereas some good arguments have been made that the seven horns and eyes are symbolic of Christ's attributes, this verse specifi-cally states that they represent the seven Spirits of God, comparable to the lamps of fire mentioned in chapter four. *"Seven lamps of fire were burning before the throne, which are the seven Spirits of God." (Revelation 4.5b)* In the first three chapters of Revelation, the seven spirits spoke to the seven churches in Asia Minor, and in this verse, the ministry of the seven spirits appears to have expanded such that they addressed the entire earth.

Verse 7- Then He came and took the scroll out of the right hand of Him who sat on the throne.

In a gesture which both asserted His supreme authority and answered earlier concerns that the contents of the scroll might not be revealed, the Lamb removed the scroll from the right hand of Almighty God. Jesus, the Lamb of God, was the only One worthy to do this, and the only One *able* to do this. Though Jesus *is* God and is *of* God as one Person of the divine Trinity, this action illustrates that Christ is worthy by virtue of what He accomplished at Calvary. God became man in the form of Jesus Christ, Who came to earth, lived the sinless life, died for the atonement of mankind's sins, and rose again, thereby defeating sin and death forevermore.

Notes/Applications

This passage identifies the Lamb, the Lord Jesus Christ, to be the only One worthy to open the seals of the judgment scroll. Why is Christ esteemed worthy? He is the Son of God, the likeness and essence of God, yet with perfect humility, He yielded Himself to become the sacrificial Lamb through a sinless life, undeserving death, and glorious, redemptive resurrection. *"16'For God so loved the world that He gave His only begotten Son, that whoever believes in Him should not perish but have everlasting life. 17For God did not send His Son into the world to condemn the world, but that the world through Him might be saved.'" (John 3.16–17)*

Christ is what we could not become. *"For whoever shall keep the whole law, and yet stumble in one point, he is guilty of all." (James 2.10)* *"Christ has redeemed us from the curse of the law, having become a curse for us." (Galatians 3.13a)* The spotless Lamb willingly shed His blood for our corrupt souls. Such determination overwhelms our feeble ponderings. Such divinity pierces our hearts with its saving intents. Such demonstration requires our zealous response:

5But He was wounded for our transgressions, He was bruised for our iniquities; the chastisement for our peace was upon Him, and by His stripes we are healed. 6All we like sheep have gone astray; we have turned, every one, to his own way; and the Lord has laid on Him the iniquity of us all. 7He was oppressed and He was afflicted, yet He opened not His mouth; He was led as a lamb to the slaughter, and as a sheep before its shearers is silent, so He opened not His mouth...10Yet it pleased the Lord to bruise Him; He has put Him to grief. When You make His soul an offering for sin, He shall see His seed, He shall prolong His days, and the pleasure of the Lord shall prosper in His hand. 11He shall see the labor of His soul, and be satisfied. (Isaiah 53.5–7, 10–11a)

Revelation 5.8–14

Verse 8- Now when He had taken the scroll, the four living creatures and the twenty-four elders fell down before the Lamb, each having a harp, and golden bowls full of incense, which are the prayers of the saints.

In response to the Lamb receiving the scroll from the Father, the four beings and the twenty-four elders fell prostrate before the Lamb to exalt and worship Him. In addition, each of the elders and each of the four beasts strummed their harps and expressed their worship through music. They also had golden vials that contained incense, which is described as "the prayers of the saints." *"Then another angel, having a golden censer, came and stood at the altar. He was given much incense, that he should offer it with the prayers of all the saints upon the golden altar which was before the throne." (Revelation 8.3)* This particular allusion likely serves to illustrate how the prayers of believers flow upward to God like smoke that rises from incense.

Verses 9, 10- ⁹And they sang a new song, saying: "You are worthy to take the scroll, and to open its seals; for You were slain, and have redeemed us to God by Your blood out of every tribe and tongue and people and nation, ¹⁰and have made us kings and priests to our God; and we shall reign on the earth."

These twenty-four elders and four beasts sang a new song unto the Lamb for being worthy of opening the seals of the scroll. Traditionally, this has been explained as a "new song" of redemption in contrast to the song of Moses that the Israelites sang beyond the Red Sea. *"Then Moses and the children of Israel sang this song to the LORD, and spoke, saying: 'I will sing to the LORD, for He has triumphed gloriously! The horse and its rider He has thrown into the sea!'" (Exodus 15.1)* More specifically, twenty-four elders and four beasts worshiped Him for Who He is and the things He has done that make Him worthy to open the scroll. The perfect cleansing power of Christ's blood has made redemption available to every person of any nation, tribe, or language. *"'Therefore take heed to yourselves and to all the flock, among which the Holy Spirit has made you overseers, to shepherd the church of*

God which He purchased with His own blood.'" (Acts 20.28) "'For God so loved the world that He gave His only begotten Son, that whoever believes in Him should not perish but have everlasting life.'" (John 3.16)

The Lord Jesus Christ, Redeemer of all believers, made His followers kings and priests unto God. *"And has made us kings and priests to His God and Father, to Him be glory and dominion forever and ever. Amen." (Revelation 1.6)* That we are described as "kings and priests" in this and other verses generally suggests two aspects of our relationship with God resulting from our redemption through Jesus Christ: 1) we have direct access to God, our High Priest; and, 2) we will reign with Him on the earth in His future Kingdom.[12] *(Revelation 20.6)*

Verses 11, 12- ¹¹Then I looked, and I heard the voice of many angels around the throne, the living creatures, and the elders; and the number of them was ten thousand times ten thousand, and thousands of thousands, ¹²saying with a loud voice: "Worthy is the Lamb who was slain to receive power and riches and wisdom, and strength and honor and glory and blessing!"

A choir of innumerable angels then joined in song with the four beasts and the twenty-four elders gathered around the throne. This multitude of heavenly beings loudly proclaimed that the Lamb slain from the foundation of the world was worthy of all exaltation because He is the only One who possesses all power, provisions, wisdom, strength, honor, and glory.

Verse 13- And every creature which is in heaven and on the earth and under the earth and such as are in the sea, and all that are in them, I heard saying: "Blessing and honor and glory and power be to Him who sits on the throne, and to the Lamb, forever and ever!"

Every living being in Heaven and on earth then joined this countless and magnificent choir. John witnessed all creation giving blessing, honor, glory, and power unto God the Father and unto the Lord Jesus Christ.

Verse 14- Then the four living creatures said, "Amen!" And the twenty-four elders fell down and worshiped Him who lives forever and ever.

The four beings declared, "Amen," thereby affirming the praise and worship that had been offered unto God the Father and the Lamb. The twenty-four elders then dropped to the ground again and poured out their worship to Him Who is worthy.

As is true of even the shortest and simplest verses in the Book of Revelation, much speculation is made about the deeper significance in even the smallest of details. Though many have sought to explain the identity of those represented in this passage, it should be more than sufficient to contend that more important than those who offered their worship is the One to Whom their worship was offered. The emphasis of these verses should never stray from the worthiness of the Lamb Who, as stated in this new song of praise, "[has] redeemed us to God." *(verse 9)*

Notes/Applications

Whereas the first passage revealed the Lamb, the Lord Jesus Christ, to be the only One worthy to open the seals of the scroll, this passage reveals Him to be the only One worthy to receive praise and glory.

He is worthy to receive all power, for He will never misuse it. He is worthy of all of the world's riches, for His riches are incorruptible. He is worthy of all wisdom, for all true wisdom comes from Him. He is worthy of all strength, for He is the source of strength and power. How can mortal words express due adoration to such a great Lord and Savior? Our most eloquent whispers or shouts fail in expressing the praise and glory due His name, for He Who is great has done great things. Isaac Watts, named the father of hymnody, has expressed the blessed dilemma of our loss for words when glimpsing Jesus:

What equal honors shall we bring
to Thee, O Lord our God, the Lamb,
When all the notes that angels sing
are far inferior to Thy Name?

Worthy is He that once was slain,
the Prince of Peace that groaned and died;
Worthy to rise, and live, and reign
at His Almighty Father's side.
Power and dominion are His due
Who stood condemned at Pilates' bar;
Wisdom belongs to Jesus too,
though He was charged with madness here.
All riches are His native right,
yet He sustained amazing loss;
To him ascribe eternal might,
Who left His weakness on the cross.
Honor immortal must be paid,
instead of scandal and of scorn;
While glory shines around His head,
and a bright crown without a thorn.
Blessings forever on the Lamb
Who bore the curse for wretched men;
Let angels sound His sacred Name,
and every creature say, Amen.[13]

Chapter Six

Revelation 6.1–8

Verse 1- Now I saw when the Lamb opened one of the seals; and I heard one of the four living creatures saying with a voice like thunder, "Come and see."

John witnessed Jesus opening the first seal, and a great, thunderous noise resounded. The opening of these seals signaled the beginning of the final judgments upon the earth and all of its inhabitants, a time unlike any creation would ever know.[1] *"'For then there will be great tribulation, such as has not been since the beginning of the world until this time, no, nor ever shall be.'" (Matthew 24.21)*

Some Greek texts contain only the word *come,* ερχου (erchou), while other texts employ the entire phrase *come and see,* και βλεπε (kai blepe). Therefore, many scholars debate the validity of the words as part of the original text, and as a result, the person being addressed by this command remains obscure.[2] Nevertheless, whether John was being summoned to come and observe these events as they unfolded or whether the horsemen appeared as a result of hearing this command, the result would be the same, and the events would remain unaffected. Jesus alone opened the seal, one of the four beings (introduced in 4.6) bellowed the command, and judgment immediately followed.

Verse 2- And I looked, and behold, a white horse. He who sat on it had a bow; and a crown was given to him, and he went out conquering and to conquer.

John saw a man carrying a bow and sitting upon a white horse. Some commentators ascribe this rider's identity as Jesus Christ in some veiled reference to His Second Coming as described in chapter nineteen.[3] This comparison, however, seems unlikely since it was the Lamb Himself Who opened the seal which brought forth this rider. Furthermore, this rider's authority, represented by the crown, was "given to him," signifying the sovereignty of a higher authority over this figure. The Lord would not need such permission since there exists no higher authority than His own. *"And Jesus came and spoke to them, saying, 'All authority has been given to Me in heaven and on earth.'" (Matthew 28.18)* Still other interpreters render this rider's identity as that of the antichrist, acknowledging that this being cannot be Christ yet contending that the similarities (primarily that of the white horse) cannot be ignored.[4]

Wisdom is perhaps best exercised while interpreting this verse by not requiring that the identity of the rider be established since this cannot be done with any certainty. Doing so, in fact, may assign more implication and consequence to this rider than was intended by the text. On the other hand, it can be said that this horse and rider symbolize that which we are told—a prevailing lust for ambitious conquests which will characterize the judgment that ensues the opening of the first seal.

Verses 3, 4- [3]When He opened the second seal, I heard the second living creature saying, "Come and see." [4]Another horse, fiery red, went out. And it was granted to the one who sat on it to take peace from the earth, and that people should kill one another; and there was given to him a great sword.

Jesus opened the second seal, and another of the four creatures exclaimed, "Come and see," whereupon John witnessed a second horse and rider. The color of the horse was red, which some commentators theorize signifies the color of blood and slaughter.[5] With the power of the great sword he was given, this rider instigated war all around the world. He did not directly battle with the inhabitants of the earth but initiated war throughout the world by removing all peace from it.

Verse 5- When He opened the third seal, I heard the third living creature say, "Come and see." So I looked, and behold, a black horse, and he who sat on it had a pair of scales in his hand.

The Lord opened the third seal, and the third creature like the others before it called out "Come and see." John observed a third rider sitting upon a black horse and gripping a set of balances in his hand. Balances weigh the exchange of merchandise and, in this verse, possibly serve as a symbol of the economy.

Verse 6- And I heard a voice in the midst of the four living creatures saying, "A quart of wheat for a denarius, and three quarts of barley for a denarius; and do not harm the oil and the wine."

John heard a voice emerge from amidst the four beasts seated around the throne, indicating that this was the Lamb's voice. The prevailing interpretation advocates that the black horse and its rider symbolize famine and economic destitution.[6] Most would also agree that the measurements mentioned in this verse show that one day's wages were only sufficient to attain one day's sustenance.[7]

Scholars agree less, however, on the interpretation of the command, "Do not harm the oil and the wine." Some argue that this emphasizes the economic and social inequality affecting the earth during this period of the final judgment.[8] It seems faithful to the text to maintain that the oil and wine symbolize the excessive availability of luxury items (which, of course, few could afford) concurring with the shortage of necessities.[9] This verse paints a picture of an abundance of luxurious items for those influential individuals who could afford them while life's basic provisions, such as bread, would become so scarce that people of average income would only be able to meet their needs on a day-by-day basis.

Verses 7, 8- ⁷When He opened the fourth seal, I heard the voice of the fourth living creature saying, "Come and see." ⁸So I looked, and behold, a pale horse. And the name of him who sat on it was Death, and Hades followed with him. And power was given to them over a fourth of the earth, to kill with sword, with hunger, with death, and by the beasts of the earth.

Jesus opened the fourth seal, and the last of the four creatures said, "Come and see." The fourth and final horseman appeared riding a pale horse. This is the first and only of the horsemen whose name we are told—Death. Unlike the other riders before him, Death was accompanied by another figure, identified as Hades. The mention of these two together suggests that Death was given the power to destroy one quarter of the world's population, and Hades followed closely behind to gather the victims.

Death was given power to kill one fourth of the world's population by four means: the sword, which describes man-made military weapons; hunger, which includes famine and perhaps a deliberate rationing of food supplies by those in authority; death, which denotes disease and pestilence having far-reaching effects; and finally, wild animals, which apparently become desperate for new food sources in a world devastated by war and famine. This description seems to be the fulfillment of a prophecy foretold by Ezekiel. *"For thus says the Lord God: 'How much more it shall be when I send My four severe judgments on Jerusalem—the sword and famine and wild beasts and pestilence—to cut off man and beast from it?'" (Ezekiel 14.21)*

Notes/Applications

The reprobate inhabitants of the earth will one day be judged for their unrepentant sinfulness. However, God also judges His faithful believers. Judgment is as much a part of God's love for His children as is blessing, but we often want to reject the truth. It is more pleasant for us to focus upon God's love than upon the fact that God is righteous and that righteousness fuels His judgment of sin. God is a just God. He does not reprimand sin because He is egocentric or egotistic or because He wants to spoil our fun. He disciplines us because He loves us. He wants us to be able to partake fully of His abundance, and He knows that our sinfulness yields heartache and destruction, thereby robbing us of lasting fulfillment and peace. When we sin, there are consequences, and we should expect to be reprimanded just as a child receives discipline from a parent. *"⁶Then the Lord answered Job out of the whirlwind, and said: ⁷'Now prepare yourself like a man; I will question you, and you shall answer Me: ⁸Would you indeed annul My judgment? Would you condemn Me that you may be justified? ⁹Have you an arm like God? Or can you thunder with a voice like His? ¹⁰Then adorn yourself with majesty and splendor, and array yourself with glory and beauty.'" (Job 40.6–10)*

God's perfect nature requires Him to discipline disobedience. However, God is longsuffering before He sends judgment, but when judgment does come, it is fixed and appropriate. Therefore, we must live in obedience to God's will even when it requires us to stand alone for the truth. *"⁹Therefore we make it our aim, whether present or absent, to be well pleasing to Him. ¹⁰For we must all appear before the judgment seat of Christ, that each one may receive the things done in the body, according to what he has done, whether good or bad." (2 Corinthians 5.9–10)*

Revelation 6.9–17

Verse 9- When He opened the fifth seal, I saw under the altar the souls of those who had been slain for the word of God and for the testimony which they held.

The Lord opened the fifth seal, and there appeared under the heavenly altar the souls of those who were martyred for their resolute faith in Jesus Christ. This was the only time that the opening of a seal did not prompt a specific act of judgment upon the world. Rather, it seems that this seal was deliberately opened to recognize those who had been martyred for the cause of Christ. The significance of them being under the altar is uncertain, but the scene paints a vivid picture of the sacrifice paid these martyrs, as if at the altar itself.[10] This group should not be understood to include all of God's elect because they have been specifically identified as martyrs. Obviously, all Christians should uphold a testimony that confirms the truth of God's Word, yet certainly not all Christians are killed because of it.

However, not all questions about this verse are answered by this conclusion. Some commentators believe that this group will consist only of those who are martyred between Christ's ascension and an expected pre-tribulation rapture while others suppose these to be tribulation martyrs only.[11] No part of this description suggests that this group is limited to anything less than *all* of those killed "for the Word of God and for the testimony which they held." Surely, those martyred for the sake of the gospel will be rewarded *(verse 11)*, but they will not receive their reward until their number is complete, that is, until the very last martyr gives his life as explained in the following verses.

Verse 10- And they cried with a loud voice, saying, "How long, O Lord, holy and true, until You judge and avenge our blood on those who dwell on the earth?"

The souls of these martyred believers gathered beneath the altar questioned how long it would be before the Almighty dispensed His justice. Even in the safety of Heaven's refuge, it appears that they were still able to remember the earthly horrors that they endured at the hands of those who opposed their faith. Naturally, they wanted justice. They petitioned the Lord, Who is holy and true, to "judge and avenge" their deaths upon the ungodly.

Verse 11- Then a white robe was given to each of them; and it was said to them that they should rest a little while longer, until both the number of their fellow servants and their brethren, who would be killed as they were, was completed.

White robes were presented to each of these souls that were under the altar, just as all those who have received the righteousness of Christ will one day be clothed:

'He who overcomes shall be clothed in white garments, and I will not blot out his name from the Book of Life; but I will confess his name before My Father and before His angels.' (Revelation 3.5) After these things I looked, and behold, a great multitude which no one could number, of all nations, tribes, peoples, and tongues, standing before the throne and before the Lamb, clothed with white robes, with palm branches in their hands. (Revelation 7.9)

These souls were told to "rest a little while longer," which appears to be the only answer God provided to their question regarding how long it would be until the Lord avenged their deaths. *(verse 10)* In a simple manner, it seems the response urged patience, for that time had not yet come.

Verse 12- I looked when He opened the sixth seal, and behold, there was a great earthquake; and the sun became black as sackcloth of hair, and the moon became like blood.

The Lord Jesus Christ opened the sixth seal, and the whole earth felt the result. There was an earthquake so sizeable and so violent that it affected the entire planet. Evidently, this earthquake disrupted the normal atmosphere, thereby influencing the climate and making the moon appear as the color of blood. *"'The sun shall be turned into darkness, and the moon into blood, before the coming of the great and awesome day of the Lord.'" (Acts 2.20)* Sackcloth is a material woven from goat or camel hair, generally very dark in color, and it is used here to describe the totality and depth of the darkness that covered the entire earth.[12]

Verses 13, 14- [13]***And the stars of heaven fell to the earth, as a fig tree drops its late figs when it is shaken by a mighty wind.*** [14]***Then the sky receded as a scroll when it is rolled up, and every mountain and island was moved out of its place.***

The stars of heaven fell to earth, resembling a tree losing its leaves in a strong wind. This could possibly describe a meteor shower breaking through a deteriorated atmosphere and having a devastating impact on the earth.[13] On the other hand, this verse might describe John's perception of the events more than serve as a literal, scientific explanation of what actually occurred.

The heavens rolled open as a scroll, and every mass of land shook from its foundation. All of the events described in these verses would occur in a self-perpetuating, self-sustaining series of reactions resulting in universal catastrophe. *"*[25]*'And there will be signs in the sun, in the moon, and in the stars; and on the earth distress of nations, with perplexity, the sea and the waves roaring;* [26]*men's hearts failing them from fear and the expectation of those things which are coming on the earth, for the powers of heaven will be shaken.'" (Luke 21.25–26)*

When the dust settled, the landmasses of the earth would look nothing like their former selves. Mountain ranges would be leveled, and islands would be moved miles from where they once rested.

Verses 15, 16- [15]***And the kings of the earth, the great men, the rich men, the commanders, the mighty men, every slave and every free man, hid themselves in the caves and in the rocks of the mountains,*** [16]***and said to the mountains and rocks, "Fall on us and hide us from the face of Him who sits on the throne and from the wrath of the Lamb!***

The sixth seal, unlike the five preceding it, affected all of mankind. This list, though not comprehensive, generally accounts for every person on earth.

People tried to hide themselves in the dens, caves, and crevasses of the mountains to escape the oncoming destruction.

However, the widespread devastation left no safe hiding place. *"Then they will begin 'to say to the mountains, "Fall on us!" and to the hills, "Cover us!"'" (Luke 23.30)* As a result, the earth's inhabitants could neither deny Who had caused this upheaval nor deny why these calamities had befallen them. The events which followed the breaking of these six seals would serve as indicators that God's judgment was imminent.

Verse 17- "For the great day of His wrath has come, and who is able to stand?"

As dreadful as these first six seals would be, they served only as the precursors to the coming judgment that John would witness. Declarations such as this were not a response to the devastation that had come upon the earth but rather were an acknowledgment that the worst was yet to come:

> *[14]The great day of the Lord is near; it is near and hastens quickly. The noise of the day of the Lord is bitter; there the mighty men shall cry out. [15]That day is a day of wrath, a day of trouble and distress, a day of devastation and desolation, a day of darkness and gloominess, a day of clouds and thick darkness, [16]a day of trumpet and alarm against the fortified cities and against the high towers. [17]'I will bring distress upon men, and they shall walk like blind men, because they have sinned against the Lord; their blood shall be poured out like dust, and their flesh like refuse.' [18]Neither their silver nor their gold shall be able to deliver them in the day of the Lord's wrath; but the whole land shall be devoured by the fire of His jealousy, for He will make speedy riddance of all those who dwell in the land. (Zephaniah 1.14–18)*

Men cannot conceive of the horrors that will befall them when the Day of the Lord approaches, yet God must deliver such judgment because He is eternally holy and just. This judgment, therefore, will be poured out in perfect righteousness. "Because He has appointed a day on which He will judge the world in righteousness by the Man whom He has ordained." (Acts 17.31a)

DIG DEEPER: *THE DAY OF WRATH*

The Day of the Lord is revealed as a day of terrible judgment when God's wrath will be poured out on His rebellious creation. This theme permeates the literature of the prophets and is found most often in the short book of Joel. *(Joel 2 and 3)* Joel also saw this day as a time when all of the elements of the universe would tremble at the voice of God's anger. Nothing can stand in the face of such fury, for *"who can endure the day of His coming? And who can stand when He appears? For He is like a refiner's fire and like a launderer's soap."* *(Malachi 3.2)*

Notes/Applications

A group of martyrs, those slain because of their testimony in Christ gathered under the altar in Heaven. These martyrs were given a very special blessing in Heaven for sacrificing their lives while they were upon the earth. In addition, the martyrs were presented white robes, garments of righteousness, yet they were told not to put them on until their fellow servants and their brethren were killed for their faith as well.

How valuable is Jesus to us? What price is too high to pay for a soul?

May we always live our Christian lives with the boldness to keep the testimony of our Redeemer upon our lips and, if necessary, be willing to pay the ultimate price of our lives for the same rather than deny the One Who paid the ultimate sacrifice for our salvation.

Chapter Seven

Revelation 7.1–8

Verse 1- After these things I saw four angels standing at the four corners of the earth, holding the four winds of the earth, that the wind should not blow on the earth, on the sea, or on any tree.

Sometime after the sixth seal had been opened and worldwide catastrophes had begun, an angel was seen standing at each of the four corners of the world. These angels kept the winds from blowing anywhere over the lands or seas. For the time being, all motion stopped, and not even a breeze fell upon a single tree. These four angels accomplished this at the command and by the will of Almighty God and the Lamb. In a sense, it was the calm before the storm.

Verses 2, 3- ²Then I saw another angel ascending from the east, having the seal of the living God. And he cried with a loud voice to the four angels to whom it was granted to harm the earth and the sea, ³saying, "Do not harm the earth, the sea, or the trees till we have sealed the servants of our God on their foreheads."

The purpose for this momentary calm was revealed. John saw an angel approaching from the east, and the angel had "the seal of the living God" with him. This seal was to be used to mark the foreheads of specific "servants of our God," whose identity will be explained in later verses. We cannot be sure about the form of this seal, but it was clearly the method by which Almighty God would distinguish this group from all others.

This angel commanded the other four angels not to hurt the earth or sea until God's servants had been sealed with this distinctive mark. The implication is that all people on the earth would be hurt when these angels were allowed to proceed, but God's servants were to be marked for protection.

Verse 4- And I heard the number of those who were sealed. One hundred and forty-four thousand of all the tribes of the children of Israel were sealed:

Unlike occasions where John was shown a multitude of countless beings described as "ten thousand times ten thousand, and thousands upon thousands" *(Revelation 5.11)* and "a great multitude which no one could number" *(Revelation 7.9)*, in this case, John heard an exact number of people who would have this seal of God on their foreheads. The number was 144,000, which was comprised of twelve thousand members from each of the twelve tribes of Israel. During this period of tribulation, these 144,000 would be sealed by God, so the entire world would know to Whom they belonged, and no one would be able to harm them. *(Revelation 9.4)*

There are some commentators who reject a literal interpretation of this group as being specifically 144,000 in number or Jewish in identity, and they instead consider this group to include the entire sum of believers on the earth during this time of judgment.[1] However, rarely is the Book of Revelation so clear and precise in its wording as it is in this passage, so it seems most logical in such cases to adhere to a literal interpretation.[2] Furthermore, most commentators tend to speculate about the significance of this group even though the Bible has very little to say about it. In reality, once the sealing has taken place, no more mention of this group is made until chapter fourteen, where we are given a little more detail about the character of those who comprised this group but are still told little about why they were ultimately singled out.

Verse 5- of the tribe of Judah twelve thousand were sealed; of the tribe of Reuben twelve thousand were sealed; of the tribe of Gad twelve thousand were sealed;

The individual tribes were named, which further supports the Jewish ethnicity of these 144,000.[3] Much conjecture arises from the difference in the order by which these tribes are listed in this passage as compared to the Old Testament. *(Exodus 1)* Again, wisdom is probably exercised by refraining from speculating about what we are not told.

The name *Judah* means "He shall be praised."[4] This tribe might be mentioned first because it is the one through which the Messiah came. The second tribe mentioned was *Reuben,* which means "See ye, a son," and the third tribe mentioned was *Gad,* which means "an invader."[5] Reuben and Gad fought alongside the other tribes on the western side of the Jordan until they conquered the land of Canaan, and they then returned to live on the eastern side. *(Numbers 32)* From each of these three tribes, God sealed the foreheads of twelve thousand people.

Verse 6- of the tribe of Asher twelve thousand were sealed; of the tribe of Naphtali twelve thousand were sealed; of the tribe of Manasseh twelve thousand were sealed;

The fourth tribe named was *Asher,* which means "happy," and the fifth tribe was *Naphtali,* which means "my wrestling."[6] These were some of the original tribes to settle in the land of Canaan. *(Numbers 34)* The sixth tribe was *Manasseh,* which means "causing to forget."[7] Manasseh was one of two sons of Joseph to be named a tribe and to receive a territorial allotment. *(Numbers 34.23–24)* Half of this very large tribe took its inheritance on the eastern side of the Jordan River with the tribes of Reuben and Gad, and the other half remained to occupy the western side of the Jordan River. *(Numbers 34.14)* From each of these three tribes, God sealed the foreheads of twelve thousand people.

Verse 7- of the tribe of Simeon twelve thousand were sealed; of the tribe of Levi twelve thousand were sealed; of the tribe of Issachar twelve thousand were sealed;

The seventh tribe named was *Simeon,* which means "hearkening."[8] This tribe was also among Canaan's original settlers. The tribe of Levi was listed eighth. *Levi* means "joined."[9] This tribe did not receive any territorial inheritance in the land of Canaan because it was appointed as the tribe of priests, and as such, the Lord was its inheritance. *"Then the LORD said to Aaron:'You shall have no inheritance in their land, nor shall you have any portion among them; I am your portion and your inheritance among the children of Israel.'" (Numbers 18.20)* The ninth tribe was *Issachar,* which means "there is a reward" or "he will bring reward."[10] From each of these three tribes, God sealed the foreheads of twelve thousand people.

Verse 8- of the tribe of Zebulun twelve thousand were sealed; of the tribe of Joseph twelve thousand were sealed; of the tribe of Benjamin twelve thousand were sealed.

The last three tribes listed were *Zebulun,* which means "dwelling;" *Joseph,* which means "let him add;" and *Benjamin,* which means "son of my right hand."[11] Joseph was listed instead of Ephraim because Ephraim was Joseph's second son. His first son was Manasseh, and Joseph's inheritance was divided between the two sons. *(Numbers 34.23–24)* From each of these three tribes, God sealed the foreheads of twelve thousand people. Each of the twelve tribes had equal representation of twelve thousand people.

DIG DEEPER: *WHERE'S DAN?*

The tribe of Dan is not among the tribes listed in Revelation even though it was one of the original twelve tribes of Israel. *(Numbers 1, 2, and 10)* One possible reason for this omission is that they despised their appointed heritage and pursued false gods. *(Judges 18)* Others believe that the antichrist will arise from the tribe of Dan because of certain biblical prophecies. *(Genesis 49:17; Jeremiah 8:16)*

Notes/Applications

One hundred forty-four thousand were sealed with the mark of God upon their foreheads, which revealed to Whom they belonged. We do not minimize that this mark confirmed God's special anointing upon a specific group of His followers; nevertheless, parallels may be drawn between the unique sealing of this group and every believer. At salvation, we are sealed with the Holy Spirit of God, and therefore, our lives will undeniably identify us as His children. *"26'I will give you a new heart and put a new spirit within you; I will take the heart of stone out of your flesh and give you a heart of flesh. 27I will put My Spirit within you and cause you to walk in My statutes, and you will keep My judgments and do them.'" (Ezekiel 36.26–27)*

When Christ illuminates our understanding, the Holy Spirit takes residence in our being. Our thought patterns, choices, values, priorities, and actions change as we live in response to His prompting in our lives. This sealing, however, does not only initiate the work of the Holy Spirit in our lives as our guide but also serves as our spiritual guarantee. It secures our souls so that no person, including ourselves, or evil force can separate us from God's love or from the work that He desires to accomplish in us. *"13In Him you also trusted, after you heard the word of truth, the gospel of your salvation; in whom also, having believed, you were sealed with the Holy Spirit of promise, 14who is the guarantee of our inheritance until the redemption of the purchased possession, to the praise of His glory." (Ephesians 1.13–14)* No matter what physical harm we may encounter, we are assured that our eternal destiny is with Him in His glory. *"3For you died, and your life is hidden with Christ in God. 4When Christ who is our life appears, then you also will appear with Him in glory." (Colossians 3.3–4)*

Can we trace the hand of the Holy Spirit's guidance in our life? Do we rest in the assurance that we are sealed with the Holy Spirit for all eternity?

Revelation 7.9–17

Verse 9- After these things I looked, and behold, a great multitude which no one could number, of all nations, tribes, peoples, and tongues, standing before the throne and before the Lamb, clothed with white robes, with palm branches in their hands,

After John had witnessed the sealing of the 144,000, he saw a great multitude of people standing before the Lamb and before the throne of God Almighty. These were people of various nationalities, races, and countries, Jews and Gentiles alike, and their number was so great that they could not be counted.

Conflicts surface in almost every attempt to specify the identity of this group. It seems unfounded to presume that this is the one and same group as the 144,000, given the difference in their countless numbers and the inclusion of "all nations, tribes, peoples, and tongues."[12] Identifying this group as only tribulation martyrs seems an injustice to other Scriptures of hope intended for martyrs throughout the ages and to the entire sum of faithful believers. *(Ephesians 1.18–21; 1 Peter 1.3–5; and Revelation 3.1–5)* Perhaps the best explanations are those which place the timing of this vision beyond the tribulation events yet to be explained. With an interpretation as heartening as any available, nineteenth-century commentator Albert Barnes observes:

> The design seems to be to carry the mind forward quite beyond the storms and tempests of earth...to that period when the church should be triumphant in heaven. Instead, therefore, of leaving the impression that the hundred and forty-four thousand would be all that would be saved, the eye is directed to an innumerable host, gathered from all ages, all climes, and all people, triumphant in glory...The object of the vision is to cheer those who are desponding in times of religious declension and in seasons of persecution, and when the number of true Christians seems to be small, with the assurance that an immense host shall be redeemed from our world, and be gathered triumphant before the throne.[13]

These believers were in their resurrected bodies, as evidenced by their situation before the throne and their being clothed in white robes, which signifies the righteousness that they had received through salvation in Christ Jesus. The palm fronds in their hands appear to be symbolic of Christ's royalty and victory.[14]

Verse 10- and crying out with a loud voice, saying, "Salvation belongs to our God who sits on the throne, and to the Lamb!"

This multitude had been rescued from the consequences of sin and from the clutches of the curse. They praised God Almighty, Who sits upon His heavenly throne, and the Lamb, Who bought their salvation with His blood at Calvary.

Verses 11, 12- [11]All the angels stood around the throne and the elders and the four living creatures, and fell on their faces before the throne and worshiped God, [12]saying: "Amen! Blessing and glory and wisdom, thanksgiving and honor and power and might, be to our God forever and ever. Amen."

The angels, the elders, and the four beasts were also gathered around the throne and joined the multitude in worship. The angels began and concluded their worship by declaring, "Amen," thereby confirming the truth of what they said. They thanked God for salvation and acknowledged Him as being all-powerful. Because of Who He is and what He has done, God alone is worthy of all blessing, glory, wisdom, thanksgiving, honor, power, and might.

Verse 13- Then one of the elders answered, saying to me, "Who are these arrayed in white robes, and where did they come from?"

One of the elders inquired about the identity and origin of those wearing the white robes. Perhaps it was a rhetorical question posed to John, a witness of this vision, so that the answers to this question could be verbally explained to remove any doubt and speculation about the identity of this group arrayed in white.[15]

Verse 14- And I said to him, "Sir, you know." So he said to me, "These are the ones who come out of the great tribulation, and washed their robes and made them white in the blood of the Lamb.

John replied to the elder, "Sir, you know," which allowed the elder to answer his own question and, in turn, explain the scene to John.

The elder informed John that the ones dressed in the white robes were those who had "come out of the great tribulation." Despite the use of the definite article the before great tribulation, some commentators insist that this multitude included all believers saved throughout history by Jesus Christ's atonement at Calvary.[16] Others contend that this group consists of the same martyrs mentioned in chapter six, including the "fellow-servants" and "brethren" for whom they were waiting. Notwithstanding the elder's account of this group, it remains uncertain just which and how many of Heaven's host comprised this countless multitude. At the very least, the wording of this description supports an interpretation that this vision, though witnessed by John in the first century, is a scene of Heaven some time after the close of the tribulation period.[17]

Verse 15- "Therefore they are before the throne of God, and serve Him day and night in His temple. And He who sits on the throne will dwell among them.

Only because this multitude had the righteousness of Christ were they even able to stand before the throne both day and night to worship Him without ceasing. To be in His presence was the indescribable joy and peace with which they worshipped Him both day and night. These saints remained faithful and loyal to God while in their earthly bodies, and they now received their reward of eternal life in His presence.

Verses 16, 17- [16]"They shall neither hunger anymore nor thirst anymore; the sun shall not strike them, nor any heat; [17]for the Lamb who is in the midst of the throne will shepherd them and lead them to living fountains of waters. And God will wipe away every tear from their eyes."

These worshippers would never again feel the pains of hunger and thirst as they had in their mortal bodies. There are two reasonable interpretations. First, they would no longer experience physical hunger or thirst for the food and water that sustained the lives of their earthly bodies. The implication is that believers will never want for sustenance in Heaven because it is simply not required. Their lives are no longer physical, and therefore, they will not need physical nourishment.[18] Second, the multitude no longer hungered or thirsted spiritually as they had in their physical lives on earth because they were in the presence of the Lord. In their mortal bodies, they craved a closer fellowship with their Creator, but in Heaven, this desire would be fulfilled by perfect communion with God Almighty. These believers were secure in the care of the Good Shepherd.

Also, the sun's light no longer shined upon the inhabitants in Heaven because the light in Heaven was God Himself. He is the source of all light and *is* light; therefore, in Heaven, the sun will not be necessary. *"The city had no need of the sun or of the moon to shine in it, for the glory of God illuminated it. The Lamb is its light." (Revelation 21.23)*

The Lamb would lead them unto the living fountains of water. *"'But whoever drinks of the water that I shall give him will never thirst. But the water that I shall give him will become in him a fountain of water springing up into everlasting life.'" (John 4.14) "And the Spirit and the bride say, 'Come!' And let him who hears say, 'Come!' And let him who thirsts come. Whoever desires, let him take the water of life freely." (Revelation 22.17)* God would also wipe away the tears from their eyes. *"And God will wipe away every tear from their eyes; there shall be no more death, nor sorrow, nor crying. There shall be no more pain, for the former things have passed away.'" (Revelation 21.4)*

Notes/Applications

What exactly is Heaven like? Early twentieth century evangelist William E. Bierderwolf said, "Heaven would hardly be heaven if we could define it."[19] Although Scripture does not disclose a detailed pictorial of Heaven's panorama, these verses give characteristics of the glorious, unparalleled place where believers will spend eternity:

⁹For we know in part and we prophesy in part. ¹⁰But when that which is perfect has come, then that which is in part will be done away. ¹¹When I was a child, I spoke as a child, I understood as a child, I thought as a child; but when I became a man, I put away childish things. ¹²For now we see in a mirror, dimly, but then face to face. Now I know in part, but then I shall know just as I also am known. (1 Corinthians 13.9–12)

Heaven is the eternal dwelling for Christ followers of all ethnicities and many denominations. There, believers will eternally dwell within the Father's presence and worship Him as the glorious Creator, Sustainer, and Redeemer. As Puritan pastor Ezekiel Hopkins (1634–1690) said, Heaven is "where the unveiled glories of the Deity shall beat full upon us, and we forever sun ourselves in the smiles of God."[20]

Hunger, thirst, and physical ailment—they will fade with every other lingering vapor of this life. Even still, one of the most comforting messages about our heavenly home is the sweet assurance that "God will wipe away every tear from their eyes." *"²²'Therefore you now have sorrow; but I will see you again and your heart will rejoice, and your joy no one will take from you.'" (John 16.22)* Sorrows that have darkened the corridors of our present lives will have no reign over our days in the new heaven and new earth where the light of God's righteousness will be our delight:

There is a land
Of pure delight.
Where saints immortal reign.
Infinite day excludes the night
And pleasure banish pain.

There everlasting spring abides
And never withering flowers.
Death, like a narrow sea
Divides this heavenly land from ours.

Sweet fields beyond
This swelling floods
Stand dressed in living green.[21]

When we ponder with wonder the magnificence of our eternal home, how can we not join the heavenly beings' song of worship? *"Salvation belongs to our God who sits on the throne, and to the Lamb…Blessing and glory and wisdom, thanksgiving and honor and power and might, be to our God forever and ever."* (Revelation 7.10b, 12)

Chapter Eight

Revelation 8.1–6

Verse 1- When He opened the seventh seal, there was silence in heaven for about half an hour.

Chapter seven reads somewhat like an intermission. It explains an event (the sealing of the 144,000) that had to take place before God's judgment would continue. The Lamb had opened six seals *(chapter 6)*, and now, at last, He opened the final seal whereupon there was a pause in Heaven. It is not clear whether this silence, lasting about half an hour, was noticeable upon the earth. If so, it served as a dramatic pause, a brief respite between the destruction of the first six seals and the calamities that would follow the opening of the seventh.[1]

Some scholars propose that the seven seals, seven trumpets, and seven bowls are concurrent judgments of God.[2] It appears more probable that these sets of seven would occur consecutively and follow a chronological progression of increasing intensity.[3] The opening of five of the first six seals would result in devastation, and the opening of the seventh seal would usher in the trumpet judgments.

Verse 2- And I saw the seven angels who stand before God, and to them were given seven trumpets.

Upon the opening of the seventh seal, John observed seven angels who stood before the Lord with seven trumpets. Evidently, these trumpets announced impending judgment.

Verse 3- Then another angel, having a golden censer, came and stood at the altar. He was given much incense, that he should offer it with the prayers of all the saints upon the golden altar which was before the throne.

Another angel, not one of the seven angels with trumpets, came with a golden censer before God's altar in Heaven. The angel's role in this scene should be understood merely as offering the prayers to the Lord and not as making the prayers acceptable to Him. Our prayers need no such intervention.[4] *"'For the eyes of the LORD are on the righteous, and His ears are open to their prayers.'"* (1 Peter 3.12a) The emphasis that there was *much* incense given to the angel may be indicative of the volume of prayers rising toward God.

Verse 4- And the smoke of the incense, with the prayers of the saints, ascended before God from the angel's hand.

The smoke rose from the angel's hands toward God. This indicates that God's throne was positioned significantly higher than the altar and higher than the elders, the four beasts, the angels, and the multitude of glorified believers gathered around His throne.

Verse 5- Then the angel took the censer, filled it with fire from the altar, and threw it to the earth. And there were noises, thunderings, lightnings, and an earthquake.

The angel filled the censer with fire from the altar, cast the fire to earth, and brought an end to the silence that followed the opening of the seventh seal. This action resulted in thunder and lightning and another great earthquake, yet all of this was mere preparation for what was yet to come.

Verse 6- So the seven angels who had the seven trumpets prepared themselves to sound.

God's seven angels with the seven trumpets assembled together and readied themselves to sound their trumpets individually at His command. With that, the next series of judgments was ready to begin.

Notes/Applications

This passage draws a dismal picture of God's judgment that will befall the earth and the ensuing destruction. However, fears are assailed by the assurance of knowing that God has heard and collected the prayers of His saints in much the same way one keeps treasured love-letters in a keepsake box. *"18If I regard iniquity in my heart, the Lord will not hear. 20Blessed be God, Who has not turned away my prayer, nor His mercy from me!" (Psalm 66.18, 20)*

God's will is that we pray whether or not we get our way. Our main motivation should not be to unload a shopping list of our desires when we pray. Thankfully, we serve a compassionate God Who allows us to vent our frustrations and petitions, but nevertheless, prayer should be considered as an active expression of our worship. As a result of blessed fellowship in His presence, our thoughts, emotions, attitude, and total being can be brought into conformity with His will. That is the type of praying modeled by our Lord Jesus Christ as He anticipated His own death the cross. *"41He knelt down and prayed, 42saying, 'Father, if it is Your will, take this cup away from Me; nevertheless not My will, but Yours, be done.'" (Luke 22.41b–42)*

Perhaps we wonder if God hears our prayers, if they get past the ceiling, or if they do any good. God is a faithful Father Who does hear the prayers of His children—those who have committed their lives to Him—and Who does answer petitions according to His timing. A response may not be immediately obvious to us or come in the form of "handwriting in the sky." Those moments when Heaven appears to be silent try our faith and trust in a God Who is alive and loving, just, and holy. We may find ourselves in one of life's waiting rooms where we have a choice to make. We can choose to draw closer to the Lord than we ever dared, or we can become a willing target for Satan's attempts to plant doubts in our mind with questions: *Does God really care for me? Why is God allowing this to happen when I have served Him the best I know how? God, do you really love me?*

God does love us—immensely and unfathomably. His silence is evidence that He intentionally takes His time, His perfect time, to craft the best for His children. He does not settle for what is only good for us; He designs the best.

When we get to Heaven, how many love-letters will God have from us? What joy we would gain just by being in communion with the God of the universe, and what an amazing spiritual adventure we forfeit when we do not pray as we should. Let us not allow Satan to convince us otherwise. Our time in prayer is well spent. We do not pray in vain, and our Heavenly Father values the prayers of His saints. "*³'Now we know that God does not hear sinners; but if anyone is a worshiper of God and does His will, He hears him.'*" (John 9.31)

Revelation 8.7–13

Verse 7- The first angel sounded: And hail and fire followed, mingled with blood, and they were thrown to the earth. And a third of the trees were burned up, and all green grass was burned up.

The sounding of the first angel's trumpet unleashed hail and fire that was mingled with blood falling from the sky. This hail and fire storm destroyed one third of the world's vegetation, including fruits and vegetables. Such an occurrence would surely affect the subsistence of all living beings. Perhaps this occurred simultaneously with the violent thunderstorms and devastating earthquake that were already ravaging the earth. These afflictions were evidently heaped one upon the other as the soundings of the trumpets progressed.[5]

The description of these elements as being "mingled with blood" has roused many diverse theories. Though men often go to great lengths to account for divine experiences with rational, physical explanations, there is no reason to disregard the possibility that there could be literal blood falling from above with hail and fire. Such terrifying signs would surely attest that these events would be direct judgments from the hand of Almighty God. *"And I will show wonders in the heavens and in the earth: blood and fire and pillars of smoke.'" (Joel 2.30)*

Verse 8- Then the second angel sounded: And something like a great mountain burning with fire was thrown into the sea, and a third of the sea became blood.

When the second angel sounded his trumpet, a "great mountain burning with fire" was cast into the sea. Opinions differ among scholars as to what this might mean. Some believe it to be an active volcano erupting and casting unimaginable amounts of lava into the seas.[6] Others believe that this describes an asteroid or comet breaking through the atmosphere and falling into the sea.[7] Whereas the latter interpretation is preferred, it again should be understood that this would not be some rare natural phenomenon but a specific medium created by God for judgment. This mass of fire would upset the world's bodies of salt water, and upon impact, one third of the sea would turn to blood.

Verse 9- And a third of the living creatures in the sea died, and a third of the ships were destroyed.

One third of all marine life perished in the world's oceans, though this seems unlikely to be the cause for the seas turning to blood. Rather, it is evidence of divine judgment, similar to that experienced by Pharaoh at the hands of Moses as recorded in the Old Testament. *"Then the Lord spoke to Moses, 'Say to Aaron, "Take your rod and stretch out your hand over the waters of Egypt, over their streams, over their rivers, over their ponds, and over all their pools of water, that they may become blood."'" (Exodus 7.19a)* Also, a third of the world's sailing vessels were destroyed, adversely affecting travel, commerce, and naval defenses worldwide.

Verse 10- Then the third angel sounded: And a great star fell from heaven, burning like a torch, and it fell on a third of the rivers and on the springs of water.

When the third angel sounded his trumpet, a great star fell from the sky upon one third of the earth's fresh water sources, such as rivers, lakes, and streams. A third of the earth's saltwater bodies had just been destroyed with the second trumpet judgment, and now a third of the fresh water bodies were also destroyed. Mankind could manage for a while without food, but it could not last very long without water.

Verse 11- The name of the star is Wormwood. A third of the waters became wormwood, and many men died from the water, because it was made bitter.

Wormwood is a poisonous plant, and it is used figuratively to name this star of destruction.[8] Apparently, the water contamination caused by this event infiltrated even into wells and reservoirs, and many people died as a result of consuming water that they evidently assumed to be safe.

Verse 12- *Then the fourth angel sounded: And a third of the sun was struck, a third of the moon, and a third of the stars, so that a third of them were darkened. A third of the day did not shine, and likewise the night.*

The fourth angel blew his trumpet, and celestial bodies were changed, thereby affecting the earth. A third of the sun, moon, and stars were impacted. Seasons and tides were likely altered because of the lunar changes. As a result, days would only be two-thirds as bright as before, and nights would become a third darker as well. Some have interpreted this passage to mean that one third of the day and one third of the night (approximately sixteen of every twenty-four hours) would be shrouded in total darkness.[9]

Verse 13- *And I looked, and I heard an angel flying through the midst of heaven, saying with a loud voice, "Woe, woe, woe to the inhabitants of the earth, because of the remaining blasts of the trumpet of the three angels who are about to sound!"*

The Greek word translated in this verse as *angel* would be more accurately interpreted as *eagle*.[10] However, neither interpretation changes the meaning of the verse.

This being flew around Heaven and loudly proclaimed that the people of the earth were doomed not by those calamities that had already come upon them but by those that were still appointed for them. As horrific as these catastrophes that had befallen the earth were, this dreadful pronouncement warned that the judgments yet to occur would be far worse. Once again, it seems that such a declaration was made more for the benefit of John and his readers than for those inhabitants of the earth during this period of judgment.[11]

DIG DEEPER: *WOE!*

"Woe" is the ancient cry of Israel's prophets. It is the cry of judgment against those who have disobeyed God. It occurs sixty-three times in the Bible from Isaiah through Zechariah. Jesus Himself warned of impending judgment throughout the gospels. There are thirty-one occurrences in which Jesus pronounced, "Woe." This one exclamation is the most consistent theme of judgment throughout the Bible and culminates here in Revelation as final judgment is pronounced on unbelievers.

Notes/Applications

God's holy judgment will fall upon the earth as justice for man's sins. However, despite catastrophic events that should propel mankind to seek Almighty God's forgiveness, people will still refuse to submit to Him in repentance. Instead, they will harden their hearts with hatred toward Him. As a consequence, God's wrath will continue to visit them. When the time of this tribulation comes, people will realize that the destruction befalling them is the judgment of the Almighty, but they will still not turn from their wicked ways. *"²⁰But the rest of mankind, who were not killed by these plagues, did not repent of the works of their hands, that they should not worship demons, and idols of gold, silver, brass, stone, and wood, which can neither see nor hear nor walk. ²¹And they did not repent of their murders or their sorceries or their sexual immorality or their thefts." (Revelation 9.20–21)*

This passage serves as a sober reminder that today is the day of salvation. *"Behold, now is the accepted time; behold, now is the day of salvation." (2 Corinthians 6.2b)* The time for responding to the Lord's call upon our lives is now. When we are confronted by the truth of the gospel, whether that call is unto salvation or a deeper commitment, we should yield to the Spirit without expecting another opportunity. Future opportunities may or may not come, for we ourselves do not control the Spirit's power. *"'The wind blows where it wishes, and you hear the sound of it, but cannot tell where it comes from and where it goes. So is everyone who is born of the Spirit.'" (John 3.8)*

The present is the only time that we have to be obedient to God and to do His will as He directs us. We are never promised another tomorrow. *"Do not boast about tomorrow, for you do not know what a day may bring forth." (Proverbs 27.1)* Any and every day could be the last day of our own life or the life of another to whom we should be offering hope through sharing the good news that salvation in Jesus Christ, our Blessed Hope, alone can preserve and protect us no matter the circumstances that we face.

Chapter Nine

Revelation 9.1–12

Verse 1- Then the fifth angel sounded: And I saw a star fallen from heaven to the earth. To him was given the key to the bottomless pit.

The fifth angel sounded his trumpet, and the first of the final three woes began. *(Revelation 8.13)* Unlike the star that fell from Heaven after the third trumpet sounded *(Revelation 8.10)*, it is commonly agreed upon that this star depicts an angel. Since the angel is described as "fallen from heaven," some believe that this angel is Satan or another fallen angel.[1] However, it seems more likely that this angel is one of God's own because the key was given to him presumably by the One Who holds the keys and has the authority to delegate such responsibilities.[2] *(Revelation 20.1–3)* Once the angel was given the key, he was sent to the earth to open the bottomless pit.

Verse 2- And he opened the bottomless pit, and smoke arose out of the pit like the smoke of a great furnace. So the sun and the air were darkened because of the smoke of the pit.

As the angel opened the bottomless pit, a huge cloud of smoke erupted and bellowed out of the abyss. This massive cloud of smoke choked out the already diminished sunlight of day, causing the skies to become dark from its magnitude. It was as though an enormous furnace had been opened whose smoke had inundated the earth and swallowed up much of its light.

Verse 3- *Then out of the smoke locusts came upon the earth. And to them was given power, as the scorpions of the earth have power.*

From this immense cloud of smoke emerged a swarm of locusts. It is likely that John witnessed a multitude of locusts so dense and so vast that they appeared as a great cloud of smoke.

In the past, God sent a plague of locusts upon Egypt to judge Pharaoh for not releasing the Israelites from captivity. *(Exodus 10.3–6)* These locusts, however, were far different than those in Moses' day. The locusts described in this verse were given the ability to inflict painful stings like that of a scorpion. The description of these creatures, given in verses seven through ten, further supports that these were not some mutant variety evolved from common locusts but a specific creation well-suited to fulfill this purpose.

Verse 4- *They were commanded not to harm the grass of the earth, or any green thing, or any tree, but only those men who do not have the seal of God on their foreheads.*

These locusts were commanded not to consume any of the earth's vegetation, which would be their natural diet. God created this cloud of locusts to execute His judgment—to afflict mankind. However, they were told not to hurt those bearing the seal of God on their foreheads.

The specific habitation (bottomless pit) and task (torment) of these creatures suggest that they were demonic in nature. Nevertheless, they were controlled by Almighty God, Who alone held the sovereign authority both to empower them with the capacity to cause anguish and also to limit the scope of their attack.[3]

Verse 5- And they were not given authority to kill them, but to torment them for five months. Their torment was like the torment of a scorpion when it strikes a man.

These locusts were further commanded not to kill the ungodly men and women but rather only to torture them. Their stings caused painful, severe welts from which there was no relief for five months. This means either that the venom that they had caused pain and illness to the victim for five months or that these creatures would be loosed upon the earth for five months. In either case, the hardship upon mankind would be overwhelming and nearly unbearable during this period. God had appointed a very specific duration of suffering in which these locusts swarmed the earth and afflicted the entire population of unbelievers.

Verse 6- In those days men will seek death and will not find it; they will desire to die, and death will flee from them.

The pain and agony caused by these locusts would be so intense that men would want to die to obtain relief from their torment. They would envision death as an escape from the pain of the world, but God would not allow any to escape His judgment before the duration of its appointed time. It appears that many will even consider taking their own lives, though such attempts would also be futile since life and death are under the sovereign control of Almighty God. *"Now see that I, even I, am He, and there is no God besides Me; I kill and I make alive; I wound and I heal; nor is there any who can deliver from My hand." (Deuteronomy 32.39)*

Verses 7, 8- ⁷The shape of the locusts was like horses prepared for battle. On their heads were crowns of something like gold, and their faces were like the faces of men. ⁸They had hair like women's hair, and their teeth were like lions' teeth.

The locusts appeared as horses dressed in full war armor as though prepared to go into battle. On their heads sat crowns that looked like gold. Their faces were as those of men, meaning that they had human features, likely eyes, noses, and mouths. They had something that resembled long, flowing hair like that of a woman.

They also had teeth like a lion for ripping and tearing. These locust-like creatures probably ate flesh since they were denied a diet of vegetation and were told instead to hurt mankind.

Verses 9, 10- ⁹And they had breastplates like breastplates of iron, and the sound of their wings was like the sound of chariots with many horses running into battle. ¹⁰They had tails like scorpions, and there were stings in their tails. Their power was to hurt men five months.

These strange locusts were arrayed in armor. They possessed breastplates that were as strong as, and may have even looked like, iron. The sounds of their wings, unlike the chirping song of a common locust, were as a galloping stampede of horses charging into battle.

As explained in verse five, their main weapons were the tails with which they were given power to hurt mankind for five months. Again, despite mankind's intense, unrelenting anguish, they would be made to endure this suffering and would not be allowed any relief through death.

Verse 11- And they had as king over them the angel of the bottomless pit, whose name in Hebrew is Abaddon, but in Greek he has the name Apollyon.

The locusts had a leader, the "angel of the bottomless pit." The name for the king of these demons in Hebrew is *Abaddon,* which means "destruction," and in Greek, *Apollyon,* which means "destroyer."[4] The locusts over which he ruled were truly equipped for inflicting destruction, sorrow, and pain. They would physically, mentally, and emotionally torment by destroying the peace, comfort, and health of the ungodly.

Verse 12- One woe is past. Behold, still two more woes are coming after these things.

The first of the final three woes was completed, and two more were still pending. The woes would grow progressively worse, each one more intense and horrific than the last.

Notes/Applications

During the tribulation, God will seal a remnant of 144,000 with His mark in their foreheads. *"²Then I saw another angel ascending from the east, having the seal of the living God. And he cried with a loud voice to the four angels to whom it was granted to harm the earth and the sea, ³saying, 'Do not harm the earth, the sea, or the trees till we have sealed the servants of our God on their foreheads.'" (Revelation 7.2–3)*

Similarly, as Christians, we are sealed with the Holy Spirit of promise. *"In Him you also trusted, after you heard the word of truth, the gospel of your salvation; in whom also, having believed, you were sealed with the Holy Spirit of promise." (Ephesians 1.13)* God will not lose any of His own because His sealing remains eternally secure. Neither human hands nor spiritual being can break the King's signet upon the souls of His heirs. *"'My Father, who has given them to Me, is greater than all; and no one is able to snatch them out of My Father's hand.'" (John 10.29)*

If we do not grieve the Holy Spirit by Whom we are sealed, we will be strong in Christ and able to pass the tests when they come. Our strength comes from a daily empowering from the Holy Spirit, whereas our readiness depends upon our obedience to His precepts. Let us live every day honoring the One Who has sealed us from His wrath and judgment by emulating to others the grace, mercy, and forgiveness that He has demonstrated to us. *"³⁰And do not grieve the Holy Spirit of God, by whom you were sealed for the day of redemption. ³¹Let all bitterness, wrath, anger, clamor, and evil speaking be put away from you, with all malice. ³²And be kind to one another, tenderhearted, forgiving one another, even as God in Christ forgave you." (Ephesians 4.30–32)*

Revelation 9.13–21

Verses 13, 14- ¹³Then the sixth angel sounded: And I heard a voice from the four horns of the golden altar, which is before God, ¹⁴saying to the sixth angel who had the trumpet, "Release the four angels who are bound at the great river Euphrates."

The sixth angel sounded his trumpet and ushered in the second woe. As the trumpet sounded, a voice echoed from the four horns of the golden altar. He told the angel that blew the sixth trumpet to release the four angels that were bound at the River Euphrates. These were apparently fallen angels that had been bound and restrained from causing destruction until this very moment of judgment.[5] We observe again that the commands given were authoritative in facilitating the execution of the order, and so we must conclude that this voice belonged to the Lord Jesus Christ, Who is sovereign over all judgments in occurrence, timing, and intensity.

DIG DEEPER: *EUPHRATES RIVER*

The Euphrates River plays a major role in several biblical events. It was one of the four original rivers that flowed through the Garden of Eden. *(Genesis 2.10, 14)* Abraham was living in the area of the Euphrates when he was chosen to be the father of God's people. *(Genesis 15.18)* God spoke to the prophet Jeremiah by the Euphrates River. *(Jeremiah 51.60–64)* This river has been fruitful both in blessings and in curses, depending on God's purposes.

Verse 15- So the four angels, who had been prepared for the hour and day and month and year, were released to kill a third of mankind.

The four angels released from the Euphrates River had been prepared for this specific moment in time. *(Isaiah 54.16)* Each element of God's judgment always begins exactly at its preordained time and only lasts for its determined duration. This sixth trumpet judgment would be far worse than any that preceded it. These four angels were commanded to kill one third of mankind.

The historicist viewpoint suggests that this judgment coincides with the eleventh-century conquests of the Turks throughout western Asia.[6] However, wars are a natural consequence of a sinful world, and the judgments described in this passage reveal events of a supernatural magnitude and outcome that greatly transcend the extent of any historical event.[7]

Verse 16- Now the number of the army of the horsemen was two hundred million; I heard the number of them.

The four angels brought with them an army of two hundred million soldiers mounted on horses. Some commentators insist that this number is to be taken figuratively and serves only to illustrate the enormity of the group.[8] The emphasis of this verse, though, seems to dispute such suppositions. It is uncertain whether the Holy Spirit made the number known to John or whether a nearby angel directly told him the number. Whatever the case, in order to remove any speculation that John exaggerated the scale of this army, he informed his readers that he "heard the number of them." This would be the largest army ever assembled in the history of the world, though it has been debated whether this army would be comprised of human forces or spiritual agents.[9]

Verse 17- And thus I saw the horses in the vision: those who sat on them had breastplates of fiery red, hyacinth blue, and sulfur yellow; and the heads of the horses were like the heads of lions; and out of their mouths came fire, smoke, and brimstone.

Most commentators agree that the descriptions given in the following verses depict an army of demons and not of actual men.[10] The riders wore breastplates of red, blue, and yellow. The heads of the horses resembled lions, which again indicates that these were not mutations of actual animals but were demons. They were creations not of this world, and their purpose was strictly and solely to destroy. Out of their mouths emerged fire, smoke, and brimstone, drawing some comparisons to the description of the leviathan in the Old Testament. *"19'Out of his mouth go burning lights; sparks of fire shoot out. 20Smoke goes out of his nostrils, as from a boiling pot and burn-*

ing rushes. ²¹His breath kindles coals, and a flame goes out of his mouth.'"
(Job 41.19–21)

Verse 18- By these three plagues a third of mankind was killed—
by the fire and the smoke and the brimstone which came out of
their mouths.

Whereas the first woe brought anguish upon the world, this second woe brought death. It was by these three elements that one third of all mankind would be slain. Many people would be burned to death, and some would die as a result of smoke inhalation or, perhaps, by the absorption of brimstone into their lungs. It appears that the horse-like beasts did the actual killing and not the riders themselves.

One quarter of the world's population would be killed by "Death and Hades" during the judgment of the fourth seal *(Revelation 6.8)*, and one third of the remaining population would be killed by this vast army during the judgment of the sixth seal. Regardless of the size of the world's population at the time of these events, the mathematical equation yields staggering results—the death of one half of the world's total population as a result of these two judgments.

Verse 19- For their power is in their mouth and in their tails; for
their tails are like serpents, having heads; and with them they do
harm.

These demons were given power to destroy with their mouths and also with their serpent-like tails. Although they were able to inflict injury with their tails, their ability to kill came from the fire, smoke, and brimstone of their mouths. We can assume that, though not all would be killed, most of the world's population would be injured.

Verses 20, 21- ²⁰But the rest of mankind, who were not killed by
these plagues, did not repent of the works of their hands, that
they should not worship demons, and idols of gold, silver, brass,
stone, and wood, which can neither see nor hear nor walk. ²¹And
they did not repent of their murders or their sorceries or their
sexual immorality or their thefts.

Despite the unimaginable death and destruction caused by these first two woes, those that were not killed by these beasts still did not repent of their wicked ways and seek after the Lord God Almighty. In fact, their hearts were only further hardened against God. They continued to worship false idols made of gold, silver, brass, stone, and wood—idols that could not respond to their worshippers. When they sought help from these gods, none would be found. Likewise, they refused to repent of their murder, sorcery, immorality, and thievery, which only serves as further evidence of their utterly corrupt hearts.

Some speculate that this lack of repentance shows that these judgments did not generate the anticipated response.[11] To believe such, however, suggests that God's extensive display of His power would have no effect. Nevertheless, time and again, man's only response is a similar lack of repentance. *(Revelation 9.20–21; 16.9, 11)* Are we, then, to believe that the "great day of the Lord," this culmination of God's final judgment upon His reprobate creation, would be in some way ineffectual? No. We must understand that the purpose of God's judgment is to carry out justice not to evoke repentance. *"⁵Therefore put to death your members which are on the earth: fornication, uncleanness, passion, evil desire, and covetousness, which is idolatry. ⁶Because of these things the wrath of God is coming upon the sons of disobedience." (Colossians 3.5–6) "But in accordance with your hardness and your impenitent heart you are treasuring up for yourself wrath in the day of wrath and revelation of the righteous judgment of God." (Romans 2.5)* Therefore, it seems more accurate to conclude that the judgment of God was upon the inhabitants of the earth, and the opportunity for repentance had passed.

DIG DEEPER: *REPENT*

Repentance is a fundamental tenet of Christian doctrine. Without repentance, man cannot be reconciled to God. The summation of Jesus' proclamation to the masses was centered on this theme of repentance. *(Matthew 4.17)* In the Book of Revelation, the consequences of continued rebellion against the Creator and Redeemer are fully described—failure to repent demands inescapable judgment.

Notes/Applications

When we read the above passages, it is hard to imagine a world of people so callused against God that they refuse to repent even when confronted with the reality that their punishment has ensued due to their disobedience. John Donne, a sixteenth century poet, said it well:

So fond are mortal men

Fall'n into wrath divine,

As their own ruin upon themselves to invite.

Such presumptuous attitudes are the undercurrents carrying our society from the distant shores of truth. Sinful lifestyles have become tolerable and even *acceptable* within every aspect of modern culture. Consider the boldness of evil—widespread violence, thoughtless and spontaneous murders, countless abortions, increasing acceptability of euthanasia, rampant sexual perversity, and reckless disregard for others' lives and property. Such indifference for human life has become so commonplace that we do not even blink when we hear of such trespasses against the Creator's original design. Even Christians have become desensitized to such acts and adopt the worldly attitude of "live and let live" rather than stand against sin.

We must never allow society's moral decay to become our standard for living or to become a release from our responsibilities as Christians. The Lord remains the same yesterday, today, and forever, and so, too, His commission remains unaltered. Regardless of the moral state of the world around us and of the overwhelming nature of the task, we must boldly testify of the love and grace of the Lord Jesus Christ to a lost, complacent, and dying world.

The only way to even consider accomplishing such a task remains the same today as it was a thousand years ago. We must reach people individually, one soul at a time, by telling them of the good news—the Lord Jesus Christ is alive, He *does* hear and see, and He is always present by the Holy Spirit. As the first century Roman author Valerius Maximus noted, "The divine wrath is slow indeed in vengeance, but it makes up for its tardiness by the severity of the punishment."[12] As His redeemed, let us obey our Lord and not incur His chastisement upon ourselves.

Chapter Ten

Revelation 10.1–7

Verse 1- I saw still another mighty angel coming down from heaven, clothed with a cloud. And a rainbow was on his head, his face was like the sun, and his feet like pillars of fire.

A mighty angel descended from Heaven to earth. Commentators disagree about this angel's identity. Some of them offer evidence to suggest that this being is Gabriel or another heavenly archangel.[1] Others see him as just another angel, such as appears in previous chapters.[2] *(Revelation 7.2, 8.3)* However, all indications given in this passage suggest that this was not a typical angel or any other created being but that this was an appearance of the Lord Jesus Christ Himself.[3] That the Lord should be described as an angel and not specifically identified as Jesus Christ should no more forbid such an interpretation than His being called "One like the Son of Man" *(Revelation 1.13)* or a Lamb *(Revelation 5)*. Neither should His making an oath to "Him who lives forever and ever" *(verse 6)* be considered something inappropriate or out of character.[4] *"For when God made a promise to Abraham, because He could swear by no one greater, He swore by Himself." (Hebrews*

6.13) Furthermore, in reading the continuation of this passage in the next chapter, we observe the angel declaring, "*I will give power to my two witnesses" (Revelation 11.3)*, thereby revealing this same Being as a source of both authoritative empowerment and divine association.

The description further supports the conclusion that this angel is the Lord Jesus Christ.[5] He was "clothed with a cloud" *(Exodus 13.21; Numbers 10.34; Luke 21.27; and Revelation 14.14–15)*; His head was encircled by a rainbow, symbolizing the covenant between God and His creation *(Ezekiel 1.28 and Revelation 4.3)*; His face was "like the sun," another familiar description of Christ in Scripture *(Matthew 17.1–2 and Acts 26.13)*; and His feet were dazzling in radiance like "pillars of fire." *(Daniel 10.6 and Revelation 1.15)*

Verse 2- He had a little book open in his hand. And he set his right foot on the sea and his left foot on the land,

The Angel stood upon the earth with one foot upon land and the other upon the sea, which demonstrates the Lord's sovereignty over the entire earth, including all land masses and all bodies of water as great as the oceans and as small as brooks and streams. *"5For I know that the Lord is great, and our Lord is above all gods. 6Whatever the Lord pleases He does, in heaven and in earth, in the seas and in all deep places." (Psalm 135.5–6)* He held a small, opened book in His hand. As we will see later in this chapter, there were prophecies in this book that were to be revealed.

Verse 3- and cried with a loud voice, as when a lion roars. When he cried out, seven thunders uttered their voices.

The Angel called out with a loud voice like that of a roaring lion, which again draws parallels to other scriptural references that depict the voice of the Lord. *(Jeremiah 25.30; Hosea 11.10; Amos 3.8; and Joel 3.16)* As the Angel cried out, John heard seven distinct "thunders" speak, possibly in response to the call. It is possible that these seven thunders, like the seven seals and six of the seven trumpets that preceded them, were elements of judgment ordained by Almighty God.[6]

Verse 4- Now when the seven thunders uttered their voices, I was about to write; but I heard a voice from heaven saying to me, "Seal up the things which the seven thunders uttered, and do not write them."

John apparently understood the message uttered by the seven thunders because he was prepared to record them like he did everything else he had seen and heard to that point. However, a voice from Heaven instructed John not to write down what the thunders had revealed. Rather, the voice told John to seal up those things that he had heard the thunders disclose and not to include them as part of his message.

It cannot be determined with any certainty why John would even mention a situation about which he was not permitted to elaborate. It is possible that what he heard was so sacred or so dreadful that it would be beyond our ability to comprehend.[7] It should suffice, though, to recognize that God is under no obligation to disclose everything that He will bring to pass but only those things that He wants us to know.[8] *"'The secret things belong to the LORD our God, but those things which are revealed belong to us and to our children forever, that we may do all the words of this law.'" (Deuteronomy 29.29)*

Verses 5, 6- [5]The angel whom I saw standing on the sea and on the land raised up his hand to heaven [6]and swore by Him who lives forever and ever, who created heaven and the things that are in it, the earth and the things that are in it, and the sea and the things that are in it, that there should be delay no longer,

As He stood across the land and sea, the Angel lifted up His hand to Heaven and vowed that all John saw and heard was true and certain. He declared this oath before the eternal Creator of the heavens, the earth, the seas, and everything living within them. As stated earlier, it should not be presumed by this act that this Angel could not be an appearance of the Lord. *"For when God made a promise to Abraham, because He could swear by no one greater, He swore by Himself." (Hebrews 6.13)* As His hand was raised toward Heaven, the Angel announced that there should not be any further delay, which affirmed that the time of God's final judgment was at hand.

Verse 7- but in the days of the sounding of the seventh angel, when he is about to sound, the mystery of God would be finished, as He declared to His servants the prophets.

The stage is set. Six angels had sounded their trumpets *(Revelation 8.6–9.21)*, and the sounding of the seventh trumpet was imminent. It was time for the "mystery of God" to be completed. Time had almost run out, and the final judgment had come due. All that the Lord had made known through the prophets about the events of the final days would be revealed and fulfilled. The atrocious events to this point were but a foretaste of the impending calamities to be ushered in with the sounding of the seventh trumpet.

DIG DEEPER: *THE MYSTERY OF GOD*

This mystery is not unknown to the people of God. The mystery had been declared hundreds of years earlier to the prophets. Paul told the church at Colossi, "The mystery which has been hidden from ages and from generations, but now has been revealed to His saints. To them God willed to make known what are the riches of the glory of this mystery among the Gentiles: which is Christ in you, the hope of glory." *(Colossians 1.26–27)* With the sounding of the seventh trumpet, the mystery of God would be revealed to those who do not believe, and they will at last understand their judgment.

Notes/Applications

The Angel told John not to record anything that he saw and heard uttered by the seven thunders. The Angel's instructions likely related to man's inability to believe such incredible things escorting creation closer toward the final days of this world.

Sand continually slips through the slender neck of time's hourglass, and with every passing moment go forfeited opportunities. There will not always be opportunities to obey God, to speak a kind word, to write a letter, or to touch a life by investing ourselves in others.

Scripture admonishes us to redeem time because the present day is our only ample opportunity to serve the Lord God Almighty.

"15See then that you walk circumspectly, not as fools but as wise, 16redeeming the time, because the days are evil." (Ephesians 5.15–16) May the following poem remind us to cherish the time God has appointed for us by being wise stewards of it:

My Name Is Time

My name is Time; I am the present moment,
I am on the move, I measure out life.
Some men welcome me, some men fear me,
Some could not care less, but none can stop me
I have not always been, nor will I always be.
God says I am running out
and He is in control.
When I stop, when I am no longer now,
Eternity keeps on going
and it will be too late for getting right with God,
too late for faith in Christ.
Nothing will be left
but forever and its regrets.

My name is Time. Can you tell me?
If you redeem me, you will find me good.
If you use me, you will find me precious.
My name is Time. I am nearing the end,
and I shall take you with me into eternity.

–selected

Revelation 10. 8–11

Verses 8, 9- *⁸Then the voice which I heard from heaven spoke to me again and said, "Go, take the little book which is open in the hand of the angel who stands on the sea and on the earth." ⁹So I went to the angel and said to him, "Give me the little book." And he said to me, "Take and eat it; and it will make your stomach bitter, but it will be as sweet as honey in your mouth."*

John was directed to go and take the little book from the Angel's hand. This was an authoritative command, presumably by God Himself, directing John to do something that he likely would not have otherwise done, being intimidated by such a magnificent and powerful Angel.[9] John demonstrated obedience while facing such a troubling and overwhelming experience. He approached the Angel and asked for the book, whereupon the Angel gave him the book and instructed John to eat it. It is generally agreed that this was a symbolic gesture whereby John was to absorb the book's contents with complete understanding.[10] *"But you, son of man, hear what I say to you. Do not be rebellious like that rebellious house; open your mouth and eat what I give you."' (Ezekiel 2.8)*

The Angel warned John that the book would be very sweet in his mouth but bitter in his stomach. Many expositors suggest that the book epitomizes the Word of God, which contains the joy of the gospel message and the path of salvation as well as the certain and inescapable judgment and wrath of God.[11] It seems clear within the context of the entire passage that John was instructed to understand fully the contents of the book, so he could convey them to others at a later time.[12]

Verse 10- Then I took the little book out of the angel's hand and ate it, and it was as sweet as honey in my mouth. But when I had eaten it, my stomach became bitter.

John obeyed what the Lord had told him to do, and the Angel's warning proved to be true. He ate the book, and although it was sweet in his mouth, it soon became bitter in his stomach. *"Moreover He said to me, 'Son of man, eat what you find; eat this scroll, and go, speak to the house of Israel.' ²So I opened my mouth, and He caused me to eat that scroll. ³And He said to me, 'Son of man, feed your belly, and fill your stomach with this scroll that I give you.' So I ate, and it was in my mouth like honey in sweetness." (Ezekiel 3.1–3)* It was surely thrilling for John to "eat" the book and be directly involved in the divulgence of the truth contained within. However, upon "digesting" its contents, the reality of its truth and its corresponding judgments soon weighed heavily upon him.

Verse 11- And he said to me, "You must prophesy again about many peoples, nations, tongues, and kings."

The Angel told John that he would prophesy again, though opinions differ regarding whether he would be prophesying "to" or "about" these many nations and leaders. The preposition translated as *about* in this version is perhaps better expressed as *against*, such that John would testify both "to" *and* "about" these many people.[13] He recorded everything he had seen and heard in this great vision so that all mankind throughout the ages could likewise be able to understand the message and be warned of the impending judgment.

Notes/Applications

A lesson can be learned from John's experience in the preceding passage to the impact that the Word of God has on believers' lives. God has gifted us with the Bible as an instruction book concerning His principles and precepts by which we should conduct our lives. The Word is always sweet to us as we read it because it registers a true witness within our spirits. However, when we "digest" the Holy Word, when we seek to apply it to our lives, it becomes bitter as it clashes with our human nature. *"For the word of God is living and powerful, and sharper than any two-edged sword, piercing even to the division of soul and spirit, and of joints and marrow, and is a discerner of the thoughts and intents of the heart." (Hebrews 4.12)* The Word corrects us as it cuts away the chaff of selfishness and self-centeredness. It implores us to trust and obey that which is godly rather than that which is human.

Praise the Lord that He has given us a glimpse of His script for the end of the world, and He is victorious! We can celebrate the ending yet still mourn the events that creation must endure before this ending will be realized. Surely, this must have been similar to what John experienced when he took and ate the little book the Angel presented to him. Such truth is bitter to experience but, oh, so sweet to know:

Come, divine Interpreter,
Bring me eyes Thy book to read,
Ears the mystic words to hear,
Words which did from Thee proceed,
Words that endless bliss impart,
Kept in an obedient heart.
All who read, or hear, are blessed,
If Thy plain commands we do;
Of Thy kingdom here possessed,
Thee we shall in glory view
When Thou comest on earth to abide,
Reign triumphant at Thy side.[14]

Chapter Eleven

Revelation 11.1–2

Verse 1- Then I was given a reed like a measuring rod. And the angel stood, saying, "Rise and measure the temple of God, the altar, and those who worship there.

Despite the numerous interpretive difficulties found in the Book of Revelation, many consider this passage to be the most challenging to explain.[1] Though this chapter is a continuation of the previous chapter, we are immediately confronted with a shift of events that provokes many questions and stirs vast controversy while inspiring few substantial resolutions. Verses one and two, specifically, appear almost as an isolated incident in which a command is given that reveals no obvious relationship with the events preceding it or with those following it.

As with the little book he had been commanded to take from the Angel's hand and eat, John was again required to play an active role in these prophetic visions. Rather than merely observing and recording the events that he witnessed, he was instructed to participate in them as they unfolded. The Angel introduced in the previous chapter handed John a reed, likely a cane stem similar to those common in the Jordan valley which grew upward to twenty feet in height.[2] With this reed, John was instructed to measure "the temple of God, the altar, and those who worship there."

What does this "temple of God" refer to? This is a question that has perplexed scholars and commentators for centuries. How one attempts to explain the issue can have inescapable bearing on the interpretation of other scriptural passages from Old and New Testaments alike.

Determining whether this is a literal temple or a symbolic one lies at the core of any interpretation. Most scholars who favor a literal interpretation of these two verses suggest that they refer to a temple that has yet to be rebuilt in the last days for the reinstitution of Jewish offering and sacrifices.[3] In this scenario, then, John was commanded to take a physical measurement of a future temple in Jerusalem. Some preterists also view this as a literal temple, though they see it as the first-century temple before its destruction in AD 70 by Titus, the notorious Roman emperor.[4] However, it seems highly improbable that the temple referred to in this passage should be understood as literal or physical.[5] The primary difficulty in supporting a literal interpretation lies in the difficulty of proving the biblical substantiation for an end-times temple since the Lord has rendered the temple sacrifices ineffectual with His own sacrifice at Calvary. *"In that He says, 'A new covenant,' He has made the first obsolete."* *(Hebrews 8.13a)* Furthermore, it seems very unlikely that John would be instructed to measure people ("those who worship") with a measuring rod, the same tool with which he was to measure the temple and the altar.

It seems more plausible, therefore, that this temple is to be understood in a spiritual sense. *(1 Peter 2.4–5)* Even many preterists, who might find more reasons than most to view this as a literal temple, agree.[6] The strongest and most common interpretation is that the three elements, "the temple of God, the altar, and those who worship there," comprise one unit representing the universal Church— the body of true believers on the earth.[7] This interpretation also benefits from more New Testament support, wherein the temple is redefined as the body of every believer indwelled with the Holy Spirit. *"Do you not know that you are the temple of God and that the Spirit of God dwells in you?" (1 Corinthians 3.16) "For you are the temple of the living God. As God has said: 'I will dwell in them and walk among them. I will be their God, and they shall be My people.'" (2 Corinthians 6.16b)*

The command to measure, therefore, is not to be accomplished in a physical sense but a judicial one.[8] The Angel instructed John to account for all those included within the body of Christ—the true believers. This explanation does not necessarily answer the question of *why* John was commanded to measure. Many commentators argue that this act of measuring in some way implies the protection of God over His people during the tribulation.[9] However, based on the text itself, this or any other explanation is simply speculation.

Verse 2- "But leave out the court which is outside the temple, and do not measure it, for it has been given to the Gentiles. And they will tread the holy city underfoot for forty-two months.

The Angel further instructed John not to measure the court outside the temple. Again, this should be taken as a symbolic gesture, though what exactly is represented is uncertain. Some commentators argue that the outer court refers to those professing to belong to the church but who are not true believers, such as those addressed in chapter two for adhering to the doctrines of Balaam *(2.14)* and Jezebel *(2.20)*.[10] Others insist that both delineations refer to the church but from two different perspectives—the temple of God depicting the spiritual preservation of God's faithful in troublesome times and the outer court illustrating the imminent hostility of the antichrist against them.[11] Finally, many believe that the court represents not just imposters within the true church but the entire sum of unbelievers.[12] The Greek word rendered as "Gentiles" in this verse is more accurately translated as "nations," denoting groups of people that are not necessarily segregated by ethnicity.[13] This lends more support to the credibility of the third interpretation. Such an explanation implies that this is not a separation of Jews from non-Jews but of believers from unbelievers.

The reference to forty-two months, as with every other aspect of this passage, has received vastly differing interpretations. Some scholars have allocated these as 1,260 days of years (1,260 years) in an allusion to the rise of the Roman papacy.[14] Others altogether dismiss this as being a specific period of time and instead suggest that these forty-two months symbolize the limitation of evil's free reign over God's faithful.[15] However, this is the first of many times that this specific time period is mentioned in the Book of Revelation, and the duration is depicted in several different ways: forty-two months *(11.2, 13.5)*, 1,260 days *(11.3, 12.6)*, and three and a half years *(12.14)*. It appears that this is done to avoid confusion. Therefore, it seems most likely that this refers to a literal three-and-a-half year period of time during which the antichrist will rise to power and persecute all believers. Again, we have evidence of God's preordained limitation to this persecution.

Many commentators designate "the holy city" as another representation of the true Church.[16] However, the Scriptures specifically refer to Jerusalem as the holy city. *(Nehemiah 11.1; Isaiah 52.1; Daniel 9.24; and Matthew 27.53)* Nevertheless, this could be both a physical and symbolic element of the prophecy. For forty-two months, the nations (the unbelievers) would trample (with violent aggression) the holy city (the believers and/or the city of Jerusalem) under foot (having dominion over them).

Notes/Applications

Whether the reader ascribes to the interpretation that this would be a literal or symbolic temple, the predominant theme of this passage is that the temple of God is more than buildings of physical matter. It is comprised of people that matter to God, and God Himself "measures" the hearts of His people. He weighs their thoughts, motives, and deeds. He determines them as lacking or growing. He discerns them as committed or carnal.

What is the condition of our temple? As individuals, we are either a house of God or a house of Satan. Our lives will tell the story. *"[16]Do you not know that you are the temple of God and that the Spirit of God dwells in you? [17]If anyone defiles the temple of God, God will destroy him. For the temple of God is holy, which temple you are." (1 Corinthians 3.16–17) "For you are the temple of the living God. As God has said: 'I will dwell in them and walk among them. I will be their God, and they shall be My people.'" (2 Corinthians 6.16b)*

Revelation 11.3–8

Verse 3- "And I will give power to my two witnesses, and they will prophesy one thousand two hundred and sixty days, clothed in sackcloth."

Obviously, the One speaking to John was also the One who would empower these two witnesses. It should not be presumed that such authority exists in any created being, and therefore, this verse is the best evidence that the speaker was indeed the Lord Jesus Christ.

God would empower "two witnesses" to prophesy for 1,260 days (three and a half years), the same duration of time that Jerusalem would be trodden under foot. *(verse 2)* One commonly accepted interpretation proposes that these two witnesses would not actually be two individuals but are a symbolic representation of the witnessing church.[17] Many who endorse this position point to biblical principles requiring two witnesses for legal testimony.[18] *(Deuteronomy 19.15)* This argument aside, there seems little convincing evidence to nullify the straightforward presentation of this passage. It is apparent that these would be two specific individuals prepared and empowered by God to fulfill a unique purpose during an appointed time.[19]

These two witnesses were dressed in sackcloth, which was a dark, coarse material usually made of goat or camel hair.[20] It was customarily worn as a gesture of mourning. *(Genesis 37.34; 2 Samuel 3.31; 1 Kings 21.27; Esther 4.1; and Isaiah 15.3)* Though we are not specifically told about their message, we can safely presume that these two warned people about God's impending judgment and urged them to repent.

Verse 4- These are the two olive trees and the two lampstands standing before the God of the earth.

This verse parallels an Old Testament prophecy of Zechariah concerning Joshua and Zerubbabel:

[11]Then I answered and said to him, 'What are these two olive trees—at the right of the lampstand and at its left?' [12]And I further

answered and said to him, 'What are these two olive branches that drip into the receptacles of the two gold pipes from which the golden oil drains?' [13]Then he answered me and said, 'Do you not know what these are?' And I said, 'No, my lord.' [14]So he said, 'These are the two anointed ones, who stand beside the Lord of the whole earth.' (Zechariah 4.11–14)

It is unclear whether this verse is simply a reference to the earlier prophecy or the ultimate fulfillment of it. At the very least, the similarities between these two passages are unmistakable. The entire world would know that these two witnesses were servants of the Lord.

Verse 5- And if anyone wants to harm them, fire proceeds from their mouth and devours their enemies. And if anyone wants to harm them, he must be killed in this manner.

During the three and a half years that these two witnesses prophesy, no one would be allowed to hurt them. Any who tried would be killed by fire expelled from the witnesses' mouths. If this is to be understood literally, we should not doubt that God is certainly able to defend His prophets with such a remarkable phenomenon. *"So Elijah answered and said to the captain of fifty, 'If I am a man of God, then let fire come down from heaven and consume you and your fifty men.' And fire came down from heaven and consumed him and his fifty."* (2 Kings 1.10) However, it seems equally plausible to understand this as a figurative expression similar to that spoken of by the prophet Jeremiah.[21] *"Therefore thus says the LORD God of hosts: 'Because you speak this word, behold, I will make My words in your mouth fire, and this people wood, and it shall devour them.'"* (Jeremiah 5.14)

Verse 6- These have power to shut heaven, so that no rain falls in the days of their prophecy; and they have power over waters to turn them to blood, and to strike the earth with all plagues, as often as they desire.

The two witnesses would be given the power to stop rain from falling and to summon other types of plagues upon the earth during the 1,260 days that they would be prophesying. To compound the innumerable problems caused by such a great drought, they would be able to turn whatever waters remained into blood. These powers were given to them to be used at their discretion.

Many scholars have devised theories regarding the identity of these two witnesses. Some speculate that the witnesses will be Moses and Elijah, two Old Testament figures who appeared at Jesus' transfiguration, as witnessed by Peter, James, and John. *(Matthew 17)* This conclusion is also drawn because of the similar powers that Moses and Elijah possessed while on the earth.[22] *(Exodus 7.17; Exodus 8.12; and 1 Kings 17.1)* Other commentators agree that Elijah will be one of the two witnesses based upon the Old Testament prophecy concerning him. *(Malachi 4.5)* However, because Moses died *(Deuteronomy 34.5)*, many conclude that the other witness must be Enoch since neither he nor Elijah ever experienced a physical, earthly death.[23]

Whereas either of these theories are legitimate possibilities, the fact remains that God has chosen these two witnesses from the beginning of time and their identity is known only to Him. They could just as easily be Christians that arise from among those living during this period of time. They need not be powerful, influential men, for it is the Lord Who will empower them.

Verse 7- *When they finish their testimony, the beast that ascends out of the bottomless pit will make war against them, overcome them, and kill them.*

Once the two witnesses had completed their three-and-a-half-year mission, the beast of the bottomless pit would execute them. Based on previous references in Revelation, one might be inclined to identify this beast as the same "angel of the bottomless pit" named Apollyon. *"And they had as king over them the angel of the bottomless pit, whose name in Hebrew is Abaddon, but in Greek he has the name Apollyon." (Revelation 9.11)* However, this is the first of thirty-six references in Revelation to a different beast that plays a major role in the events of the last days and who is commonly identified as the antichrist.[24] In this verse, the allusion to the bottomless pit should be understood in a broader sense as an indicator of this beast's Satanic origin.[25]

For 1,260 days, these two witnesses were invincible under the power of God's protection. At the appointed time, though, God would withdraw His safeguard and allow the antichrist to triumph over them.

Verse 8- And their dead bodies will lie in the street of the great city which spiritually is called Sodom and Egypt, where also our Lord was crucified.

The two witnesses were not given proper burial, but instead, their corpses were laid upon the streets of "the great city" for all to see. The clarification of this city as being the same one "where also our Lord was crucified" seems to leave little room to doubt that this could be any place other than Jerusalem.[26] Nevertheless, some expositors insist that this city is Rome or at least represents a revived Roman empire.[27] Others believe that this should not be identified with any particular city but that it is indicative of the paganism existing throughout all civilizations.[28]

This city was compared spiritually to Sodom and Egypt. In the Old Testament, evil and perversion abounded in Sodom and its sister city Gomorrah. *(Genesis 13.13, 18.20–21)* Sodom, then, represents the profusion of wickedness in the city, whereas the spiritual comparison to Egypt typifies unrestrained persecution and oppression of God's people. *(Exodus 3.7–9)*

Notes/Applications

Although our human curiosities bid the contrary, it is not necessary to reach an absolute conclusion regarding the identity of these two witnesses, for phenomenal results transpire not from superior people accomplishing such miracles but from a supernatural Almighty God empowering His vessels to perform the wondrous things for which He has preordained them.

We may shrink when we consider the witnesses' mission. We would probably even deem their assignment to be undesirable. Perhaps we would dodge such spiritually weighty tasks, ones requiring our bowing to the Lord's calling, yet Scripture reminds us not only to be obedient in our willingness to serve but to be content in the area of service the Lord prescribes for us as well. *"¹²I know how to be abased, and I know how to abound...¹³I can do all things through Christ who strengthens me." (Philippians 4.12a–13)*

We unwittingly pray according to our perception of how the Lord should use us. We unintentionally live according to our perception of reasonable commitment. How entangled we become by the limits we place upon the Sovereign God and His power.

God's plan surpasses human analysis. His righteousness never fails, and His perfection never ends. He will intricately weave together the events of our lives into a significant witness, but such significance begins with ministry founded upon obedience, surrender, and service. Some areas of ministry will be less glamorous, less comfortable, and even less safe. Nevertheless, Christ followers must willingly give themselves, trusting that the Lord will achieve His purposes through them.

Revelation 11.9–19

Verse 9- Then those from the peoples, tribes, tongues, and nations will see their dead bodies three-and-a-half days, and not allow their dead bodies to be put into graves.

The corpses of the two witnesses would lie in the street for three and a half days where the whole world could see them. How much these two must have been despised! How offensive their message of judgment must have been that their deaths would be treated with such utter disregard! No one would even remove their bodies from where they lay in the streets. Of course, they were hated not only for the message they proclaimed but also because they kept rain from falling and poured out plagues upon the earth for three and a half years.

Verse 10- And those who dwell on the earth will rejoice over them, make merry, and send gifts to one another, because these two prophets tormented those who dwell on the earth.

People all around the world celebrated the deaths of these witnesses who had tormented them for so long. The two corpses remained in the street serving as symbols of victory. Both the elated response of the people and the duration of time that these witnesses lay dead in the streets draw an evident parallel to the death and resurrection of Jesus Christ. *(John 16.19–20; Mark 8.31)* The most obvious similarity, though, was about to take place.

Verse 11- Now after the three-and-a-half days the breath of life from God entered them, and they stood on their feet, and great fear fell on those who saw them.

At the end of three and a half days, God's power again fell upon the two witnesses, whereupon life reentered their bodies. They stood to their feet where moments earlier their lifeless bodies had been. The people's rejoicing came to an abrupt halt, and those who witnessed the miracle were gripped with paralyzing fear.

Verse 12- And they heard a loud voice from heaven saying to them, "Come up here." And they ascended to heaven in a cloud, and their enemies saw them.

Upon being summoned to "come up here" by a voice which was surely that of the Lord, the two witnesses disappeared into a cloud and were taken into Heaven. This, too, seems to parallel the account of the Lord's own ascension. *"Now when He had spoken these things, while they watched, He was taken up, and a cloud received Him out of their sight." (Acts 1.9)* Upon watching the two miraculously ascend into the sky, the crowd surely must have reconsidered some of the things that these two had preached.

Verse 13- In the same hour there was a great earthquake, and a tenth of the city fell. In the earthquake seven thousand people were killed, and the rest were afraid and gave glory to the God of heaven.

Within the same hour that the two witnesses were called up into Heaven, a devastating earthquake rocked the great city, resulting in the deaths of seven thousand people and in the destruction of one tenth of the city. "The rest," all those who were spared from the anni- hilation, were motivated by fear to glorify Almighty God in Heaven.

Verse 14- The second woe is past. Behold, the third woe is com- ing quickly.

The second woe, the judgment of the sixth trumpet, was com- pleted. The third and final woe, the judgment of the seventh trum- pet, was imminent.

Verse 15- Then the seventh angel sounded: And there were loud voices in heaven, saying, "The kingdoms of this world have become the kingdoms of our Lord and of His Christ, and He shall reign forever and ever!"

The seventh angel blew the seventh trumpet, unleashing God's final judgments upon the earth. The sounding of this last trumpet initiated the pouring out of the seven bowls of God's wrath, as described in chapter sixteen.

Loudly, but in one accord, many voices in Heaven responded, proclaiming that the kingdoms of earth belonged to the Lord Jesus Christ. There was tremendous excitement and anticipation that this long-awaited moment was finally at hand.

Verses 16, 17- ¹⁶And the twenty-four elders who sat before God on their thrones fell on their faces and worshiped God, ¹⁷saying: "We give You thanks, O Lord God Almighty, the One who is and who was and who is to come, because You have taken Your great power and reigned.

The twenty-four elders gathered around God's throne fell prostrate before the Lord in worship. *(Revelation 4.10–11)* The elders praised the Lord with thanksgiving for asserting His rightful position as King of kings. The elders also rejoiced that the reign of evil upon the earth approached completion, and the time for the Lord Jesus Christ to rule the earth was at hand. *"Which He will manifest in His own time, He who is the blessed and only Potentate, the King of kings and Lord of lords." (1 Timothy 6.15)*

Verse 18- The nations were angry, and Your wrath has come, and the time of the dead, that they should be judged, and that You should reward Your servants the prophets and the saints, and those who fear Your name, small and great, and should destroy those who destroy the earth."

At this point, mankind had not responded to God's judgments with repentance but with anger. Though the final outpouring of God's wrath had yet to take place, the result was as fixed and certain as though it had already occurred, and the elders rejoiced over the outcome.[29]

Those who endured persecution for Christ, labored for Christ, prophesied for Christ, lived for Christ, and died for Christ would receive their reward—eternal life in Heaven. Those who lived in their sin and rejected the salvation of Christ would also receive their just punishment. The saints would triumph over those who had exacted violence and destruction upon God's people while on the earth.

Verse 19- Then the temple of God was opened in heaven, and the ark of His covenant was seen in His temple. And there were lightnings, noises, thunderings, an earthquake, and great hail.

Whereas the temple in Heaven which John beheld can be understood as a literal temple, it should not necessarily be understood as some colossal, physical structure situated in the clouds. Within this heavenly temple, opened wide for John to see, sat the "ark of His covenant." It should not be presumed that this was the tangible, historical ark, which had long since been destroyed, lost, or concealed from the world. Rather, this object seems most likely to serve as some reminder of God's covenant with His people.[30]

The sounding of the seventh trumpet also resulted in an extensive display of great atmospheric upheaval. Thunder, lightning, earthquakes, and hail were also unleashed at the opening of the seventh seal *(Revelation 8.1–5)* and would be observed again at the pouring out of the seventh bowl *(Revelation 16.17–18)*.

DIG DEEPER: *ARK OF THE COVENANT*

This imagery finds its roots in Old Testament history. The ark of the covenant was housed in the tabernacle and later in the Temple in a place called the Holy of Holies. No one was allowed to enter this place except for the high priest on one day of the year, the Day of Atonement, in which he entered with sacrificial blood as the atonement for the sin of God's people. In this verse, the ark of the covenant is fully visible to everyone and is no longer hidden. Now, the truth of Jesus Christ will be made known to everyone.

Notes/Applications

Mankind's reaction of mankind over the deaths of the two witnesses is almost like that of an international holiday. There is widespread rejoicing and celebration that these two will no longer be able to "torment" the world's inhabitants with their testimony. The thing so offensive about the two witnesses is that they testify to the truth of the Lord Jesus Christ. The world enjoys its sin and does not want to be told or reminded that its actions are indeed sinful. For three and a half years, these two witnesses will be hated by the world simply because they will reveal sin for what it is—evil and unacceptable in the sight of God.

Though opposition to the truth will be epidemic in the end times, it is prevalent even now. Certainly, it is easier for mainstream culture to label Christians as radical, closed-minded, and eccentric simply because believers hold steadfastly to a certain moral standard than it is for them to acknowledge that behavior they deem acceptable is, in fact, sin, abhorrent in the sight of God. In like manner as the two witnesses in this passage, we must testify to the truth of Christ in a world that does not recognize sin as sin or Christ as the Deliverer.

Harsh rejection never hindered these witnesses from doing what they were called to do. Unfortunately, even the *fear* of rejection is often enough to impede many Christians from witnessing to others. It is vital for us to recognize that the Great Commission is more than a suggestion. We need to see it for what it is—a holy calling to all Christians to stand upon the truth of their salvation. *"¹⁹'Go therefore and make disciples of all the nations, baptizing them in the name of the Father and of the Son and of the Holy Spirit, ²⁰teaching them to observe all things that I have commanded you; and lo, I am with you always, even to the end of the age.' Amen." (Matthew 28.19–20)*

We must rise above the petty excuses hindering us from fulfilling our spiritual responsibility, even at the cost of our frail human egos. Though every Christian is uniquely called to different areas of service based upon individual spiritual gifts, we have *all* received a common, privileged calling from the Lord Jesus Christ Himself—to share our faith with the lost and dying world in which we live.

Chapter Twelve

Revelation 12.1–6

Verse 1- Now a great sign appeared in heaven: a woman clothed with the sun, with the moon under her feet, and on her head a garland of twelve stars.

John witnessed a vision that was both an integral part of the revelation of the seventh trumpet and also different than that which he had thus far experienced. This chapter describes a vision within a vision, and though the passage might at first seem disconnected, it is intricately interwoven into the events of the chapters surrounding it. The figurative language used in this chapter is typical of prophetic literature *(Daniel 7; Isaiah 27; and Hosea 3)* wherein familiar icons are often used to depict events of greater significance; therefore, John's emphasis of a "sign" urges readers to look beyond the physical description of the vision to grasp the deeper meaning.

John saw a woman clothed in the golden glory of the sun and crowned with twelve stars around her head, and the moon lay under her feet. Speculations about this woman's identity range from the Virgin Mary to the universal Church.[1] The most convincing arguments seem to be made by those who insist that this woman represents Israel, as based on imagery found in other Scriptures. *(Genesis 37.9; 1 Kings 18.31)* Within this passage, however, this interpretation is better appreciated by viewing the woman as portrayed throughout the chapter rather than relying upon any particular verse. Even so, differences persist concerning whether she embodies the nation of Israel (strictly those of Jewish heritage) or whether she also includes a "spiritual Israel" as defined by the apostle Paul.[2] *(Romans 2.28–29; Romans 9.6–8)* However, it is perhaps most judicious not to insist on adhering solely to one interpretation or the other at this point in the text but rather to simply acknowledge that the woman most likely represents Israel in God's greater cosmic plan. More telling details about this woman will become apparent in later verses.

Verse 2- Then being with child, she cried out in labor and in pain to give birth.

Those who approach the interpretation of Revelation from a historicist viewpoint (see Introduction) are among the few who refute that this child was the Son of God, the Lord Jesus Christ.[3] The description given in verse five leaves little doubt that the child was Israel's long-awaited Messiah. This verse, however, offers more evidence of the mother's identity than of the child's. The imagery of a woman crying out "in labor and in pain" is a familiar theme in Old Testament references to Israel:

> *As a woman with child is in pain and cries out in her pangs, when she draws near the time of her delivery, so have we been in Your sight, O LORD. (Isaiah 26.17) 'Before she was in labor, she gave birth; before her pain came, she delivered a male child.' (Isaiah 66.7) [9]Now why do you cry aloud? Is there no king in your midst? Has your counselor perished? For pangs have seized you like a woman in labor. [10]Be in pain, and labor to bring forth, O daughter of Zion, like a woman in birth pangs. (Micah 4.9–10a)*

Verse 3- And another sign appeared in heaven: behold, a great, fiery red dragon having seven heads and ten horns, and seven diadems on his heads.

The identity of this dragon is far less obscure than that of the woman since verse nine clearly distinguishes it as Satan. Just as common in Jewish writing as the image of the pregnant woman which portrays Israel is the dreadful beast that depicts her enemies:

> You broke the heads of Leviathan in pieces, and gave him as food to the people inhabiting the wilderness. (Psalm 74.14) In that day the LORD with His severe sword, great and strong, will punish Leviathan the fleeing serpent, Leviathan that twisted serpent; and He will slay the reptile that is in the sea. (Isaiah 27.1) ³'Speak, and say, "Thus says the Lord GOD: 'Behold, I am against you, O Pharaoh king of Egypt, O great monster who lies in the midst of his rivers, who has said, "My River is my own; I have made it for myself." ⁴But I will put hooks in your jaws, and cause the fish of your rivers to stick to your scales; I will bring you up out of the midst of your rivers, and all the fish in your rivers will stick to your scale.'"' (Ezekiel 29.3–4)

That the dragon is red probably holds less significance than the number of his heads, horns, and crowns, about which much has been conjectured. Comparisons have been made between this dragon and the fourth beast that appeared to the prophet Daniel in a vision (Daniel 7.23–24) despite a lack of consistent interpretation linking the two creatures.[4] The use of the number seven is a common and recurring thread throughout Revelation, so it should not surprise the reader that this dragon has seven heads and seven crowns. However, since no obvious relevance of these heads, horns, or crowns is apparent within the text, it is perhaps wisest to avoid speculation about their significance altogether. Suffice it to say, the dragon represents Satan, and seldom in Revelation does the reader benefit from more solid and indisputable clarification than in this instance.

Verse 4- His tail drew a third of the stars of heaven and threw them to the earth. And the dragon stood before the woman who was ready to give birth, to devour her Child as soon as it was born.

The dragon caused "a third of the stars of heaven" to be cast to the earth. Since we have been told that this vision was a sign, we may conclude that these stars of Heaven possess significance greater than that of mere celestial bodies. These "stars of heaven" likely represent those angels of the heavenly host that were cast out of Paradise with Satan for rebelling against God.[5] *"And the angels who did not keep their proper domain, but left their own abode, He has reserved in everlasting chains under darkness for the judgment of the great day."* *(Jude 6)* *"For if God did not spare the angels who sinned, but cast them down to hell and delivered them into chains of darkness, to be reserved for judgment." (2 Peter 2.4)*

It should not be presumed that this event occurred later along a timeline of creation simply because this vision occurred as part of apocalyptic revelation. Rather, John received a succinct, compact vision of the loathing and malice that Satan has always possessed against God and His chosen people. Satan lurked around Israel and sought to destroy this Child Who was to be her Deliverer. These "stars" thrown to earth perhaps denote, as some commentators have suggested, the many earthly channels, such as Herod, through which Satan attempted to kill the Child.[6] Nevertheless, the birth of the Messiah, the Savior for the entire world from Israel's seed, could not be impeded despite Satan's best efforts.

Verse 5- She bore a male Child who was to rule all nations with a rod of iron. And her Child was caught up to God and His throne.

When a Son was born unto the woman, a Redeemer was born unto Israel:

6For unto us a Child is born, unto us a Son is given; and the government will be upon His shoulder. And His name will be called Wonderful, Counselor, Mighty God, Everlasting Father, Prince of Peace.
7Of the increase of His government and peace there will be no end, upon the throne of David and over His kingdom, to order it and establish it with judgment and justice from that time forward, even forever. The zeal of the Lord of hosts will perform this. (Isaiah 9.6–7)

The identity of this "male Child" as the Lord Jesus Christ is verified by His description as the One who would "rule all nations with a rod of iron":

⁷I will declare the decree: the Lord has said to Me, 'You are My Son, today I have begotten You. ⁸Ask of Me, and I will give You the nations for Your inheritance, and the ends of the earth for Your possession. ⁹You shall break them with a rod of iron; You shall dash them to pieces like a potter's vessel.' (Psalm 2.7–9) Now out of His mouth goes a sharp sword, that with it He should strike the nations. And He Himself will rule them with a rod of iron. (Revelation 19.15a)

That this vision portrays Jesus' ascension as occurring immediately after His birth is not intended in any way to minimize the importance of His sinless life, His earthly teachings and miracles, or His atoning death and resurrection. Rather, it appears the intention is to stress the significance of the Child as pertaining to this particular vision—the triumph of the Child and the utter failure of the dragon. Shortly after sealing the victory over Satan with His death and resurrection, the Lord Jesus was "caught up" unto God the Father and unto Heaven from where He came. *"Now when He had spoken these things, while they watched, He was taken up, and a cloud received Him out of their sight." (Acts 1.9) "Looking unto Jesus, the author and finisher of our faith, who for the joy that was set before Him endured the cross, despising the shame, and has sat down at the right hand of the throne of God." (Hebrews 12.2)*

Verse 6- Then the woman fled into the wilderness, where she has a place prepared by God, that they should feed her there one thousand two hundred and sixty days.

The "wilderness," as used in this verse, probably is not intended to depict any literal topographical description or geographical location. As with the other metaphors prevalent throughout this passage, it should be taken figuratively. The wilderness is simply, as clarified, "a place prepared by God," imagery for the Lord's safety and refuge.[7]

Despite the metaphorical imagery used in verses one through five to depict Satan's contention with Jesus the Messiah, the reference to 1,260 days in this verse seems to lead the reader back to the eschatological relevance of the overall scene, serving somewhat as a link between Israel's past and her future. Especially given the context of the vision, there appears no reason to suppose that the mention of this specific period, which is identical to the timeframe mentioned in chapters eleven and thirteen, should refer to any span other than the three and a half years of tribulation which will befall mankind in the final days.

It should come as little surprise that many scholars are determined to identify this woman as the universal Church (a "spiritual" or "ideal" Israel), wherein this verse would serve as biblical evidence of God's protection over all believers during the final period of tribulation described throughout the Book of Revelation.[8] However, as we will later study, a clear distinction is made in verse seventeen between this woman and "the rest of her offspring, who keep the commandments of God and have the testimony of Jesus Christ." Therefore, it seems doubtful that the group depicted by this woman includes all believers, or consequently, the universal Church.[9]

Notes/Application

This passage gives an overview of Satan's efforts to thwart God's plan for sending His Son to earth. Satan has done everything within his strength to impede Christ's birth, death, resurrection, and especially the transforming power that this miracle of love has on individual lives. Nevertheless, nothing can ever obstruct God's perfect plan and sovereign purpose. God has proven His love for us by exerting His supremacy over the powers of darkness.

Satan desires to thwart God's plan for our lives, so he daily attempts to deceive us as individuals to deviate from the Father's course. He wants to intimidate us; he wants to confuse us; he wants to frustrate us. Simply, he wants to destroy us. *"Be sober, be vigilant; because your adversary the devil walks about like a roaring lion, seeking whom he may devour." (1 Peter 5.8)* However, God Almighty, through His Holy Spirit, indwells believers' lives, and He is infinitely greater than Satan and his demons. *"³And every spirit that does not confess that Jesus Christ has come in the flesh is not of God. And this is the spirit of the Antichrist, which you have heard was coming, and is now already in the* world. *⁴You are of God, little children, and have overcome them, because He who is in you is greater than he who is in the world."* (1 John 4.3–4) Therefore, Satan cannot devour us if we remain soberly plugged into the power source of our lives, Almighty God, by never allowing our selfish wills to dictate our path. We must always yield to God's total control over even the minute facets of our everyday lives.

Too many times, we feel defeated before we get started because the battle seems already lost, drawing a bleak future forecast. Have we forgotten that in the end God wins? Just as Satan could not overthrow God's plan and purpose for Christ's first advent, the same will be true for the King of kings' return and His eternal reign. If we are obedient to God's Holy Word, living daily in God's will and in continual communion with Him, Satan will have no power over us either. *"What then shall we say to these things? If God is for us, who can be against us?"* (Romans 8.31)

Revelation 12.7–12

Verse 7- And war broke out in heaven: Michael and his angels fought with the dragon; and the dragon and his angels fought,

At first glance, it may appear that we are thrust back to events which, according to other biblical evidence, occurred near or before the creation of the world. *"He who sins is of the devil, for the devil has sinned from the beginning. For this purpose the Son of God was manifested, that He might destroy the works of the devil." (1 John 3.8)* *"How you are fallen from heaven, O Lucifer, son of the morning! How you are cut down to the ground, you who weakened the nations!" (Isaiah 14.12)* However, this passage seems to suggest that these events, though similar to events traditionally associated with Satan's initial rebellion or his defeat by Christ's resurrection, depict a momentous occurrence yet unfulfilled.[10] Especially in consideration of verse six, this appears to be an explanation of an eschatological event foretold by the prophet Daniel. *"At that time Michael shall stand up, the great prince who stands watch over the sons of your people; and there shall be a time of trouble, such as never was since there was a nation, even to that time. And at that time your people shall be delivered, every one who is found written in the book." (Daniel 12.1)*

The archangel Michael and the angels of Heaven battled Satan, the red dragon, and his legion of fallen angels. Michael, as we are told in this and other Scriptures, is the chief prince of angels and the guardian angel over the children of Israel. *"But the prince of the kingdom of Persia withstood me twenty-one days; and behold, Michael, one of the chief princes, came to help me, for I had been left alone there with the kings of Persia." (Daniel 10.13)* *"Yet Michael the archangel, in contending with the devil, when he disputed about the body of Moses, dared not bring against him a reviling accusation, but said, 'The Lord rebuke you!'" (Jude 9)*

DIG DEEPER: *MICHAEL*

Michael, the archangel, appears five times in Scripture. He is first mentioned in the apocalyptic book of Daniel as the angel that protects the nation of Israel. *(Daniel 10.13, 21; 12.1)* He is one of two angels that are named in the Bible, the other being Gabriel. In these few snapshots, we see a warrior prince who serves at the command of the Almighty God.

Verse 8- but they did not prevail, nor was a place found for them in heaven any longer.

Many commentators point to this verse as further support that this celestial battle does not describe Satan's initial rebellion against the Lord but an end-times event which will precede God's final judgments upon the earth.[11] Assisting this view are Scriptures that seem to suggest that Satan had still been afforded, at least to some degree, access to Heaven even after his uprising:

> *⁶Now there was a day when the sons of God came to present themselves before the LORD, and Satan also came among them. ⁷And the LORD said to Satan, 'From where do you come?' So Satan answered the LORD and said, 'From going to and fro on the earth, and from walking back and forth on it.' (Job 1.6–7) Then he showed me Joshua the high priest standing before the Angel of the LORD, and Satan standing at his right hand to oppose him. (Zechariah 3.1)*

The specific mention that they "did not prevail" suggests that the war would be initiated by Satan. His aggressive endeavor, however, would be doomed to failure before it ever began. Surely, even Satan must have realized the futility of his goal, yet his obstinate ambition and atrocious malice would nonetheless drive him to attempt the impossible.[12] After the clash, Satan and his angels would forevermore be denied access to Heaven.

Verse 9- So the great dragon was cast out, that serpent of old, called the Devil and Satan, who deceives the whole world; he was cast to the earth, and his angels were cast out with him.

The dragon is also referred to as the old serpent, likely in reference to a passage from the Book of Genesis. *"And the Lord God said to the woman, 'What is this you have done?' The woman said, 'The serpent deceived me, and I ate.'" (Genesis 3.13)* He was also called the Devil and Satan so that there could be no confusion that these are all the one and same being. Satan would be cast out into the world with all of his followers, and the door to Heaven would be closed behind him forevermore.

Verses 10, 11- ¹⁰*Then I heard a loud voice saying in heaven, "Now salvation, and strength, and the kingdom of our God, and the power of His Christ have come, for the accuser of our brethren, who accused them before our God day and night, has been cast down. ¹¹And they overcame him by the blood of the Lamb and by the word of their testimony, and they did not love their lives to the death.*

The heavens burst in exuberant praise with what has become a familiar response to the victories attained in the heavenly realms. *(Revelation 4.8–10; 7.9–12; and 11.15–18)* The identity of the speaker is uncertain but is also inconsequential to the full appreciation of this verse.

John heard a loud voice proclaiming that salvation and strength in the Lord had been accomplished as had the kingdom of God and the power of Christ. Satan was overcome "by the blood of the Lamb and by the word of their testimony," which seems to indicate that there was not much of a physical conflict at all. The victory was determined before the clash began—those on the Lord's side would be triumphant, and those who fought alongside Satan would be conquered and cast out with their evil leader, the "accuser of our brethren." It was not by the might of Michael or his angels that this battle was won but by the sacrifice of the Lord Jesus Christ and His shed blood at Calvary.

Most commentators generally agree that the description of "they [who] did not love their lives to the death" obviously signifies martyrs, those persons willing to give their lives for the cause of Christ.¹³ The war fought in Heaven is of a spiritual nature, but it has earthly ramifications. Whatever the hardships endured by believers in the world, the victory is certain and irreversible and is not dependent upon the triumphs over evil in the earthly realm but upon those achieved in the spiritual realm.[14]

Verse 12- "Therefore rejoice, O heavens, and you who dwell in them! Woe to the inhabitants of the earth and the sea! For the devil has come down to you, having great wrath, because he knows that he has a short time."

There was great joy in Heaven because the devil had been defeated. However, there was still great misery in store for those who remained on the earth, for the devil was now among them. The devil's absolute failure in Heaven would only incite his anger and wrath against the earth's inhabitants. Further provoking Satan's fury would be his awareness that his time was almost up. God would only allow Satan's unprecedented outpouring of wrath upon the earth for a limited time, and during this period, believers would be encouraged to persevere with great confidence and hope.[15]

Notes/Applications

Satan was overcome "by the blood of the Lamb and by the word of their testimony," the most powerful weapons necessary in fighting the adversary. Both offensive weapons originate in the completed work of the Lord Jesus Christ and His victory over death and Hell. The Lord Jesus Christ shed His precious blood on Calvary's cross. When we unite with Him by accepting His gift of love, broken and spilled out for us, we become warriors enlisted in His army by the "word" of our testimonies.

All Christians, by nature of their redeemed beings, will be subjected to spiritual warfare throughout their lives because those living in obedience to God will inherently be at odds with the enemy. *"For we do not wrestle against flesh and blood, but against principalities, against powers, against the rulers of the darkness of this age, against spiritual hosts of wickedness in the heavenly places." (Ephesians 6.12)* Therefore, it is vitally important that believers equip themselves with the armor of God on a daily basis to be prepared for both subtle and blatant spiritual attacks. The more we strive to live according to God's ways, the more Satan will come against us in resistance, which is all the more reason we must daily "dress" for combat:

> *¹³Therefore take up the whole armor of God, that you may be able to withstand in the evil day, and having done all, to stand. ¹⁴Stand therefore, having girded your waist with truth, having put on the breastplate of righteousness, ¹⁵and having shod your feet with the preparation of the gospel of peace; ¹⁶above all, taking the shield of faith with which you will be able to quench all the fiery darts of the wicked one. ¹⁷And take the helmet of salvation, and the sword of the Spirit, which is the word of God. (Ephesians 6.13–17)*

Take a moment to consider the spiritual battles in our lives. If it is difficult to point out regular spiritual battles taking place, it is time to ask ourselves why that is the case. The answer may be that Satan has deceived us into becoming complacent with our spiritual walk. Make a serious effort, starting today, to shed the apathy that might be hindering spiritual victory by utilizing the tools God has provided for us—the power of His blood and the word of our testimony in Him.

Revelation 12.13–17

Verse 13- Now when the dragon saw that he had been cast to the earth, he persecuted the woman who gave birth to the male Child.

Satan, unable to defeat Christ Jesus, redirected His wrath against Israel, God's chosen, who had bore the Messiah. Since the devil could not touch God and no longer even possessed access to Heaven, he would act out his fury upon God's people.

Verse 14- But the woman was given two wings of a great eagle, that she might fly into the wilderness to her place, where she is nourished for a time and times and half a time, from the presence of the serpent.

As discussed in verse six, a place of safety and refuge (the wilderness) was prepared for the woman so that she would not be harmed by the dragon's tactics. The Lord God also provided "two wings of a great eagle" to carry her to that place of sanctuary. This phrasing is similar to imagery used in the Old Testament to depict God's active safekeeping of His faithful. *"You have seen what I did to the Egyptians, and how I bore you on eagles' wings and brought you to Myself." (Exodus 19.4) "¹¹As an eagle stirs up its nest, hovers over its young, spreading out its wings, taking them up, carrying them on its wings, ¹²so the LORD alone led him." (Deuteronomy 32.11–12a)*

Again, we are told about the specific duration that the Lord's protection of the woman would be necessary, in this verse referred to as "a time and times and half a time." Most scholars agree that the word "time" as used in this verse denotes one year, thereby affirming this as a span of three and a half years and as being the same end-times period of tribulation specified in several other passages of Revelation.[16]

Perhaps the greatest difficulty in understanding this chapter rests in the interpretation of the woman. As already explained, the strongest case can be made that the woman represents Israel. In consideration of arguments that the woman likely does not represent a "spiritual" Israel, thus embodying the universal Church (see comments on verse six), how does this interpretation endure the expanded boundaries of New Testament principles such as "there is no distinction between Jew and Greek"? *(Romans 10.12)* It seems unsuitable to conclude that the woman symbolizes the total sum of natural Israel—each and every ethnic Jew throughout history— whereby such conclusions might insinuate that all Jews automatically gain an inheritance into Heaven based solely upon their ethnicity because such would be contradictory to God's Word. *(Romans 9, 10, and 11)* So, where does one draw the line between inclusion and exclusion? The solution for some commentators is to refer to this woman as a "faithful" Israel, all those who are Jewish believers in the Lord Jesus Christ.[17] This group may refer to what some scholars argue will be a mass conversion of Jews to Christianity in the last days.[18] Perhaps they are those referred to in Scripture as the "remnant" of Israel. *"Isaiah also cries out concerning Israel: 'Though the number of the children of Israel be as the sand of the sea, the remnant will be saved.'" (Romans 9.27) "'I say then, has God cast away His people? Certainly not! For I also am an Israelite, of the seed of Abraham, of the tribe of Benjamin. ⁵Even so then, at this present time there is a remnant according to the election of grace." (Romans 11.1, 5)* Still, the only description within Revelation that is evident of any such protection provided to a specific group of Jews occurs in chapter seven with the sealing of the 144,000. *"And I heard the number of those who were sealed. One hundred and forty-four thousand of all the tribes of the children of Israel were sealed." (Revelation 7.4)* Consequently, within the limitations of what we are told in this chapter, it is difficult to identify with absolute certainty the exact makeup of the group depicted by this woman.

Nevertheless, whether the woman consists of the 144,000 Jews or includes all Jewish believers alive during this period of tribulation or even whether she embodies a group of people not accurately defined within this book or any other, we can rest assured that God is in control and that all events will occur precisely as He has ordained. *"²⁴Shall the prey be taken from the mighty, or the captives of the righteous be delivered? ²⁵But thus says the Lord: 'Even the captives of the mighty shall be taken away, and the prey of the terrible be delivered; for I will contend with him who contends with you, and I will save your chil-dren.'" (Isaiah 49.24–25)*

Verses 15, 16- **¹⁵So the serpent spewed water out of his mouth like a flood after the woman, that he might cause her to be car-ried away by the flood. ¹⁶But the earth helped the woman, and the earth opened its mouth and swallowed up the flood which the dragon had spewed out of his mouth.**

Satan was able to cause some sort of a deluge in an attempt to stifle the flight of the woman. This flood likely represents an out-pouring of the dragon's wrath toward the woman, perhaps an allu-sion to Old Testament imagery of evils perpetrated against the children of God. *(Psalm 124; Isaiah 43.2)* However, once again Satan's schemes would be foiled when God's hand protected the fleeing Israelites, allowing them to remain unharmed. Determining the exact meaning of the imagery used in these two verses is unneces-sary. The scene primarily elucidates upon God's protection of the woman from Satan's attempts to destroy her.

Verse 17- And the dragon was enraged with the woman, and he went to make war with the rest of her offspring, who keep the commandments of God and have the testimony of Jesus Christ.

Because the dragon was unable to vent his rage against either the Child or the woman, he sought to redirect his vehement rage— this time against "the rest of her offspring." This wording does not necessarily imply, as some suppose, that this would be a limited group specifically selected for martyrdom.[19] Rather, it refers to those *not* included in the group previously mentioned. The woman's seed, as indicated in previous verses of this passage, was her Deliverer and Redeemer, the Lord Jesus Christ. The "rest of her offspring," therefore, refers to those who would be included among the redeemed but who were not counted among those represented by the woman (Israel). Further description identifies them as those "who keep the commandments of God, and have the testimony of Jesus Christ." There can be little doubt, therefore, that these would indeed be Christians of this tribulation period.[20]

What John witnessed in this concentrated vision was the exclusive relationship that God had with His chosen people, the Israelites. It almost seems as though this passage reveals a possible, if partial, fulfillment of prophecy wherein the Lord would one day restore that relationship:

> *⁵'And now the Lord says, Who formed Me from the womb to be His Servant, to bring Jacob back to Him, so that Israel is gathered to Him (for I shall be glorious in the eyes of the Lord, and My God shall be My strength), ⁶Indeed He says, "It is too small a thing that You should be My Servant to raise up the tribes of Jacob, and to restore the preserved ones of Israel; I will also give You as a light to the Gentiles, that You should be My salvation to the ends of the earth."' (Isaiah 49.5–6) ⁶'For the Lord has called you like a woman forsaken and grieved in spirit, like a youthful wife when you were refused,' says your God. ⁷'For a mere moment I have forsaken you, but with great mercies I will gather you. ⁸With a little wrath I hid My face from you for a moment; but with everlasting kindness I will have mercy on you,' says the Lord, your Redeemer. (Isaiah 54.6–8)*

As He had in the past, God would protect this group from the hands of her oppressors. As a result, though, Satan would inflict his wrath upon those he could. He would accomplish this, as we will read in the chapter that follows, through the oppression administered by the beast and the false prophet.

Notes/Applications

In this passage, the dragon determined to attack the seed of the woman's offspring, the redeemed. The only hope individuals have to stand against the devil's schemes is to employ the tools made available to those who believe in Jesus Christ as Lord and Savior and accept His sacrificial death and glorious resurrection. *"'Most assuredly, I say to you, he who hears My word and believes in Him who sent Me has everlasting life, and shall not come into judgment, but has passed from death into life.'" (John 5.24)*

Only then can we raise the offensive weapons necessary to counterattack—"the word" of our testimony and an attitude that we "love not [our] lives unto death." When attacks befall us and the enemy wears us down, we can stand firmly upon our salvation and claim victory over the devil, confidently proclaiming that Satan no longer owns us, for we belong to Christ, and His Spirit empowers us to reject Satan's ways and to live victoriously. *"I have written to you, fathers, because you have known Him who is from the beginning. I have written to you, young men, because you are strong, and the word of God abides in you, and you have overcome the wicked one." (1 John 2.14)*

As believers, who among us would want to forfeit our eternal destiny in glory in order to live a longer earthly life? Therefore, we should strive for such an eternal perspective on our lives that we would be willing to die before denying the God that we serve. Satan will never be able to have a hold on those who claim their victory in Christ Jesus and truly live for Him and daily die to themselves. *"'But seek first the kingdom of God and His righteousness, and all these things shall be added to you.'" (Matthew 6.33) "For to me, to live is Christ, and to die is gain." (Philippians 1.21)*

Chapter Thirteen

Revelation 13.1-6

Verse 1- Then I stood on the sand of the sea. And I saw a beast rising up out of the sea, having seven heads and ten horns, and on his horns ten crowns, and on his heads a blasphemous name.

This verse seems suitable as an introduction of the dominant figure whose rise to prominence will be manifested before Christ's return, as foretold in Scriptures:

> [24]*'For false christs and false prophets will rise and show great signs and wonders to deceive, if possible, even the elect. [25]See, I have told you beforehand. [26]Therefore if they say to you, "Look, He is in the desert!" do not go out; or "Look, He is in the inner rooms!" do not believe it. [27]For as the lightning comes from the east and flashes to the west, so also will the coming of the Son of Man be.' (Matthew 24.24-27) [3]Let no one deceive you by any means; for that Day will not come unless the falling away comes first, and the man of sin is revealed, the son of perdition, [4]who opposes and exalts himself above all that is called God or that is worshiped, so that he sits as God in the temple of God, showing himself that he is God. [9]The coming of the lawless one is according to the working of Satan,*

with all power, signs, and lying wonders, [10]and with all unrighteous deception among those who perish, because they did not receive the love of the truth, that they might be saved. (2 Thessalonians 2.3–4, 9–10)

This figure is traditionally referred to as the ultimate incarnation of antichrist. However, many disparities exist within the interpretation of the details, and some of these differences become immediately evident.

For instance, many translations interpret the subject standing by the sea as the dragon instead of John.[1] To many scholars, this distinction is relatively important for linking this chapter with the previous one, whereby the dragon introduced in chapter twelve, after being cast to the earth and prevented from harming the woman, stormed forward to make war with "the rest of her seed" according to the events described in this chapter.[2] Whereas it is not necessary to precisely identify this being as either John or the dragon in order to accommodate this interpretation, the more chilling of the two scenarios situates the atrocious dragon on the seashore summoning forth a beast from the depths of the sea to carry out its plan of destruction upon those who follow Almighty God.

Whether this ocean refers to a literal or figurative body of water is uncertain. Most likely, the significance of this description illustrates the manner of the beast's emanation, symbolizing that it would arise from within the tumultuous sea of humanity.[3] The antichrist would not be sent from above or from any other spiritual realm where the importance of his existence would be obvious to the inhabitants of the world.

Because this scene is a continuation of the previous chapter, these events should also be understood as symbolic. As previously mentioned, it is commonly accepted that the grotesque monster emerging from the waters of the sea represents the physical embodiment of what is traditionally referred to as the antichrist, yet for centuries, scholars have debated whether this beast is intended to depict a specific individual or a group of leaders which comprise a governmental alliance. Biblical evidence seems to substantiate the employment of both ideas. *(Matthew 24.24; 2 Thessalonians 2.3; 1 John*

2.18–22; and 2 John 1.7) The systematically violent behavior demonstrated by the beast in this chapter suggests that this spirit of antichrist, though at work throughout history, will manifest its ultimate fulfillment through the life of one particularly corrupt yet globally influential individual serving as the head of an administration likely comprised of ten administrators.[4] It seems probable that these heads, horns, and crowns symbolize leaders who will govern under the authority of the beast.[5] *"The ten horns which you saw are ten kings who have received no kingdom as yet, but they receive authority for one hour as kings with the beast." (Revelation 17.12)*

Whatever the case, the description of the beast so closely resembles that of the dragon itself that we must conclude that the manifestation of the beast is Satan's ploy to imitate Jesus Christ, God incarnate. As such, the beast must be viewed as more than just a spirit of antichrist that will flow unrestrained in the last days but will also encompass the physical materialization of one who will embody all the characteristics of the dragon and will be the agent through which Satan will carry out his ultimate plot to make war with the saints *(Revelation 12.17)* and make war with the Lord Himself *(Revelation 19.19).* He will achieve some success in his campaign against God's faithful *(Revelation 13.7)*, but his efforts against Almighty God will be met with utter defeat and will ultimately lead to his own eternal destruction *(Revelation 19.20, 20.10).*

Verse 2- Now the beast which I saw was like a leopard, his feet were like the feet of a bear, and his mouth like the mouth of a lion. The dragon gave him his power, his throne, and great authority.

Many have attributed significance to similarities between the description of this beast and those described in a vision by the prophet Daniel. *(Daniel 7.4–6)* However, with a lack of compelling evidence linking the two visions, it is perhaps most practical to recognize that the attributes of this beast's authority could most aptly be compared to those found in these common animals. Accordingly, the beast may rise to power with the great speed of a leopard, exercise his dominion with the brute strength of a bear, and conquer with the ravenous appetite of a lion. If, on the other hand, this verse does serve as John's attempt to describe the beast's physical appearance, we can still maintain that this description, while unique in its extreme grotesqueness, is complete as intended by the writer, and it remains unnecessary to reconcile any similarities to the Daniel account for proposing some greater significance.

The beast was given its power and position of great authority by the dragon. The beast could do nothing within its own power and was solely reliant upon Satan for the authority and influence that it possessed.

Verse 3- And I saw one of his heads as if it had been mortally wounded, and his deadly wound was healed. And all the world marveled and followed the beast.

One of the beast's heads was mortally wounded. This "head" could be representative of one of the world leaders that would reign under the hierarchy of the antichrist and under the power of Satan. It is unclear whether this is indeed some supernatural phenomenon precipitated by the power of the dragon (under the sovereignty of Almighty God) or whether John's specific use of words should be taken more literally, indicating that this being *appeared* "as if [he] had been mortally wounded," while such was not in fact the case. Regardless of the circumstance, the outward effect would be the same. To the public eye, this beast (or an element of the beast) would display its power and authority by defying death and returning to life after receiving some manner of fatal injury. This appears to be another instance of Satan mimicking Christ, specifically in this case, the Lord's resurrection.

In response, the entire world would be utterly amazed at the wonder of its beast's healing, and out of respect or fear or perhaps both, people would fully devote themselves to the beast. In whatever social or political manner this being arose from among the people, the relationship was about to change, as described in the following verse.

Verse 4- So they worshiped the dragon who gave authority to the beast; and they worshiped the beast, saying, "Who is like the beast? Who is able to make war with him?"

With the occurrence of this and other "miracles" yet to come, the world would be deceived into following the beast. *"The coming of the lawless one is according to the working of Satan, with all power, signs, and lying wonders." (2 Thessalonians 2.9)* The world's inhabitants would first worship the dragon who empowered the beast. They knew that this "miracle" was from a power higher than the beast itself, though their conclusions were misguided. They then also worshipped the beast, which they now perceived as being all-powerful. Insomuch as they accepted him as some incarnate manifestation of deity, they believed that none could ever oppose him and that he was invincible in all things, including, as it seems they were specifically concerned, war. Their reply mocked that of God's people in the Old Testament.[6] *"'Who is like You, O LORD, among the gods? Who is like You, glorious in holiness, fearful in praises, doing wonders?'" (Exodus 15.11)*

Verse 5- And he was given a mouth speaking great things and blasphemies, and he was given authority to continue for forty-two months.

The beast was given "a mouth," a means by which he could communicate to many people. More important to note, however, is that this mouth "was given" to him and was not earned by the beast's own accomplishments, indicating the beast's empowerment by a higher power. Though the details of his words are not divulged, we are told that the message the beast promoted was blasphemous. By other biblical accounts, it seems likely that his message included the proclamation of himself as God. *(Daniel 11.36; 2 Thessalonians 2.3–4)* Everything the antichrist spoke would be a lie, but the people of the world would still willingly follow him, unaware of his true identity.

The word *continue*, as used in this verse, is translated from the Greek word ποιῆσαι, (poieō) which means "to make or to do."[7] This simply indicates that the beast would only be allowed to carry out these blasphemous acts for a preordained period of forty-two months (three and a half years), a time span which correlates with that mentioned in other passages of Revelation *(11.2–3; 12.6, 14)* and Daniel. *"He shall speak pompous words against the Most High, shall persecute the saints of the Most High, and shall intend to change times and law. Then the saints shall be given into his hand for a time and times and half a time.'" (Daniel 7.25)*

Verse 6- Then he opened his mouth in blasphemy against God, to blaspheme His name, His tabernacle, and those who dwell in heaven.

The detail of the beast's blasphemies is disclosed in this verse, and they were leveled not only against God but also directed toward any and all things related to God, including the redeemed of Heaven. It is generally agreed that the "tabernacle" mentioned in this verse likely refers to Heaven and all those who dwell there.[8]

Notes/Applications

As seen in the above passage, the earth is a place where Satan has been allowed limited power in his quest to frustrate, destroy, divide, and astound the work of God and His people. The evil one is not some animator's creation but a very real force, and his primary tool is deception. Satan mimics the miracles and ways of truth in order to possess the hearts and minds of people and to destroy their lives. *"For Satan himself transforms himself into an angel of light."* *(2 Corinthians 11.14b)*

We may wonder why the dragon was allowed the authority that he then extended to the beast. In essence, why would God permit this beast to blaspheme His holy name, His tabernacle, and those residing in Heaven? God will allow His adversary to prowl wickedly according to this rebellious being's vile nature for only a season in order to bring about the end of Satan and his evil influence over the earth.

The enemy is a mocker and an imposter. Nevertheless, his time is limited, and praise God, his end is in sight. As we study these disturbing chapters of this world's destiny, we cannot forget the promised conclusion. The adversary and his ways are of no avail against the power of Almighty God and His Son, the Lord and Savior Jesus Christ. Satan, too, will one day bow to the Holy Father and Son!

While we, as believing children of God, still abide during these times when Satan continues to roam as a lion seeking whom he may devour, we must combat the lion's tactics and spiritual oppression by drawing near to the victorious and sovereign Almighty God, and to His Son with the Name above all others, the Lord Jesus Christ. *"⁷Therefore submit to God. Resist the devil and he will flee from you. ⁸Draw near to God and He will draw near to you."* (James 4.7–8)

Revelation 13.7–12

Verse 7- It was granted to him to make war with the saints and to overcome them. And authority was given him over every tribe, tongue, and nation.

As we read in the previous chapter, the dragon would wage war against believers throughout the earth because he would be unable to destroy the woman. *"And the dragon was enraged with the woman, and he went to make war with the rest of her offspring, who keep the commandments of God and have the testimony of Jesus Christ." (Revelation 12.17)* We now see that the dragon's means of making war with the saints still upon the earth would be through the manifestation of this beast.

During the end times as throughout history, Satan will only be able to do that which is "granted to him" by God Almighty. Though we understand that the dragon would wage war against believers through the antichrist, the manner in which the antichrist would implement war with the saints remains unclear. It might have meant actual war, as in military battles, though such was not likely unless all the saints had banded together to form their own communities or forces of resistance. More likely, as indicated by the remainder of this passage, the war waged against the saints would come in the form of intolerable persecution, which would result in the deaths of many believers worldwide without regard to nationality or race. No matter where they were located throughout the world, all Christians would feel the impact of the beast's persecution against them.

Also, whatever his method, we are told that the beast would not only be given the power to make war with Christians but also the power to *succeed* in this campaign. He would appear to have total control of the world during this period of time.

Verse 8- All who dwell on the earth will worship him, whose names have not been written in the Book of Life of the Lamb slain from the foundation of the world.

This verse likely indicates the means by which the beast would wage his war against the redeemed. Every living person upon the earth would be required to worship the beast, and the only people who would refuse to worship him would be the faithful believers of Christ Jesus. All unbelievers would worship the beast without exception as emphasized by the phrases "*all* who dwell on the earth," which include *all* "whose names have not been written in the Book of Life." Only those having received the salvation of God's grace have their names written in the Book of Life, and only these would have the power to resist the enticing lure of the antichrist. The believers would have the power within them from the indwelling Holy Spirit to be able to withstand this evil command. *"Because He who is in you is greater than he who is in the world." (1 John 4.4b) "And anyone not found written in the Book of Life was cast into the lake of fire." (Revelation 20.15)* True believers would see the antichrist for what he was—an adversary of the Lord Jesus Christ.

In the phrase "the Lamb slain from the foundation of the world," we are given interesting insight that could be overlooked by the impact of the first part of the verse. This is another evidence of Jesus' eternal co-existence with the Father and Spirit. The Lord Jesus Christ was not introduced onto the scene in the middle of the world's history as a reactionary decision by God to redeem mankind unto Himself. The Lord God Almighty had already purposed in His heart to send His Son as the sacrifice for mankind's sins before the creation of the world. He had determined to send Himself into the world as the solution (Christ's sacrificial atonement) before the problem (the fall of man into sin) was ever manifested.

Verse 9- If anyone has an ear, let him hear.

Similar to the warnings given to the seven churches in chapters two and three, we are again admonished to listen intently with our spiritual ears and not just our physical ears. The "if" implies that not all people have spiritual ears. All who read this portion of Revelation have been admonished not to simply read but to study, understand, meditate upon, and assimilate the warnings that are given herein.

Verse 10- He who leads into captivity shall go into captivity; he who kills with the sword must be killed with the sword. Here is the patience and the faith of the saints.

Herein lays a promise given to the believers who stand against the fury of the antichrist. The saints are assured that their endurance in faith and patience would not be in vain. Truth and righteousness would eventually and ultimately prevail. Their captor would eventually be the captive, and those who had killed as part of this war waged against Christians would likewise be killed. *"Woe to you who plunder, though you have not been plundered; and you who deal treacherously, though they have not dealt treacherously with you! When you cease plundering, you will be plundered; when you make an end of dealing treacherously, they will deal treacherously with you." (Isaiah 33.1)* This promise would not lessen the agony of the Christians' persecution, but it would serve as assurance amid great suffering that their endurance would be rewarded, and justice would have its day.[9]

Verse 11- Then I saw another beast coming up out of the earth, and he had two horns like a lamb and spoke like a dragon.

John witnessed the emergence of a second beast, not arising from within the sea like the first but from within the earth. This beast had two horns like a lamb. It was again a direct reflection of Satan's response to the things of Almighty God. This second beast spoke as the dragon because the dragon was the source for all he said and did. Consequently, this meant that he blasphemed and lied just like the dragon, the father of lies. This verse marks the introduction of the one generally referred to as the false prophet. *(Revelation 16.13, 19.20, and 20.10)*

Verse 12- And he exercises all the authority of the first beast in his presence, and causes the earth and those who dwell in it to worship the first beast, whose deadly wound was healed.

The false prophet was given the same power as his predecessor, the beast, also known as the antichrist. Both received their power from Satan but were ultimately allowed to execute their actions only by the sovereign will of Almighty God. The second beast directed all the world's inhabitants to worship the first beast, the global figure miraculously restored to life from a mortal wound. Evidently, the false prophet did not promote the worshiping of himself.

The phrasing of this and related verses suggest that this control would be exercised throughout the earth. The entire world system, including all operations of currency, media, and vital provisions, would submit to the control of the antichrist at this point, and it would also be expected that all the world's inhabitants would place their trust and loyalties solely upon this individual.

Notes/Applications

Many people contend that the antichrist will actually emerge as a result of technological advancements. Though there are many arguments for this and other similar theories, the clear implication throughout Revelation and other Scriptures is that the antichrist is a living, breathing person. Such evidence includes the healing of the antichrist's physical wound, the use of the demonstrative pronoun *who,* and the constant use of personal pronouns *he, him,* and *his.* The attributes describing the antichrist and the false prophet are also distinctive expressions of animate beings. These beings are given physical descriptions, possess willful, evil intentions, and have the *desire* to be worshipped. Furthermore, they demonstrate a supernatural ability to enforce their demand for worship. Therefore, it should be clearly evident that the antichrist will be an actual, physical being, most likely a very charismatic leader.

It is quite possible, however, that the antichrist will use technology as his means to control the world. If the entire world currency exchange were conducted via high-tech machinery, which alleviates the need for physical money transactions, each and every individual's provisions for food, clothing, and shelter would be solely reliant upon networked systems. The antichrist could then implement the "mark of the beast" as a required registration for individuals to be members of a global system, thus fulfilling verses sixteen and seventeen of this chapter.

Even so, it is not technology itself of which we need to remain wary but of those who have the access and ability to exploit others' dependency upon it. It is among such a group of people that the actual antichrist may emerge. We must not live under the bondage of fear and paranoia but under the freedom and confidence of the Holy Spirit which indwells us and will guard us against the enemy's deception. *(1 John 4.1–3)*

Revelation 13.13–18

Verse 13- He performs great signs, so that he even makes fire come down from heaven on the earth in the sight of men.

The false prophet possessed the ability, as did the antichrist, to perform incredible wonders. In this verse, he summoned fire down upon the earth from the heavens, perhaps in the form of lightning or a similar spectacle. He did this under the watchful eye of many witnesses in order to deceive them into believing that he was actually a man of God.

This fire was a miracle in the eyes of men but not in the eyes of God. It was a deception of Satan that would be very convincing. This seems similar to Old Testament accounts where Pharaoh's magicians reproduced several of the miracles that Moses performed. *(Exodus 7 and 8)*

Verse 14- And he deceives those who dwell on the earth by those signs which he was granted to do in the sight of the beast, telling those who dwell on the earth to make an image to the beast who was wounded by the sword and lived.

It is evident that the world would be fooled by the antichrist and false prophet. The two beasts were very persuasive because of the "miracles" that they performed. *"For false christs and false prophets will rise and show great signs and wonders to deceive, if possible, even the elect." (Matthew 24.24)* After the world had been deceived into worshipping the antichrist, it would more easily be seduced into worshipping an idol of the beast.

Because of the conflict between the beast and Christians described in verses seven and eight, we know that the beast was only able to deceive those who were not true believers. Nonetheless, the false prophet now commanded people to erect an image of the beast, which would further oppose God's laws:

> [1]*'If there arises among you a prophet or a dreamer of dreams, and he gives you a sign or a wonder, [2]and the sign or the wonder comes to pass, of which he spoke to you, saying, "Let us go after other gods"—which you have not known—"and let us serve them,"*

³you shall not listen to the words of that prophet or that dreamer of dreams, for the Lord your God is testing you to know whether you love the Lord your God with all your heart and with all your soul.'
(Deuteronomy 13.1–3)

Verse 15- He was granted power to give breath to the image of the beast, that the image of the beast should both speak and cause as many as would not worship the image of the beast to be killed.

As additional evidence of the "miraculous" powers of these servants of Satan, we see that the false prophet was given the power to summon life into the image of the beast that would be erected. In yet another effort to undermine God's might and power, Satan would mimic God's miraculous life-giving creation of Adam by bestowing life into this statue.[10] This inanimate effigy would become alive, being given the ability to speak and to kill anyone who refused to worship it. The false prophet would have power to give life to the idol that had been built, and the idol consequently would be given power to carry out its own part of Satan's plan.

There is no clear indication that this image would be able to cause the deaths of those who refused to worship it simply by wishing such. Rather, it seems more likely that there would be a process of "weeding out" the true believers from those who worship the antichrist. One possible method of separating the deceived followers from those who refused to worship the beast might be the obligation of everyone upon the earth to receive the mark of the beast, as explained in the next two verses.

Verses 16, 17- ¹⁶He causes all, both small and great, rich and poor, free and slave, to receive a mark on their right hand or on their foreheads, ¹⁷and that no one may buy or sell except one who has the mark or the name of the beast, or the number of his name.

The antichrist and his ruling system would make it essential for anyone hoping to carry on life's normal activities to receive a specific mark on his right hand or forehead.[11] This mark would be a necessary prerequisite for transacting both personal and professional business. We know that this "decree" would be required of every individual upon the earth because the description specified all classes of people in just a few, short words—small and great (implying everyone in between), rich and poor (also implying everyone in between), and free or bond (every living person being one or the other). This description further implies that wealth, status, and power would be of no value and no help. Only those who bore the mark of the beast would benefit from material wealth because only they would be permitted the use of such resources.

On the contrary, anyone who refused to receive the mark of the beast either in his forehead or on his right hand would not be allowed to buy or sell anything. For believers who stood firm in their faith and refused to receive the mark, provisions for health and life would be unobtainable through the world system. They would not be able to buy food, clothing, property, services, medical needs, or anything purchased by means of exchange.

This might be the method by which the beast had the power to kill the resistant, though it is implied that his power to kill was more of an active nature, such as through persecution and murder. The indications are that once a citizen who refused to receive the mark was "found out," he or she would be executed. From God's perspective, such a brazen stance would be considered an act of martyrdom, and Scriptures indicate that there would be many martyrs during this time of tribulation. *"And I saw something like a sea of glass mingled with fire, and those who have the victory over the beast, over his image and over his mark and over the number of his name, standing on the sea of glass, having harps of God." (Revelation 15.2)*

Verse 18- Here is wisdom. Let him who has understanding calculate the number of the beast, for it is the number of a man: His number is 666.

We are admonished to pay close attention to the information about to be revealed. Though we do not yet know the antichrist's name and probably will not know until further signs of the end times are revealed, we are clearly given the number that represents the beast. Herein, John offers wisdom, which is given by God for all to read and understand. The message is clear and the warning unmistakable when he writes, "Let him who has understanding calculate the number of the beast." Those who follow Christ will be able to identify the beast by his number, which is 666. Though explanations have been variously ascribed to the meanings of the number, the explanation of it being "the number of man," and its use in triplicate, it is perhaps best to trust that the Holy Spirit will intercede and guide us when such wisdom becomes necessary.

Notes/Applications

Many throughout history have tried to interpret the meaning of the number 666 and the mark of the beast through calculations such as "gematria," which is a formula of mathematics that attempts to find hidden meanings in names and numbers. As a result, countless explanations and theories concerning this number's relevance have been posed.

Still, it is fitting for us to refrain from over speculating and from placing too much emphasis upon the actual number instead of upon the warning given in this passage: "His number is 666." The number six, as explained in this verse and further supported throughout Scripture, is the number of man. The triplicate presence of the number six might represent nothing more than the unholy trinity of the dragon, the beast, and the false prophet. Therefore, as evident in most prophetic warnings in the Bible, the emphasis should be upon the applicable message presented and not upon vague intricacies. Although interesting dialogues may abound, it is generally man's futile effort to use human intellect to interpret the ways of the infinite God that convolutes the clarity of God's overall message by hypothesizing about the obscure.

What we must concentrate upon, then, is what we *do* know— those things clearly explained in the Scriptures. We are told that at the ordained time people from every vantage point and life situation will bow to the beast. All will bow except for those who belong to God. True believers will be provided the discernment necessary to recognize the beast for who and what he is. They will not be unwittingly duped into eternal damnation by the beast's deceitful ways because they will have the Holy Spirit to direct them through the treacherous channels of evil's deception, and they will be armed with God's Word and the warnings contained therein. *"You are of God, little children, and have overcome them, because He who is in you is greater than he who is in the world. ⁵They are of the world. Therefore they speak as of the world, and the world hears them. ⁶We are of God. He who knows God hears us; he who is not of God does not hear us. By this we know the spirit of truth and the spirit of error." (1 John 4.4–6)* Such assurance draws us to become soberly aware of our need for a renewed commitment to God's Word, knowing that if we remain faithful to studying His revelation He will safeguard our minds from the evil one's lies with His truth. *"Be diligent to present yourself approved to God, a worker who does not need to be ashamed, rightly dividing the word of truth." (2 Timothy 2.15)*

Chapter Fourteen

Revelation 14.1–7

Verse 1- Then I looked, and behold, a Lamb standing on Mount Zion, and with Him one hundred and forty-four thousand, having His Father's name written on their foreheads.

What a glorious opening scene we are given in chapter fourteen to contrast the terrible picture of persecution and corruption that was painted in the previous chapter. John saw the Lamb standing high upon Mount Zion with the 144,000 that had the seal of God upon their foreheads. There should be little doubt that these 144,000 comprise the same group described earlier in the book *(Revelation 7.4)* or that this Lamb was the Lord Jesus Christ *(Revelation 5.6)*.

This scene paints a wonderful picture of promise revealing the Lamb's assurance of protection to this group specifically set apart by Almighty God, which possibly depicts the beginning of Israel's restoration in the last days. *"³¹The sun shall be turned into darkness, and the moon into blood, before the coming of the great and awesome day of the LORD. ³²And it shall come to pass that whoever calls on the name of the LORD shall be saved. For in Mount Zion and in Jerusalem there shall be deliverance, as the LORD has said, among the remnant whom the LORD calls." (Joel 2.31–32)*

Verse 2- And I heard a voice from heaven, like the voice of many waters, and like the voice of loud thunder. And I heard the sound of harpists playing their harps.

A voice resounded from Heaven like the rushing currents of many waters and like the rumbling boom of great thunder. Both of these descriptions express the Lord's voice as it has been depicted in similar accounts in the Bible. *"And behold, the glory of the God of Israel came from the way of the east. His voice was like the sound of many waters; and the earth shone with His glory." (Ezekiel 43.2) "His body was like beryl, his face like the appearance of lightning, his eyes like torches of fire, his arms and feet like burnished bronze in color, and the sound of his words like the voice of a multitude." (Daniel 10.6) "'Have you an arm like God? Or can you thunder with a voice like His?'" (Job 40.9)* This description characterizes a voice that was certainly loud and mighty. Accompanying this sound, John heard music from harps. He did not say that he saw anyone playing harps but only that he was able to hear the familiar sound of many musicians playing their harps.

Verse 3- They sang as it were a new song before the throne, before the four living creatures, and the elders; and no one could learn that song except the hundred and forty-four thousand who were redeemed from the earth.

The assembly of 144,000 was heard singing a unique song of praise and worship unto the Lord God Almighty and unto the Lamb. It was a song that was exclusive to this group. No one else could understand it or learn it. The song was solely created for and sung by the 144,000 that had been protected from the persecution of the dragon. They were aptly called the "redeemed from the earth," indicating the earthly realm from which they originated. This verse provides additional confirmation of the special relationship that this group of people had with Almighty God and of their distinguished importance to Him. *"So the ransomed of the Lord shall return, and come to Zion with singing, with everlasting joy on their heads.*

They shall obtain joy and gladness; sorrow and sighing shall flee away."
(Isaiah 51.11)

Verse 4- These are the ones who were not defiled with women, for they are virgins. These are the ones who follow the Lamb wherever He goes. These were redeemed from among men, being firstfruits to God and to the Lamb.

We are told more specifically about the character and discipline of these 144,000. Many expositors contend that this group was comprised solely of men because of the mention of them being "not defiled with women" and also the masculine use of the Greek word παρθενοι (parthenoi), translated as *virgin*.[1]

Another dispute arises in the debate over whether these people were literal virgins or whether the use of the word *virgin* simply connotes those who had not defiled their bodies in either a physical or spiritual sense. Whereas there is no irrefutable scriptural basis upon which these positions can be either proved or disproved, it is clear that the characteristics of these selected people were, though not perfect, purer than most. They were not faultless in either the eyes of God or the eyes of man, but they were certainly commended for their virtuous lives. It is important to realize, however, that their chaste and moralistic attributes had not earned their position among this elite group. It was still only by God's sovereign choice that these would be redeemed and sealed for protection throughout the tribulation. In addition, throughout the duration of the tribulation, they would remain fully obedient unto the leading of the Lord Jesus Christ and would diligently follow his every command wherever He went.

Again, we are told that these 144,000 were redeemed from among mankind in the world. Much is made of their being called the "firstfruits to God and to the Lamb." Such a description would seem to indicate that this group of 144,000 cannot comprise the entire sum of the redeemed upon the earth, as some have indicated, for by the word's very definition, the implication is that those included in this group are but the first group gathered at harvest time and presented to the Lord as consecrated or set apart.[2]

Accordingly, chapter fourteen could be aptly subtitled *The Harvest* for reasons which we are about to discover.

DIG DEEPER: *FIRSTFRUITS*

Firstfruits were the very first yield from the crops gathered at harvest time. The Israelites set these aside, the first and best of every crop, and considered them as belonging to God in a special sense. They were consecrated, dedicated, and presented to God on the day of the first-fruits, a part of the celebration of Pentecost.[3] *(Numbers 28.26; 2 Chronicles 31.5)*

Verse 5- *And in their mouth was found no deceit, for they are without fault before the throne of God.*

The use of the word *deceit* goes a step further than to merely say that these people did not lie, though such should also be included within its meaning. The meaning expresses the idea that they did not stretch the truth, cleverly avoid the truth, or even say truthful things that would give false impressions. Nothing except truth came from their mouths. *"The remnant of Israel shall do no unrighteousness and speak no lies, nor shall a deceitful tongue be found in their mouth."* *(Zephaniah 3.13a)* They stood faultless before God, though not as to suggest that they were without sin, but as all Christians, they had been justified by the redemptive work of the Lord Jesus Christ on the cross of Calvary.

Verses 6, 7- *⁶Then I saw another angel flying in the midst of heaven, having the everlasting gospel to preach to those who dwell on the earth—to every nation, tribe, tongue, and people— ⁷saying with a loud voice, "Fear God and give glory to Him, for the hour of His judgment has come; and worship Him who made heaven and earth, the sea and springs of water."*

A heavenly angel flew throughout the regions of Heaven preaching to all people of every nationality and tongue on earth. The messenger's purpose was to declare the truth of the Lord Jesus Christ to everyone throughout the world, though some commentators have hinted that this moment reveals one last opportunity for repentance and one last offer of salvation to the inhabitants of earth.[4]

However, in context of this chapter and in light of the events that follow, it seems more likely that this is a pronouncement of judgment and not one of hope.[5] First, we have already witnessed how the reprobate of the earth would refuse to repent even faced with direct judgment from God. *(Revelation 9.20–21)* Second, a noticeable lack of response followed this event. There is no subsequent description of any people repenting and receiving salvation and redemption. By both the tone of the message and the context in which it was written, it can be assumed that this "everlasting gospel" message that was preached did not accompany an invitation to which the earth's population could respond. As verse seven testifies, this declaration was not a pronouncement that "the hour of His judgment" was coming but that it had come and fell, at that very moment, upon the inhabitants of the world. Once the angel announced that the hour of judgment was upon mankind, he called for all people to worship God Almighty, the Creator of the earth and everything therein.

Notes/Applications

A declaration was proclaimed for all people to fear God because His judgment was upon them. But what does it mean to fear God? *"The fear of the Lord is the beginning of wisdom." (Psalm 111.10a) "The fear of the Lord is the beginning of knowledge, but fools despise wisdom and instruction." (Proverbs 1.7)* Unbelievers become fearful of God when judgment pours forth from His just hand in response to their unrepentant hearts. They may even have a surface respect for the "higher power." But what about believers? How deeply does our fear of the Lord run? Should believers *fear* their Lord? Many Christians answer that question with the trite reply, "Fearing God really means to have a proper respect and reverence for God." Whereas reverence and respect are *proper* responses to God, they are not fully *adequate* responses. A genuine fear of the Lord expresses the totality of our response to the Almighty One. If we have not responded to Him with the totality of our being, we will probably not live in both worship and trembling.

God Almighty created the entire universe, the earth and everything contained upon it. He is perfectly sovereign and answers to no person or being. He employs every circumstance, good and bad, in fulfilling His perfect plan for creation. God reigns supremely over the entire realm of creation, and yet each person is a unique opus of His design. God interlaced the very hairs on every head, and He fills man's lungs with each needed breath. Fat grams and cholesterol counts do not ultimately ordain the longevity of lives, but the good and perfect will of God Almighty does, for He determines man's days according to His sovereign calendar.

The fear of the Lord involves not just theoretically understanding these differences between the God of the Universe and us as vessels of His creation but by accepting these truths as realities. Recall how the disciples responded to Jesus Christ. The closer they drew to the Son of God, His power, His holiness, and His love, the more they feared Him.

A holy God will judge sin. God is not merely our friend; He is our King. Therefore, He deserves our praise, our worship, and our fear. *"¹¹Teach me Your way, O Lord; I will walk in Your truth; unite my heart to fear Your name. ¹²I will praise You, O Lord my God, with all my heart, and I will glorify Your name forevermore. ¹³For great is Your mercy toward me, and You have delivered my soul from the depths of Sheol." (Psalm 86.11–13)*

Revelation 14.8–13

Verse 8- *And another angel followed, saying, "Babylon is fallen, is fallen, that great city, because she has made all nations drink of the wine of the wrath of her fornication."*

A second angel immediately followed, and like the first angel, his message was surely heard by every person throughout the earth. Though it was not the gospel message (like that of the first angel), it was a message of good news for believers and one of doom for unbelievers: "Babylon is fallen." The godless world-system had collapsed.[6] The significance of this message and the reference to Babylon will be discussed thoroughly in chapter eighteen.

This message was also a proclamation of judgment against those who had participated in the luring ways of the world and had succumbed to its temptations. *Fornication* means "unfaithfulness," and its use here does not imply unfaithfulness among people but rather exemplifies the defiance of the creation against its Creator. This had been accomplished through idolatry, atheism, and many other forms of rebellion against God. *"[6]Flee from the midst of Babylon, and every one save his life! Do not be cut off in her iniquity, for this is the time of the LORD'S vengeance; He shall recompense her. [7]Babylon was a golden cup in the LORD'S hand, that made all the earth drunk. The nations drank her wine; therefore the nations are deranged. [8]Babylon has suddenly fallen and been destroyed." (Jeremiah 51.6–8a)*

Verses 9, 10- *[9]Then a third angel followed them, saying with a loud voice, "If anyone worships the beast and his image, and receives his mark on his forehead or on his hand, [10]he himself shall also drink of the wine of the wrath of God, which is poured out full strength into the cup of His indignation. He shall be tormented with fire and brimstone in the presence of the holy angels and in the presence of the Lamb.*

A third angel followed with another proclamation of judgment and condemnation. This angel also spoke with a loud voice addressing all of those who worshipped the beast and bore his image on their right hands or foreheads, which, as evidenced in chapter thirteen, applied to all mankind except for the redeemed. *"He causes all, both small and great, rich and poor, free and slave, to receive a mark on their right hand or on their foreheads." (Revelation 13.16)*

The angel's message was a promise, though not a very favorable one for those being addressed. Without exception, all who worshipped the beast and received his mark would experience God's wrath. The description of this wrath being "poured out full strength into the cup of His indignation" depicts the extreme levels at which this judgment would ultimately be delivered. It would not be tempered in the least but would be issued in full measure and full strength. *"For in the hand of the Lord there is a cup, and the wine is red; it is fully mixed, and He pours it out; surely its dregs shall all the wicked of the earth drain and drink down." (Psalm 75.8) "Upon the wicked He will rain coals; fire and brimstone and a burning wind shall be the portion of their cup." (Psalm 11.6)* These people would be tormented with fire and brimstone in the presence of the Lord Jesus Christ and in the presence of His holy angels, which does not necessitate that the eternal consequence of their rebellion would take place in the presence of the Lord and His angels but that it was a necessary parameter at this moment in history and for this decree of judgment.

Verse 11- "And the smoke of their torment ascends forever and ever; and they have no rest day or night, who worship the beast and his image, and whoever receives the mark of his name."

The fire and brimstone will never burn out or fade away but will burn forever without being quenched. There would not be even a moment of relief or respite for those who had worshiped the beast and had accepted his mark in their right hands or foreheads. *"It shall not be quenched night or day; its smoke shall ascend forever. From generation to generation it shall lie waste; no one shall pass through it forever and ever." (Isaiah 34.10)* The mark, once taken, could never be erased. To accept the mark of the beast was to accept eternal damnation upon oneself.[7]

Verse 12- Here is the patience of the saints; here are those who keep the commandments of God and the faith of Jesus.

This statement encompasses a promise of hope to those Christians who withstand the persecution of the antichrist and maintained an unshakable faith in the Lord Christ Jesus. Those who refused to receive the mark of the beast were assured that their perseverance was not in vain. The "patience of the saints" is the vindication of the faithful at the onset of judgment.

In addition, these saints were commended for their obedience in keeping God's commandments. They were about to receive the reward of their redemption in the Lord Jesus Christ, the very hope to which they had steadfastly clung throughout their earthly hardships. They had persevered in their faith, and the prize to which they had endured the antichrist's persecution was about to be accomplished.

Verse 13- Then I heard a voice from heaven saying to me, "Write: 'Blessed are the dead who die in the Lord from now on.'" "Yes," says the Spirit, "that they may rest from their labors, and their works follow them."

John heard a voice call to him from Heaven, and the voice instructed him to write that which he was told. John obeyed and wrote: "Blessed are the dead who die in the Lord from now on," and to this statement, the Holy Spirit confirmed that these believers would finally have rest in Heaven from the persecution they had endured. This should not be understood to suggest that those who had previously been martyred for the cause of Christ were not equally blessed as those who would "die...from now on." We know from earlier chapters that they, too, already possessed their reward in Heaven and were simply awaiting the Lord's final judgment upon those who took their lives:

> [9]When He opened the fifth seal, I saw under the altar the souls of those who had been slain for the word of God and for the testimony which they held. [10]And they cried with a loud voice, saying, 'How long, O Lord, holy and true, until You judge and avenge our blood on those who dwell on the earth?' [11]Then a white robe was given to each of them; and it was said to them that they should rest a little while longer, until both the number of their fellow servants

and their brethren, who would be killed as they were, was completed. (Revelation 6.9–11)

The emphasis of the verse seems to be more upon the magnificent rest and tranquility that will be granted those who have endured so much suffering, many even unto death, at the hands of beast. The time of judgment, the great Day of the Lord, was imminent, and the tables at last would be turned. Those who had received the mark of the beast, had indulged in its fornications, and had refused to repent of their wickedness would share in the fury of God's wrath, whereas those who remained faithful to Christ in the midst of the antichrist's intolerable persecution would at last be vindicated. The final harvest was at hand!

Notes/Applications

"The patience of the saints, those who keep the commandments of God and the faith of Jesus...they may rest from their labors, and their works follow them." Cast against the backdrop of dreadful details concerning the spiritual fate of those who will partake in the mark of the beast, the Lord offers encouragement to the members of His body who will suffer horribly for His name by not submitting to the beast's mark. He will see their sorrow and remember their commitment; they will be blessed for their faithfulness. Their lives will leave His mark—a legacy of His gospel message, His power, and His authority.

We must refrain from misunderstanding how these martyrs were told their works were not in vain. *(verse 13)* Such affirmation does not support a "works theology" because the total summation of mankind's good works could never buy even one individual's entrance into Heaven. *"⁸For by grace you have been saved through faith, and that not of yourselves; it is the gift of God, ⁹not of works, lest anyone should boast." (Ephesians 2.8–9)* We are well aware that any works generated from self will never be of any use to God nor gain any rewards. Therefore, even when fulfilling small deeds that the Lord has commissioned, we must be very careful to keep our motives pure and beware of the traps set by pride, stubbornness, selfishness, and self-righteousness.

Even now amid rough times of careless disposal of human life, what could be said of us? Would the Lord find us to be His patient saints, keeping His commandments and His faith? May He find us needing rest from our labors.

Revelation 14.14–20

Verse 14- Then I looked, and behold, a white cloud, and on the cloud sat One like the Son of Man, having on His head a golden crown, and in His hand a sharp sickle.

John's vision continued with the appearance of "One like the Son of man" sitting on a cloud. There can be little doubt that this was any other than the Lord Jesus Christ Himself. *"'Then they will see the Son of Man coming in a cloud with power and great glory.'" (Luke 21.27)* John certainly recognized the very one and same Lord Whom he served and with Whom he walked during Jesus' physical presence on earth. Because of Christ's appearance with a sharp sickle and in light of the preceding verses, we now anticipate His judgment upon all people of the earth.

Verse 15- And another angel came out of the temple, crying with a loud voice to Him who sat on the cloud, "Thrust in Your sickle and reap, for the time has come for You to reap, for the harvest of the earth is ripe."

An angel appeared from within the temple in Heaven and called out to the Lord Jesus, Who sat upon the cloud with the sickle in His hand. The angel told the Son of Man that the time had come to thrust the sickle over the entire earth and reap the harvest, which was ripe and ready to be gleaned.

The fact that an angel emerged from the temple to inform the Son of Man upon the clouds that the harvest was ripe in no manner contradicts the omniscience of God. The angel was not the bearer of any information about which the Lord was not already fully aware. The purpose for the angel's declaration appears to be solely for John's sake so that understanding the significance of these unfolding events would be perfectly clear to the witness. This passage can be likened to Revelation 7.13, where one of the heavenly elders asked John, "Who are these arrayed in white robes, and where did they come from?" John responded in verse fourteen, "Sir, you know," after which the elder proceeded to explain to John what was occurring.

Verse 16- So He who sat on the cloud thrust in His sickle on the earth, and the earth was reaped.

John then watched as the Son of Man thrust His sickle over the whole earth. Prudent study of the specific word use in this verse offers much insight. The Greek word θεριζω (therizō) is translated as "reap," which is a figurative word used here to indicate "discriminating judgment."[8] Though their identity was not clearly stated, it seems most reasonable to conclude that this first harvest reaped by the Son of Man consisted of the believers that remained upon the earth.[9] This group, however, does not appear to include the 144,000, which is always explicitly specified as unique from every other group type that would be present in Heaven, such as the redeemed, the twenty-four elders, the martyrs under the altar, the four beasts that surrounded the throne, and the host of angels. This group that was harvested, therefore, plainly consisted of the remaining believers living in their physical bodies upon the earth that would complete Heaven's population. This seems a rather clear depiction of the Lord gathering His own unto Him before the final judgment.[10]

"His winnowing fan is in His hand, and He will thoroughly clean out His threshing floor, and gather the wheat into His barn; but the chaff He will burn with unquenchable fire."' (Luke 3.17)

Verse 17- Then another angel came out of the temple which is in heaven, he also having a sharp sickle.

Many commentators suggest that verses seventeen through twenty merely reflect the harvest of judgment described in verses fourteen through sixteen, and that this entire chapter depicts only one event—the judgment of the wicked.[11] However, the specific wording seems to indicate otherwise—"then" (expressing a subsequent transition of time), "another angel" (expressing a different subject), and "also having" (expressing similarity but not equivalence).

Another angel emerged from within the temple of Heaven, and he, too, carried a sharp sickle similar to that utilized by the Son of Man seated upon the cloud. All of God's angels are at His command to do His will as He requires. In this case, the angel was appointed to help carry out Almighty God's judgment upon the wicked.

Verse 18- And another angel came out from the altar, who had power over fire, and he cried with a loud cry to him who had the sharp sickle, saying, "Thrust in your sharp sickle and gather the clusters of the vine of the earth, for her grapes are fully ripe."

Another angel emerged from the altar in Heaven. This angel, who God had given the power over fire, called from the altar with a loud voice to the angel that had just emerged from the temple with a sharp sickle. He told the angel to thrust the sickle across the entire earth in the same manner as the Son of Man had just done. The angel was instructed to "gather the clusters of the vine of the earth" because the harvest was ripe. *"Put in the sickle, for the harvest is ripe. Come, go down; for the winepress is full, the vats overflow—for their wickedness is great.'" (Joel 3.13)*

The implication in the remaining verses of this chapter is that the Lord had already gathered His redeemed from the earth and that the angel with the sickle reaped those that remained. Had the Lord already harvested every person from the earth to judgment, there would be no need for a subsequent gathering. Therefore, by the evidence of what awaits those harvested by the second angel, the conclusion must be drawn that the Lord had harvested those belonging to Him. All that remained after the first harvesting were the unbelievers for whom, as later verses specify, the wrath of God had been prepared:

[30]'Let both grow together until the harvest, and at the time of harvest I will say to the reapers, "First gather together the tares and bind them in bundles to burn them, but gather the wheat into my barn." [38]The field is the world, the good seeds are the sons of the kingdom, but the tares are the sons of the wicked one. [39]The enemy who sowed them is the devil, the harvest is the end of the age, and the reapers are the angels. [40]Therefore as the tares are gathered and burned in the fire, so it will be at the end of this age. [41]The Son of Man will send out His angels, and they will gather out of His kingdom all things that offend, and those who practice lawlessness, [42]and will cast them into the furnace of fire. There will be wailing and gnashing of teeth.' (Matthew 13.30, 38–42)

Verse 19- So the angel thrust his sickle into the earth and gathered the vine of the earth, and threw it into the great winepress of the wrath of God.

John watched as the second angel fulfilled that which he had been instructed to do. The angel thrust his sickle across the entire earth, gathered up all that remained upon it, and then cast them "into the great winepress of the wrath of God." Evidently, the angel did not kill all of these people but gathered them together for the purpose of experiencing the consequences of their unrepentant sinfulness. The elements of God's wrath that were to be poured out upon these people are explained in greater detail in the following chapters.

Verse 20- And the winepress was trampled outside the city, and blood came out of the winepress, up to the horses' bridles, for one thousand six hundred furlongs.

This verse anticipates the sequence of events described in chapters sixteen through nineteen. The location where this second harvest was gathered, referred to as the "winepress," was "outside the city," likely the same city that is mentioned frequently throughout Revelation—Jerusalem. This seems to have been done so as not to violate the sanctity of the city. *(Leviticus 24.14; Numbers 5.1–3; Matthew 27.31; Acts 7.58; and Hebrews 13.12)* The winepress would yield blood so vast and widespread that it would reach the height of horses' bridles for a distance spanning sixteen hundred furlongs or about 180 miles.[12] This vividly illustrates a complete slaughter of the unrighteous in which not a trace of hope, peace, or relief can be found. With this, we approach a doorstep in the text where we will cross the threshold to the end of the world as we know it:

> [3]*'I have trodden the winepress alone, and from the peoples no one was with Me. For I have trodden them in My anger, and trampled them in My fury; their blood is sprinkled upon My garments, and I have stained all My robes. [4]For the day of vengeance is in My heart, and the year of My redeemed has come. [5]I looked, but there was no one to help, and I wondered that there was no one to uphold; therefore My own arm brought salvation for Me; and My own fury,*

*it sustained Me. ⁶I have trodden down the peoples in My anger,
made them drunk in My fury, and brought down their strength to
the earth.' (Isaiah 63.3–6)*

Notes/Applications

During the earth's final days, the world's population will experience unimaginable pain, suffering, and agony in the "great winepress" of the Holy God. *"But the Lord is the true God; He is the living God and the everlasting King. At His wrath the earth will tremble, and the nations will not be able to endure His indignation." (Jeremiah 10.10) "The Lord will cause His glorious voice to be heard, and show the descent of His arm, with the indignation of His anger and the flame of a devouring fire, with scattering, tempest, and hailstones." (Isaiah 30.30)* God's wrath is a righteous reply to man's willful disobedience and refusal to repent and worship Him, the true God. God's wrath is not an act of revenge but an expression of His holiness. God will punish the sinful and will ultimately abolish sin.

Man more readily embraces a God Who loves while rejecting a God Who is holy and just. God's wrath, however, should not be juxtaposed against His love. Both are complete attributes of His being. He has as much one as the other; He *is* as much one as the other. Man's difficulty in surrendering to such a God, the true God, lies in his rebuff to admit his sin and need. The very God Who pours out His wrath against evil is the same God Who poured out His Son as the means to restore His rebellious creation.

If we disregard God's wrath, we set up an idol—an unmerciful god with a frail and incomplete nature, and in so doing, we negate what the cross was all about. We cannot accept a portion of God's character and deny any aspect of the rest:

³And do you think this, O man, you who judge those practicing such things, and doing the same, that you will escape the judgment of God? ⁴Or do you despise the riches of His goodness, forbearance, and longsuffering, not knowing that the goodness of God leads you to repentance? ⁵But in accordance with your hardness and your impenitent heart you are treasuring up for yourself wrath in the day of wrath and revelation of the righteous judgment of

God, ⁶who 'will render to each one according to his deeds': ⁷eternal
life to those who by patient continuance in doing good seek for
glory, honor, and immortality; ⁸but to those who are self-seeking and
do not obey the truth, but obey unrighteousness—indignation and
wrath, ⁹tribulation and anguish, on every soul of man who does
evil. (Romans 2.3–9)

It is difficult to read the Book of Revelation and not be alerted
by the frightening events targeted at believers (by the antichrist)
and unbelievers (by the wrath of God) that are so vividly
described, yet still, believers often slip into apathetic slumber
within the deceiving embrace of a lost and dying world destined
for Hell. When such is the case, the Book of Revelation and its
intense prophecies concerning destruction should motivate our
souls to tell others about Christ with unparalleled fervor because
perhaps nowhere in the Bible can a more urgent reason to share
with others the message of redemption through Jesus Christ be
found. *"The Lord is slow to anger and great in power, and will not at all*
acquit the wicked."(Nahum 1.3) "¹⁹'Go therefore and make disciples of all
the nations, baptizing them in the name of the Father and of the Son and of
the Holy Spirit, ²⁰teaching them to observe all things that I have com-
manded you; and lo, I am with you always, even to the end of the age.'
Amen." (Matthew 28.19–20)

Chapter Fifteen

Revelation 15.1–8

Verse 1- Then I saw another sign in heaven, great and marvelous: seven angels having the seven last plagues, for in them the wrath of God is complete.

Chapter fifteen begins a multi-chapter explanation of the "last plagues," the final wrath of God upon mankind. Read in context, it appears that these seven vials of God's wrath are a detailed account of the "winepress of the wrath of God" that concluded the previous chapter.

John witnessed another "great and marvelous" sign in Heaven, which indicates that he was likely aware of the terrible significance of these visions. "Great and marvelous" does not imply that the sign was a good thing but that it was a momentous and critical event. *Great,* as used in this verse, is translated from the Greek word μέγα (mega), which is an adjective describing a high degree of intensity; and *marvelous,* as used in this verse, is translated from the Greek word θαυμαστόν (thaumaston), which is a word specifically used to describe a magnificent spiritual wonder of God.[1]

John saw seven angels in Heaven, each having one of the last seven plagues to afflict all mankind left on the earth, those prepared for the winepress of God's fury. Each of these plagues was filled up with God's wrath, which had come due because the world's iniquities had also reached full measure:

15That day is a day of wrath, a day of trouble and distress, a day of devastation and desolation, a day of darkness and gloominess, a day of clouds and thick darkness, 16a day of trumpet and alarm against the fortified cities and against the high towers. 17'I will bring distress upon men, and they shall walk like blind men, because they have sinned against the Lord; their blood shall be poured out like dust, and their flesh like refuse.' 18Neither their silver nor their gold shall be able to deliver them in the day of the Lord's wrath; but the whole land shall be devoured by the fire of His jealousy, for He will make speedy riddance of all those who dwell in the land. (Zephaniah 1.15–18)

DIG DEEPER: *THE WRATH OF GOD*

This term appears only ten times in Scripture, and two of those times occur in this chapter. *(verses 1 and 7)* There is only one occurrence in the Old Testament. *(Psalm 78.31)* Throughout the Book of Revelation, however, the theme appears five times, indicating that God's patient lovingkindness does reach a moment when He no longer will tolerate the rebellion of the human race. Jesus laid out the terms of His new covenant in clear, concise terms: *"He who believes in the Son has eternal life; and he who does not believe the Son shall not see life, but the wrath of God abides on him.'"* (John 3.36)

Verse 2- And I saw something like a sea of glass mingled with fire, and those who have the victory- over the beast, over his image and over his mark and over the number of his name, standing on the sea of glass, having harps of God.

John saw what he could only describe as a "sea of glass mingled with fire." According to previous accounts in Revelation, this "sea of glass" is around the throne of Almighty God in Heaven. *"Before the throne there was a sea of glass, like crystal. And in the midst of the throne, and around the throne, were four living creatures full of eyes in front and in back." (Revelation 4.6)* Upon this crystalline sea stood the redeemed who had refused to receive the mark of the beast. This group is often referred to as "tribulation saints." John also noted that they are playing "harps of God," praising Almighty God with the strums of their instruments.

Verse 3- They sing the song of Moses, the servant of God, and the song of the Lamb, saying: "Great and marvelous are Your works, Lord God Almighty! Just and true are Your ways, O King of the saints!

These martyred saints are seen singing as they played their harps. This is a song that is specifically meant for them to sing, much as the 144,000 had their own song to sing. They sing "the song of Moses." *"Then Moses and the children of Israel sang this song to the Lord, and spoke, saying: 'I will sing to the Lord, for He has triumphed gloriously! The horse and its rider He has thrown into the sea!'" (Exodus 15.1)* This song seems to be their response of praise to the Lord for His decisive and overwhelming victory. Even more so, it appears that they magnified the Lord for His mercy and deliverance upon His faithful from the times of Moses throughout history, even unto this ultimate culmination of the Lamb's final judgment.[2] They proclaimed God's ways to be "just and true," and they addressed Him as the "King of the saints." In declaring at the onset of God's final wrath that His ways are just and true, they acknowledged the perfection of God's justice for the consequences of man's sin.

Verse 4- Who shall not fear You, O Lord, and glorify Your name? For You alone are holy. For all nations shall come and worship before You, for Your judgments have been manifested."

The praise of Almighty God continued in Heaven. In a sense, these tribulation martyrs posed a rhetorical question toward both those in Heaven and those on earth by asking "Who shall not fear You, O Lord, and glorify Your name?" The word *fear* implies more than mere reverence but, more literally, expresses dread and horror.[3] *"Who would not fear You, O King of the nations? For this is Your rightful due.*

*For among all the wise men of the nations, and in all their kingdoms, there
is none like You." (Jeremiah 10.7)*

Their song also declared that all nations would worship God
Almighty. The use of the auxiliary imperative verb *shall* indicates
that this was, even at this moment of rejoicing, a future and ongoing
occurrence. The saints also proclaimed that God's judgments had
been made known unto all. Every person on earth would realize
that the suffering he or she experienced was the wrath of God and
His direct judgment on mankind for its impenitent sinfulness.

**Verses 5, 6- *⁵After these things I looked, and behold, the temple
of the tabernacle of the testimony in heaven was opened. ⁶And
out of the temple came the seven angels having the seven
plagues, clothed in pure bright linen, and having their chests
girded with golden bands.***

John saw that the temple of the Lord in Heaven was opened.
This seems to be the same temple mentioned throughout Revelation
and the same one from which the three angels in chapter fourteen
emerged. The heavenly temple was first opened after the sounding
of the seventh trumpet. *"Then the temple of God was opened in heaven,
and the ark of His covenant was seen in His temple. And there were lightnings, noises, thunderings, an earthquake, and great hail." (Revelation 11.19)*

From within the temple, seven more angels emerged, each possessing a plague from God to be administered upon mankind. The
angels wore pure white linen, and their chests were adorned in
gold. Some commentators propose particular significance to the
similarity between the descriptions of these angels' attire and that
of the Old Testament priests *(Exodus 28.22–26; Ezekiel 44.17)* as well
as to the roles that each fulfilled, but there seems little bearing to
such conclusions apart from curious observation.[4]

**Verse 7- *Then one of the four living creatures gave to the seven
angels seven golden bowls full of the wrath of God who lives forever and ever.***

Each of the seven angels that emerged from the heavenly temple was given one of seven golden bowls which contained the

wrath of God. The vials were distributed by one of the four beasts near God's throne. *(Revelation 4.6)* The golden bowls were filled to the brim with different elements that embodied God's wrath—the holy and righteousness judgment of God upon mankind.

John acknowledged the eternity of God's being; there is no indication that the description "who lives forever and ever" was stated by anyone other than the writer himself under the divine inspiration of the Holy Spirit.

Verse 8- *The temple was filled with smoke from the glory of God and from His power, and no one was able to enter the temple till the seven plagues of the seven angels were completed.*

The temple in Heaven was filled with "smoke from the glory of God and from His power." Biblically, smoke often foreshadowed judgment, as was the case at Mount Sinai. *"Now Mount Sinai was completely in smoke, because the Lord descended upon it in fire. Its smoke ascended like the smoke of a furnace, and the whole mountain quaked greatly." (Exodus 19.18)* Similarly, Isaiah saw smoke in the temple as God pronounced judgment upon the nation of Israel. *"And the posts of the door were shaken by the voice of him who cried out, and the house was filled with smoke." (Isaiah 6.4)* This essence of smoke appears eleven other times in the Book of Revelation. In this instance, the smoke of God's glory and power filled the temple so that no being could enter it until the seven golden bowls of God's wrath had been completely poured out by the seven angels. The temple was closed to all until God's judgment of mankind was complete.

Notes/Applications

Chapter fifteen begins to offer a more detailed account of the manner in which the wrath of God will be unleashed upon mankind as foretold at the end of chapter fourteen. A grim, sorrowful picture arrays the world's walls, similar to the building intensity of boiling water about to spill over a pot's rim. As we will see in the preceding chapters, this dismal prologue to the imminent wrath of God is neither miscalculated nor underrated.

Many people tend to wonder why a loving God could cause so much destruction and judgment. Perhaps a better question is found in wondering why our perfect and holy Creator has not destroyed this sinful, wayward world long before now. God's holiness demands justice, yet every moment that passes without His pouring out a full measure of holy indignation upon this world is an act of incomprehensible longsuffering mercy. *"⁸But, beloved, do not forget this one thing, that with the Lord one day is as a thousand years, and a thousand years as one day. ⁹The Lord is not slack concerning His promise, as some count slackness, but is longsuffering toward us, not willing that any should perish but that all should come to repentance." (2 Peter 3.8–9)*

Nevertheless, a day of reckoning approaches, a day of complete victory over the beast, his image, his mark, and his number. The single hope for man to bypass God's judgment is obtainable only on Holy God's terms through the means that He has already provided—the Lord Jesus Christ. Praise God for His mercy toward those who turn from their rebellion and believe in Him! *"¹⁴Therefore, beloved, looking forward to these things, be diligent to be found by Him in peace, without spot and blameless; ¹⁵and consider that the longsuffering of our Lord is salvation." (2 Peter 3.14–15)*

Chapter Sixteen

Revelation 16.1–7

Verse 1- Then I heard a loud voice from the temple saying to the seven angels, "Go and pour out the bowls of the wrath of God on the earth."

A great voice was heard from within the temple that commanded the seven angels to go fulfill their tasks. It can be presumed with relative certainty that this was the voice of God since we know from the last verse of chapter fifteen that no one could enter the temple that was filled with the smoke of God's glory and power. Furthermore, only God, the author of creation and the director of these bowls of wrath, could command the fulfillment of His wrath. Accordingly, Almighty God sent each of the angels to their respective locations to complete His all-encompassing wrath and final judgment upon the reprobate of His creation. It was perfect and fitting justice that the world deserved for its sins.

Though many scholars suggest that the judgments of the seven seals, the seven trumpets, and the seven bowls occur concurrently, the judgments hold more significance if understood as occurring progressively.[1] Each developing segment of God's judgment would increase in its intensity as the end of the age approached until, finally, these final seven bowls of wrath would be poured out with utter destruction and fierce rapidity.

Verse 2- So the first went and poured out his bowl upon the earth, and a foul and loathsome sore came upon the men who had the mark of the beast and those who worshiped his image.

The first angel poured out his first bowl of wrath upon the earth. Immediately, those bearing the mark of the beast were inflicted with "foul and loathsome" sores. A more literal translation from the Greek text is "evil and grievous."[2]

This first bowl of wrath resembles the sixth plague against Pharaoh and Egypt by God through Moses:

> [8]So the Lord said to Moses and Aaron, 'Take for yourselves handfuls of ashes from a furnace, and let Moses scatter it toward the heavens in the sight of Pharaoh. [9]And it will become fine dust in all the land of Egypt, and it will cause boils that break out in sores on man and beast throughout all the land of Egypt.' [10]Then they took ashes from the furnace and stood before Pharaoh, and Moses scattered them toward heaven. And they caused boils that break out in sores on man and beast. [11]And the magicians could not stand before Moses because of the boils, for the boils were on the magicians and on all the Egyptians. (Exodus 9.8–11)

Verse 3- Then the second angel poured out his bowl on the sea, and it became blood as of a dead man; and every living creature in the sea died.

The second angel poured out his assigned bowl of wrath into the sea, and all of the world's oceans and seas became like the contaminated blood of a dead man, wherein every living thing within them was instantly killed.

It is obvious that this plague was far worse than the previous judgment of the second trumpet, wherein only a third of the world's seas were turned into blood and only a third of the living creatures within the seas were killed. "[8]Then the second angel sounded: and something like a great mountain burning with fire was thrown into the sea, and a *third of the sea became blood.* [9]*And a third of the living creatures in the sea died, and a third of the ships were destroyed." (Revelation 8.8–9)*

This verse further specifies that the sea turned into blood like that "of a dead man." This signifies a complete contamination that ended any life-sustaining qualities of the water for the creatures that lived within the seas. It would literally be a river of diseased and decaying blood like that of a corpse.

Verse 4- Then the third angel poured out his bowl on the rivers and springs of water, and they became blood.

The third angel poured out his designated bowl of judgment upon all of the earth's fresh water sources, including rivers, streams, brooks, and springs, all of which were also turned to blood. Evidently, the very source of the earth's fresh water supply would be contaminated from even the deepest natural sources. Like the seas afflicted by the second bowl judgment, this bowl would immediately kill every creature within these waters and also bring an end to the entire world's fresh water supply needed for drinking, cooking, and cleaning.

The second and third judgments contained in these golden vessels also bear resemblance to the first plague used by Moses against Pharaoh and the Egyptians:

> [20]*And Moses and Aaron did so, just as the Lord commanded. So he lifted up the rod and struck the waters that were in the river, in the sight of Pharaoh and in the sight of his servants. And all the waters that were in the river were turned to blood.* [21]*The fish that were in the river died, the river stank, and the Egyptians could not drink the water of the river. So there was blood throughout all the land of Egypt. (Exodus 7.20–21)*

Verse 5- And I heard the angel of the waters saying: "You are righteous, O Lord, the One who is and who was and who is to be, because You have judged these things.

At this point, there was a break in the bowl judgments only long enough for the "angel of the waters" to declare that the Lord is righteous and His wrath is just. It can be assumed from John's description of the one making this proclamation as *the* angel rather than *an* angel that this was the same one that had just poured out the judgment of the third bowl.[3]

The angel acknowledged God as everlasting and eternal by describing God as One "who is and who was and who is to be." It is also important to note that the angel did not say that God is righteous *and* He has judged accordingly but rather declares that God is righteous *because* He judged accordingly, which confirms that judgment upon an unholy, unrepentant creation was not only merited but also *necessary* simply by the nature of our perfect, holy, and just Creator. Apart from surrendering to the Lord Jesus Christ's atoning work at Calvary, there is no possible way for unholy people to stand before or live forevermore in the presence of their holy Maker. Judgment, therefore, is both justifiable and essential.

Verse 6- For they have shed the blood of saints and prophets, and You have given them blood to drink. For it is their just due."

The angel of the waters continued to declare the justness of the Lord's wrath. Because these reprobate followers of the beast had shed the blood of so many "saints and prophets" of God, they were aptly given only blood to drink. The earth's drinking supply had been turned to, as it were, the blood of those they had killed. Those seeking to quench their thirst had to do so with the unsatisfying, contaminated blood that flowed from the former water sources.

There is a time of reckoning and a time to even the scales. God's vengeance would soon come against all those who had persecuted and killed His faithful.[4] *"I will feed those who oppress you with their own flesh, and they shall be drunk with their own blood as with sweet wine. All flesh shall know that I, the Lord, am your Savior, and your Redeemer, the Mighty One of Jacob."* (Isaiah 49.26)

Verse 7- And I heard another from the altar saying, "Even so, Lord God Almighty, true and righteous are Your judgments."

John heard a voice from the altar in Heaven echo the convictions of the angel of the waters. "Even so," declared the voice from the altar, presumably that of another angel or, perhaps, one of the martyred saints.[5] *"When He opened the fifth seal, I saw under the altar the souls of those who had been slain for the word of God and for the testimony which they held." (Revelation 6.9)* This conditional phrase "even so" was a manner of saying *Even as horrible and abhorrent as it all may seem, You, O Lord, are perfect and Your judgments are just.* And truly, as terrible and harsh as such wrath may appear to be, it would be the perfectly just consequence for the sins of unbelievers. Indeed, "True and righteous" are Almighty God's judgments upon the earth!

Notes/Applications

Despite the varying theories about what actual form the "creatures" of the various trumpet judgments might take or from what political or technological mode the antichrist might ascend into the world power structure, Revelation's overall message is irrefutable: God is the Almighty, the righteous and true Judge. *"God is a just judge, and God is angry with the wicked every day." (Psalm 7.11)* *"⁷But the Lord shall endure forever; He has prepared His throne for judgment. ⁸He shall judge the world in righteousness, and He shall administer judgment for the peoples in uprightness." (Psalm 9.7–8)* Most people more readily embrace love as an element of God's character but repel the idea that God is concurrently holy, righteous, and just. The Lord despises evil and how it twists its tentacles around the lives of His creation, leaving it subject to His wrath.

The Lord God will avenge sin, including the sin of murdering His saints. Those who reject the cross and follow the antichrist system in the world will experience severe tribulation greater than the world has never known and will ultimately follow the entire lost population to a final, eternal sentence in Hell.

Fortunately, if we cannot be confident that we share the same eternal destiny of those justified and preserved by their faith in the Lord Jesus Christ, there is still time to run to the Lord and, thereby, escape the utmost suffering of eternal separation from God awaiting those who rebel against Him. This day offers opportunity and hope for all who will seek His forgiveness and mercy:

Room for the penitent, burdened with sin,
Room at the open door—let him come in;
Weary and tempest tossed, where can he flee?
Jesus, Thou Lamb of God, only to Thee...

Room where the living stream flows at His feet,
Room at the throne of grace—God's mercy seat;
There may the broken heart lose all its grief,
There may the contrite soul find sweet relief...

Room at the blessed feast God has prepared,
Room where the bread of life millions have shared;
Room where the smiles of love tenderly fall;
Room in Thy arms, O Christ, room, room for all.[6]

Today is the day to make our eternal, spiritual reservation with the Father. "[30b]*'Repent, and turn from all your transgressions, so that iniquity will not be your ruin. [31]Cast away from you all the transgressions which you have committed, and get yourselves a new heart and a new spirit.'"* (Ezekiel 18.30b–31a) "[2]*'In My Father's house are many mansions; if it were not so, I would have told you. I go to prepare a place for you. [3]And if I go and prepare a place for you, I will come again and receive you to Myself; that where I am, there you may be also.'"* (John 14.2–3) We come to Him by humbly repenting and surrendering to His authority and to the full scope of His holy being, and in so doing, we can rightfully and boldly join with the heavenly proclamation, "Even so, Lord God Almighty, true and righteous are Your judgments."

Revelation 16.8–14

Verse 8- Then the fourth angel poured out his bowl on the sun, and power was given to him to scorch men with fire.

The fourth angel poured out his assigned bowl of judgment onto the sun, and immediately the intensity of the sun's heat heightened to a degree that it burned men with fire. This does not simply mean that the sun was made hotter and caused those exposed to it to receive severe sunburns. Mankind would actually be charred by the searing heat as though brought into direct contact with fire.

Whereas the fourth trumpet of judgment also affected the sun, it only did so to the point of lessening its light, as with the moon and stars, by a third. *(Revelation 8.12)* There is no mention of this bowl's effects on the stars or moon, but its ramifications were far more severe than those of the fourth trumpet judgment. Such evidences serve as further proof that the judgments of the trumpets and the bowls were progressive and not concurrent.

Verse 9- And men were scorched with great heat, and they blasphemed the name of God who has power over these plagues; and they did not repent and give Him glory.

All of mankind became scorched by the sun's great heat, but evidently, death would not result despite the fiery heat. No one would die and escape this or any of the final judgments of God's wrath. Nevertheless, rather than repent of their sinfulness, everyone instead further cursed the name of the Lord.

God's ultimate judgment will have already begun, and there would be no turning back. As such, those left behind to suffer God's wrath could only blaspheme against the only One Who had supreme control over the excruciation they experienced. This again demonstrates that everybody on earth realized from Whom this calamity had come as well as why it was being poured out upon them. *"[16]And said to the mountains and rocks, 'Fall on us and hide us from the face of Him who sits on the throne and from the wrath of the Lamb! [17]For the great day of His wrath has come, and who is able to stand?'" (Revelation 6.16–17)*

Verse 10- Then the fifth angel poured out his bowl on the throne of the beast, and his kingdom became full of darkness; and they gnawed their tongues because of the pain.

The kingdom of the beast and the kingdom of the dragon who empowered the beast should be understood as one and the same.7 Accordingly, the fifth angel poured out the bowl of wrath given to him upon the "throne of the beast," a clear reference to Satan's kingdom, which Scriptures establish as the whole world. *(John 12.31, 14.30, 16.8–11; Ephesians 2.1–2; 1 John 4.2–5; and 1 John 5.19)* Like the earth itself, Satan's kingdom is temporary, but God's kingdom is eternal. *(Psalm 145.13; Isaiah 9.7; Daniel 2.44; Hebrews 1.8; 2 Peter 1.11)* This particular designation of Satan's kingdom, however, seems to refer not to his dominion or authority but to his followers. As such, the first four bowls of God's wrath were poured out upon the physical realm of the entire world, but the last three bowls would be poured out specifically and directly upon the wicked inhabitants of the earth.[8]

Some commentators suggest that the phrase "the kingdom became full of darkness" signifies a physical darkness which would span the world, reminiscent of the ninth plague that befell Egypt by the hand of God through Moses.[9] *(Exodus 10.21–29)* A literal interpretation may be the case. However, the context of the phrase seems primarily to refer to the spiritual condition of the earth's population.[10] Those who remained upon the earth would be utterly depraved in spiritual desolation and would be plunged into the consequences of their sin. It would be too late for any of them to call upon the Lord for salvation:

> *[24]Because I have called and you refused, I have stretched out my hand and no one regarded, [25]because you disdained all my counsel, and would have none of my rebuke, [26]I also will laugh at your calamity; I will mock when your terror comes, [27]when your terror comes like a storm, and your destruction comes like a whirlwind, when distress and anguish come upon you. [28]'Then they will call on me, but I will not answer; they will seek me diligently, but they will not find me. [29]Because they hated knowledge and did not choose the fear of the Lord, [30]they would have none of my counsel and despised my every rebuke. [31]Therefore they shall eat the fruit of*

their own way, and be filled to the full with their own fancies. ³²For
the turning away of the simple will slay them, and the complacency
of fools will destroy them; ³³but whoever listens to me will dwell
safely, and will be secure, without fear of evil.' (Proverbs 1.24–33)

With a total acknowledgment of their deplorable spiritual position and because of the severe anguish of the physical pain already
inflicted upon them, people were left to "gnaw their tongues" in
response to the agony resonating throughout their bodies.

Verse 11- They blasphemed the God of heaven because of their pains and their sores, and did not repent of their deeds.

As in verse nine, mankind again cursed the name of God
because of their torment. They knew the source of and the reason
for their agony, but rather than repent, they would only further curse
the One who inflicted this pain upon them. This is the last verse in
the Book of Revelation where it is recorded that the people refused
to repent. When the Day of Judgment is present, the opportunity for
repentance is past. *"Therefore thus says the Lord: 'Behold, I will surely*
bring calamity on them which they will not be able to escape; and though
they cry out to Me, I will not listen to them.'" (Jeremiah 11.11)

Verse 12- Then the sixth angel poured out his bowl on the great river Euphrates, and its water was dried up, so that the way of the kings from the east might be prepared.

The sixth angel poured out the bowl of wrath upon the
Euphrates River, which instantly dried up. The vast banks that once
contained one of the world's greatest rivers immediately became a
dry and dusty channel so as to allow the approach of the kings from
the east. *"For this is the day of the Lord God of hosts, a day of vengeance,*
that He may avenge Himself on His adversaries. The sword shall devour; it
shall be satiated and made drunk with their blood; for the Lord God of hosts
has a sacrifice in the north country by the River Euphrates." (Jeremiah 46.10)

Though there have been many attempts to interpret the actual
identities of these "kings from the east," we can safely assume that
these would be the rulers who came from eastern countries to participate in the final battle of Armageddon. *(Revelation 19.19)*

Considering the enormous population of many of these eastern countries, the significance of this passage takes on substantial meaning. *"The Lord will utterly destroy the tongue of the Sea of Egypt; with His mighty wind He will shake His fist over the River, and strike it in the seven streams, and make men cross over dry-shod." (Isaiah 11.15)*

Verse 13- And I saw three unclean spirits like frogs coming out of the mouth of the dragon, out of the mouth of the beast, and out of the mouth of the false prophet.

As soon as the Euphrates River dried up, John saw three unclean spirits leave the dragon, the beast, and the false prophet by way of their mouths. Presumably, one unclean spirit left through the mouth of each of these hosts. To John, these spirits resembled frogs, but they were distinct spirits that possessed the supernatural power that had given these three evil beings the miraculous capabilities they had demonstrated in previous chapters.

Within this verse we see what some expositors have termed "the unholy trinity," consisting of Satan, the antichrist, and the false prophet.[11] However, this attempt by Satan to duplicate the triune existence of Almighty God failed even in its conception because these three figures existed as three completely separate entities, whereas God coexists as Father, Son, and Holy Spirit. God's three-in-one existence is unique and unable to be duplicated. It would, therefore, be more appropriate to term this threesome of Satan as a *trilogy* rather than a *trinity*.

Verse 14- For they are spirits of demons, performing signs, which go out to the kings of the earth and of the whole world, to gather them to the battle of that great day of God Almighty.

This verse further explains the frog-like spirits that emerged from the mouths of the dragon, the beast, and the false prophet. They were the spirits of particular demons empowering their host figures to perform miracles and great wonders. These spirits departed from the members of the unholy trilogy and went out unto the kings of the entire world. They wielded their power to summon the leaders into gathering together for "the battle of that great day of God Almighty." This was Satan's final effort to gather his own great army in order to wage war with the Lamb and His saints. These world leaders would be individually and corporately deceived by these spirits to believe that they could do battle with Almighty God and even claim a decisive victory. However, the mention of "the great day of God Almighty" was not just a foreshadowing of the war to come but also of the Champion of the battle and the glorious, final victory that would be won by His hands.

Notes/Applications

While men grow bold in wicked ways,
And yet a God they own,
My heart within me often says,
'Their thoughts believe there's none.'

Their thoughts and ways at once declare,
What'er their lips profess,
God hath no wrath for them to fear,
Nor will they seek His grace.

What strange self-flatt'ry blinds their eyes!
But there's a hast'ning hour,
When they shall see with sore surprise
The terrors of Thy power.

Thy justice shall maintain its throne,
Though mountains melt away;
Thy judgments are a world unknown,
A deep, unfathom'd sea...[12]

Do these words from Isaac Watts, the masterful hymnist, express our attitudes? Believers often find it difficult to understand why the lost will continue along a path of destruction, especially the lost depicted in these verses—those biting their tongues in agony yet still cursing the God of Heaven. We easily pass judgment upon them, but they respond to their situation according to their lost state of being.

As believers, we are not judged in the same manner as those who reject Christ, but we are held accountable for ignoring the Lord's instructions. How often do we take the miracle of our salvation lightly by allowing our attention to wane from Him and fall upon the world's seasonal pleasures? Most times, the Lord will send His Spirit to convict us as He confronts us through our circumstances to refocus our hearts upon Him. Such discipline hurts, and then it heals as it purges spiritual promiscuity from our lives. Are we willing to heed these warnings? *"⁶'Do not go after other gods to serve them and worship them, and do not provoke Me to anger with the works of your hands; and I will not harm you.' ⁷'Yet you have not listened to Me,' says the Lord, 'that you might provoke Me to anger with the works of your hands to your own hurt.'" (Jeremiah 25.6–7)*

Whenever we see evidence of the Lord's judgment falling upon the world around us, we must be prepared for bitter persecution by clinging to the truths that we have learned through His Word to strengthen our resolve—truths about His character, His purposes, and His plan for the world. These truths must become as real to us as the air we breathe, for they will become our nourishment when we feel weak and spiritually famished under the brunt of growing hostility and resentment against the true God, for Whom we are ambassadors.

Revelation 16.15–21

Verse 15- "Behold, I am coming as a thief. Blessed is he who watches, and keeps his garments, lest he walk naked and they see his shame."

John heard the voice of the Lord saying, "Behold, I come as a thief." This analogy was often used by Jesus to describe His Second Coming. The idea, as expressed in the Book of Matthew, was to be ready. *"43'But know this, that if the master of the house had known what hour the thief would come, he would have watched and not allowed his house to be broken into. 44Therefore you also be ready, for the Son of Man is coming at an hour you do not expect.'" (Matthew 24.43–44)*

The Lord echoed the sentiment in this verse that the one anticipating and watching for the Lord's return would be blessed. "Keeping his garments, lest he walk naked" expresses an warning to be constantly prepared, such as one sleeping in his clothing so that he could be ready at a moment's notice to go into battle or to embark upon whatever mission he might be commanded.

The idea of being ready, as spoken of here, primarily addresses the physical sense, but Christ's words surely imply that we must also be emotionally and spiritually ready. Blessed will be those who anticipate the Lord's return and are completely ready when that wonderful moment arrives. *"Finally, there is laid up for me the crown of righteousness, which the Lord, the righteous Judge, will give to me on that Day, and not to me only but also to all who have loved His appearing." (2 Timothy 4.8)*

Verse 16- And they gathered them together to the place called in Hebrew, Armageddon.

This verse serves as another reminder and blessed assurance that God is in complete control. As we have read in previous verses of this chapter, the unclean spirits that left the bodies of the dragon, the beast, and the false prophet sought to deceive the world leaders into coming together to wage war with the beast against God Almighty. In fact, we now know that this would ultimately occur according to God's plan and would have nothing to do with Satan's scheming. The armies of evil would gather at a place called *Armageddon,* which means "hill of slaughter."[13] *"And I saw the beast, the kings of the earth, and their armies, gathered together to make war against Him who sat on the horse and against His army." (Revelation 19.19)* This is the only biblical account of this place called Armageddon, and yet, much has been made of this great "battle." As the meaning of its name suggests, Armageddon would be a place of great slaughter. However, contrary to the common perception concerning Armageddon, it was not going to be the site of a great and final battle between good and evil or between God and Satan. True, the unrepentant followers of Satan and the antichrist would gather together, as this verse says, to do battle against God, but the war would be over before it ever began. Even though their numbers would be seemingly countless, God would destroy this entire gathering simply with His presence and by His will. *"And then the lawless one will be revealed, whom the Lord will consume with the breath of His mouth and destroy with the brightness of His coming." (2 Thessalonians 2.8) "And the rest were killed with the sword which proceeded from the mouth of Him who sat on the horse. And all the birds were filled with their flesh." (Revelation 19.21)* The incorrect speculation of some great battle carries with it the implication of a great struggle, which is clearly not the case. The saints would not even need to participate in order to obtain this victory. Rather, the victory would be accomplished with overwhelming results by God alone.

Verse 17- *Then the seventh angel poured out his bowl into the air, and a loud voice came out of the temple of heaven, from the throne, saying, "It is done!"*

The seventh angel poured out the bowl of wrath into the air, at which time John heard a great voice coming from the temple in Heaven and "from the throne." The voice could only be that of God Almighty, Who sat upon the throne and Whose smoke from His glory and power filled the temple. The Lord announced, "It is done." How this must have sent chills down John's spine! God's wrath upon mankind was completed, and the earth would be ready for the return of the Lord Jesus Christ as King of kings.

Verse 18- And there were noises and thunderings and lightnings; and there was a great earthquake, such a mighty and great earthquake as had not occurred since men were on the earth.

Similar to what happened after the Lord Jesus Christ said "It is finished" as He hung on the cross at Calvary and yielded His Spirit up to Heaven, so also Almighty God's decree was followed by many voices and thunder and lightning. *"Then, behold, the veil of the temple was torn in two from top to bottom; and the earth quaked, and the rocks were split." (Matthew 27.51)* In both circumstances, a boisterous, violent "amen" of nature concluded the Lord's accomplishment. In this instance, the earthquake was of greater magnitude and intensity than the world had ever before experienced. It could also be assumed that the smoke of His glory and power that filled the temple had also cleared at this moment so that those in Heaven could enter in again because the Lord had declared his wrath finished.

Verse 19- Now the great city was divided into three parts, and the cities of the nations fell. And great Babylon was remembered before God, to give her the cup of the wine of the fierceness of His wrath.

The great city, identified in this verse as Babylon, was divided into three parts by the earthquake. Also, the cities of all the nations fell, which either symbolizes or literally describes the destruction of the world power structures. These cities united in their stance against God, so they would be broken and divided as a result.

The final bowl of God's wrath was to be poured out on Babylon. For centuries, biblical scholars have debated the interpretation of *Babylon*. Some have argued that Babylon symbolizes the one world power system that would control the various nations of the world from a united structure of authority.[14] Others maintain that it should be literally interpreted that the city of Babylon would be rebuilt in the last days as the capital city of the world government.[15] Whatever the actual meaning, the intent is clear: Babylon had been disobedient to God, and therefore, the "cup of the wine of the fierceness of His wrath" would fall heavily upon that city.

Also, as we have seen in previous chapters of Revelation, the remaining visions shown to John would expound upon the details of this seventh bowl of wrath poured out against Babylon. Just as the seven trumpets expanded the details of the seventh seal and the seven bowls detailed the elements of the seventh trumpet, so, too, chapters seventeen and eighteen will explain the elements of this seventh bowl of God's wrath against Babylon. Not until the nineteenth chapter of Revelation will we return to this final "battle" scene at Armageddon, the victory of God Almighty over Satan and his armies, and the return of Christ Jesus upon the earth to reign for a thousand years.

DIG DEEPER: *BABYLON*

The ancient culture of Babylon located in Mesopotamia flourished as early as the third century BC. The city was located along the Euphrates River in what is now Iraq. It was conquered by Sennacharib of the Assyrian dynasty 689 BC. Later, in the mid-sixth century, the city achieved its greatest glory as the most powerful nation of its time under the rule of Nebuchadnezzar. This mighty king also conquered the southern kingdom of Judah, destroying Jerusalem and taking the vessels of Solomon's Temple. Since those days, Babylon has always engendered visions of an evil empire that oppose the people of God.

Verse 20- Then every island fled away, and the mountains were not found.

This verse vividly illustrates the devastating effects that this intense, worldwide earthquake would have upon the earth. "Every island fled away" seems to suggest that all the world's islands would crumble into the sea and be utterly destroyed beyond salvage. Also, the mountains would be leveled, shaken to the ground in massive piles of severed rocks and splintered lumber. *"⁴'Every valley shall be exalted and every mountain and hill brought low; the crooked places shall be made straight and the rough places smooth; ⁵the glory of the Lord shall be revealed, and all flesh shall see it together; for the mouth of the Lord has spoken.'" (Isaiah 40.4–5)* The earth was being prepared for the return of the Lord and Savior Jesus Christ.

Verse 21- And great hail from heaven fell upon men, each hailstone about the weight of a talent. Men blasphemed God because of the plague of the hail, since that plague was exceedingly great.

Another result of the seventh bowl of God's wrath would be a massive hailstorm. Enormous balls of ice, approximately one hundred pounds each, would fall from the sky to earth.[16] This phenomenon would certainly result in extensive injury and destruction above and beyond what devastation had already been caused by the worst earthquake the world had ever known. The seventh plague marked the final physical judgment God would put upon mankind, and it would be, by far, the most destructive.

Despite the intensity of the plague—and more accurately *because* of it—mankind again blasphemed God. They cursed God for their destruction and torment, though it was the just consequence of their unrepentant hearts. This verse depicts a final demonstration of man's resistance and hardness to God, even to the very end.

Notes/Applications

Though Armageddon (which loosely translated means "mount of Miggido" or "hills of Megiddo") appears only in the Book of Revelation, Megiddo is the location of many prominent events in biblical history. Around this area is where Barak conquered Sisera, King Josiah was killed, and many Old Testament battles were fought. Megiddo was once a great city fortified by King Solomon, and it had prospered under the reigns of King Ahab around 900 BC and King Jeroboam ben Joash around 800 BC. It was also of great importance because of its key location along the *Via Maris,* or "the Way of the Sea." Dating back to 3000 BC, the Via Maris has been an international roadway connecting Egypt with Damascus and Mesopotamia. Its major crossways intersect in Megiddo, which is located about halfway between the Jordan River and the

Mediterranean Sea. This region is also known as the Valley of Jezreel.

Despite the historical rise and fall of this city, it is primarily noted for only one momentous event—the final, decisive moment when the Almighty God will conquer Satan and his evil followers. Upon the victory of this great event, the Lord Jesus Christ will govern the earth for one thousand years.

Therefore, blessed are those who watch, "keep his garments," and live in a prepared state, anticipating the days when the Lord reconciles the earth with holy vengeance. *"For the day of vengeance is in my heart, and the year of My redeemed has come.'" (Isaiah 63.4)* On that day, will we be considered adversaries or allies in the Lord's army? If allies, we will reign with the King of kings for eternity in the new heaven and new earth. *"'Yours, O Lord, is the greatness, the power and the glory, the victory and the majesty; for all that is in heaven and in earth is Yours; Yours is the kingdom, O Lord, and You are exalted as head over all.'" (1 Chronicles 29.11)*

Chapter Seventeen

Revelation 17.1–6

Verses 1, 2- ¹Then one of the seven angels who had the seven bowls came and talked with me, saying to me, "Come, I will show you the judgment of the great harlot who sits on many waters, ²with whom the kings of the earth committed fornication, and the inhabitants of the earth were made drunk with the wine of her fornication."

Like the rest of the Book of Revelation, chapters seventeen and eighteen have received a wide variety of interpretations, yet they are most easily understood as following the same outline patterned throughout the book. Six seals are opened *(Revelation 6)* unveiling the precursors to God's judgment. The seventh seal is opened *(Revelation 8.1)* to usher in the seven trumpets of judgment *(Revelation 8.2–6)*. Six trumpets sound to unleash God's judgments upon the earth *(Revelation 8.7–9.21)*, and the sounding of the seventh trumpet *(Revelation 11.15)* results in the seven bowls of God's wrath *(Revelation 15.1)*. Six bowls of God's wrath are poured out against His unrepentant creation *(Revelation 16.1–16)*, and the seventh bowl was poured out upon "the great city," which received "the cup of the wine of the fierceness of His wrath" *(Revelation 16.17–21)*.

Likewise, after witnessing the outpouring of the seven bowls of God's final wrath, John was approached by one of the seven angels that had been given one of the seven bowls of wrath. The angel told John to follow him so that he could reveal the details surrounding the seventh bowl that was poured out upon the "great harlot who sits on many waters." The angel's subsequent identification of this harlot *(verse 18)* reveals that she represents the one and same "great city" mentioned in the previous chapter. We are further told that these "many waters" upon which the harlot sat embody the many "peoples, multitudes, nations, and tongues" *(verse 15)* who were "made drunk with the wine of her fornication." *Fornication* is used metaphorically in this verse and throughout Revelation as associating its participants with rampant wickedness and pagan idolatry.[1] *(Revelation 14.8, 17.4, 18.3, and 19.2)* Pagan worship is considered fornication because it is an abomination and perversion of the truth and a blatant rebellion against Almighty God. The intended sentiment seems to be that mankind had committed adultery by turning away from God, its very Creator, to adhere to a false god of absolute corruption. Therefore, mankind would also share in the wrath and the eternal judgment of its god, Satan.

The "kings of the earth" were also charged with committing fornication with the harlot and were partly responsible for leading the multitudes into the same. These kings were likely the same kings who had allied themselves with the beast and helped enforce its authority *(Daniel 7.24; Revelation 17.12)*, who had gathered with the beast to make war against God Almighty at Armageddon *(Revelation 16.14)*, and who would be thoroughly defeated upon the return of the Lord Jesus Christ *(Revelation 19.19–21)*.

Verse 3- *So he carried me away in the Spirit into the wilderness. And I saw a woman sitting on a scarlet beast which was full of names of blasphemy, having seven heads and ten horns.*

The angel carried John away in the same manner in which the apostle had been carried up into Heaven to witness the other visions. John was already present in the spirit when the angel came to escort him to "the wilderness." John simply shifted to another setting to witness another vision, and since he was carried "in the spirit," the move was virtually instantaneous.

That John saw "a woman sitting on a scarlet beast" rather than "a great harlot who sits on many waters" should cause no confusion that they are identical beings, which becomes obvious in subsequent verses. The blood-colored beast upon which she sat had names of blasphemy written on it, and it had seven heads and ten horns. Because of the matching details of this description, many commentators insist that this beast is identical to that introduced earlier in the Book of Revelation.[2] *"Then I stood on the sand of the sea. And I saw a beast rising up out of the sea, having seven heads and ten horns, and on his horns ten crowns, and on his heads a blasphemous name." (Revelation 13.1)* The only dissimilar detail in this description is that the beast was scarlet-colored. However, the beast depicted in chapter thirteen personified the characteristics of the red dragon, identified as Satan. *"And another sign appeared in heaven: behold, a great, fiery red dragon having seven heads and ten horns, and seven diadems on his heads." (Revelation 12.3)* Though the dragon and the beast in chapters twelve and thirteen appear strikingly similar in description, few commentators suggest they personify the one and same character since other verses establish clear grounds to differentiate between the two. Likewise, simply because we observe yet another beast with seven heads and ten horns, we need not limit the scope of our interpretation by unnecessarily identifying this beast as exclusively one or the other. That all three descriptions are so similar most strongly argues this beast's complete affinity with Satan. As such, it is perhaps best to recognize the beast in this chapter not solely as the figure of antichrist but also as the entire antichristian empire that led the great city into such moral demise.[3] More about this beast will be revealed in later verses.

Verse 4- *"The woman was arrayed in purple and scarlet, and adorned with gold and precious stones and pearls, having in her hand a golden cup full of abominations and the filthiness of her fornication.*

John noted that the harlot was adorned in the finest jewelry made of the most precious gems and pearls and that she was dressed in purple and scarlet garments, the colors of royalty. The city represented by this woman possessed great wealth, power, and influence. The description of her glamorous attire signifies that 1) she appeared, at least to the unbeliever, to offer all the luxuries that the world enjoyed, and that 2) she was dressed as a figure of royalty, depicting her relationship with the authorities of the world. She held in her hand a golden goblet, another emblem of her glamorous outward appearance, but the contents of the cup revealed her true ambition. Like a true harlot, she outwardly appeared beautiful and enticing, but inwardly, she overflowed with the "abominations and the filthiness of her fornication." All that she had to offer were temporary pleasures which lured her partakers far away from the eternal joy found in Christ Jesus.

Verse 5- And on her forehead a name was written: MYSTERY, BABYLON THE GREAT, THE MOTHER OF HARLOTS AND OF THE ABOMINATIONS OF THE EARTH.

Some Bible translations and commentators prefer to separate *mystery* as a description of the harlot's title rather than as a part of it.[4] The Greek word for *mystery,* as used here, is μυστήριον (musterion), which connotes an unknown thing that in this verse reflects "a spirit of disobedience to God."[5] *(2 Thessalonians 2.7; 1 Timothy 3.16)* Therefore, the treatment of this word may more easily be understood if incorporated into the title.[6] In fact, the inclusion of this word as part of her title strengthens the interpretation of the woman's symbolic representation of "that great city" which encompassed the world's deepest level of wickedness and idolatry.

One of the greatest debates in this chapter concerns the meaning of *Babylon.* Some scholars suggest that the mention of this specific name provides evidence that the city of Babylon will one day be rebuilt and serve as an internationally influential hub of corruption.[7] This seems unlikely, however, since the location where Babylon once stood has been for many centuries and still today remains primarily a deserted wasteland.[8] Further objection to this interpretation is supported by biblical prophecies regarding the city:

> *[19]And Babylon, the glory of kingdoms, the beauty of the Chaldeans' pride, will be as when God overthrew Sodom and Gomorrah. [20]It will never be inhabited, nor will it be settled from generation to generation; nor will the Arabian pitch tents there, nor will the shepherds make their sheepfolds there. [21]But wild beasts of the desert will lie there, and their houses will be full of owls; ostriches will dwell there, and wild goats will caper there. [22]The hyenas will howl in their citadels, and jackals in their pleasant palaces. Her time is near to come, and her days will not be prolonged. (Isaiah 13.19–22) [13]Because of the wrath of the LORD she shall not be inhabited, but she shall be wholly desolate. Everyone who goes by Babylon shall be horrified and hiss at all her plagues. [39]Therefore the wild desert beasts shall dwell there with the jackals, and the ostriches shall dwell in it. It shall be inhabited no more forever, nor shall it be dwelt in from generation to generation. (Jeremiah 50.13, 39)*

Among the earliest and still most prevalent interpretations is that this great city should be understood as Rome, especially because of the later reference to the "seven mountains on which the woman sits." *(verse 9)* Certainly, at the time this prophecy was written, John and his readers would recognize Rome as the obvious intention of the prophecy because of the persecution and martyrdom experienced by the Christians of the early church. Most Christians of the Reformation era also considered Rome a fitting solution to the woman primarily in light of their views of the Roman papacy.[9] Even now, several contemporary commentators uphold this interpretation, though it is done so mostly by those who see Revelation as having been fulfilled in the first century.[10] However, it is far too restrictive for any who view Revelation as having its ultimate fulfillment in the last days to interpret this great city as either Rome or a literal Babylon.[11]

Chapters sixteen, seventeen, and eighteen present a clear case for understanding this "great city" as a literal city, yet it is not necessary to determine which particular city is intended. Certainly, this description could be ascribed to many cities. By the time John recorded this book, Babylon was already a wasteland—a notorious city that was little more than a memory for the role it played in Jewish history—yet, to the Jewish mind, it would instantly evoke thoughts of unbridled paganism and sinful indulgence.[12] Similarly, it is more important for today's readers to comprehend the characteristics of the city than to attempt to identify the city itself, especially in consideration of its designation as the "mother of harlots and of the abominations of the earth." Perhaps, then, it is most sensible to presume that by the time the other events described in Revelation begin to unfold that Christians will recognize without so much debate the city that is actually portrayed.

Verse 6- I saw the woman, drunk with the blood of the saints and with the blood of the martyrs of Jesus. And when I saw her, I marveled with great amazement.

The city depicted by the woman would be the place where hostility against the followers of the one true God would not only be accepted but would be expected *(Revelation 13.15)* since she is accordingly described as being "drunk with the blood of the saints and...martyrs." The emphasis that she was drunk illustrates her ravenous and insatiable appetite for the blood of those who followed Christ. This is not a picture of passive resistance to God's will but a violently furious assault on all things of the Lord.

John was not merely awed by the sight of this woman. On the contrary, he simply could not believe the spectacle before his eyes. This vision so disturbed John that he "marveled with great amazement." In a sense, John watched with dumbfounded horror. He observed with revulsion the beautifully decorated woman who so voraciously craved the blood of Christ's faithful.

Notes/Applications

John Brown, martyr, 1413
Bartlet Green, martyr, 1521
Anne Albrighty, alias Champnes, martyr, 1556
A blind boy, and another with him, martyrs, 1556
Elizabeth Warne, martyr, year uncertain
John Philpot, preacher, martyr, 1557

The names of these martyrs reverberate with familiarity as though we might know them even though we have likely never heard of them before. We read the epitaphs of men, women, and children with common names and stations in life who all died for one cause—serving their Lord and Master Jesus Christ, and we hear the bell of truth ringing in the corridors of our hearts, "'We must through many tribulations enter the kingdom of God'" *(Acts 14.22b)*.

Throughout history, Christian saints have been persecuted and will continue to be persecuted for carrying the banner of Christ. Our Lord and Savior warned His children of impending trial and torture for His name, and during the time shortly before His return, such persecution will intensify to the point that the whore of Babylon will become drunk with the blood of the saints.

Thomas Benet, a martyr burned in Exceter in 1531 proclaimed: "I will rather die, than Worship such a Beast, the very Whore of Babylon, and a false Usurper, as manifestly doth appear by his doings...I thank Christ, and with all my heart will allow all things done and used in the Church to the Glory of God, and edifying of my Soul..."[13]

We may feel overwhelmed by the task before us because our human frame rebels against such expense to follow Christ. We are not strong enough to completely and fully accomplish this on our own, but God is faithful, and just as we can trust Him for the grace to live, we can also trust Him for the peace to die a graceful death in His name if He so requires. He will strengthen us through His Holy Spirit, our Helper, Who will empower us to eternally overcome the evil one. *"But the Lord is faithful, who will establish you and guard you from the evil one." (2 Thessalonians 3.3)*

Our trust is in our Lord and Savior, Who is greater than any enemy, Who will preserve our souls, and Who will one day raise our bodies to meet Him. The sustaining, powerful love of Almighty God will carry His saints through whatever trials they face. Like so many of our brothers and sisters before us and those left to come, we can be faithful even unto death, being held securely in the arms of an eternal God and His eternal promises:

[35]*Who shall separate us from the love of Christ? Shall tribulation, or distress, or persecution, or famine, or nakedness, or peril, or sword?* [36]*As it is written: 'For Your sake we are killed all day long; we are accounted as sheep for the slaughter.'* [37]*Yet in all these things we are more than conquerors through Him who loved us.* [38]*For I am persuaded that neither death nor life, nor angels nor principalities nor powers, nor things present nor things to come,* [39]*nor height nor depth, nor any other created thing, shall be able to separate us from the love of God which is in Christ Jesus our Lord. (Romans 8.35–39)*

Revelation 17.7–11

Verse 7- But the angel said to me, "Why did you marvel? I will tell you the mystery of the woman and of the beast that carries her, which has the seven heads and the ten horns.

John was surely appalled by the vision of the woman drunken with the blood of Christian martyrs, but the angel seems to tell the apostle that he should not have been surprised by it. The angel first questioned John about his bewilderment and then assured him that the full importance of the woman and the beast would be explained. Without delay, the angel described the significance of "the mystery," as recorded in the following verses.

Verse 8- "The beast that you saw was, and is not, and will ascend out of the bottomless pit and go to perdition. And those who dwell on the earth will marvel, whose names are not written in the Book of Life from the foundation of the world, when they see the beast that was, and is not, and yet is.

Interpretations concerning the meaning of "was, and is not" vary as readily as the interpretations concerning the symbolism of the woman. The foremost explanation merges the description of this beast with that of the beast in chapter thirteen who lived, was killed, and then was "resurrected."[14] *"And I saw one of his heads as if it had been mortally wounded, and his deadly wound was healed. And all the world marveled and followed the beast." (Revelation 13.3)* A parallel to support this explanation is found in the response of those who witnessed this "miracle" and were amazed, and those who followed the beast were only those "whose names are not written in the Book of Life from the foundation of the world." *"All who dwell on the earth will worship him, whose names have not been written in the Book of Life of the Lamb slain from the foundation of the world." (Revelation 13.8)* While this explanation satisfies many questions regarding this particular description of the beast, it is perhaps best to reserve further comment on this beast until verse eleven, when further explanation is offered by the angel.

As compelling as the preceding argument may be, another observation which should not be overlooked is that this verse con-

tains certain similarities not only to the beast of chapter thirteen
but also to the dragon of chapter twelve. First of all, as previously
noted, the dragon mimics certain aspects set forth by Almighty
God. In this case, that the beast is described as "was, and is not, and
yet is" appears to be a stark contrast if not somewhat a parody of
Jesus' description as the One "Who was and is and is to come."[15]
(Revelation 1.4, 1.8, 4.8, and 11.17) Secondly, the description of this
beast ascending "out of the bottomless pit" and ultimately going
into perdition, while often being explained away as an indication of
the beast's origination, has a stronger biblical foundation in reference to the dragon:

> *[1]Then I saw an angel coming down from heaven, having the key to
> the bottomless pit and a great chain in his hand. [2]He laid hold of
> the dragon, that serpent of old, who is the Devil and Satan, and
> bound him for a thousand years; [3]and he cast him into the bottom-
> less pit, and shut him up, and set a seal on him, so that he should
> deceive the nations no more till the thousand years were finished.
> But after these things he must be released for a little while. [7]Now
> when the thousand years have expired, Satan will be released from
> his prison… [10]The devil, who deceived them, was cast into the lake
> of fire and brimstone where the beast and the false prophet are.
> And they will be tormented day and night forever and ever.
> (Revelation 20.1–3, 7,10)*

As such, it is still probably best to proceed with caution before
identifying this beast upon which the harlot sat specifically as the
antichrist figure, though it is apparent that at least some of this interpretation is to be understood as concerning the ultimate manifestation of that evil being.

**Verse 9- "Here is the mind which has wisdom: The seven heads
are seven mountains on which the woman sits.**

The angel urged both John and ultimately all of John's readers
to understand the significance of the vision. True understanding is
not of human intelligence but requires spiritual insight, much in the
same manner as when the Lord Jesus Christ cautioned the seven
churches of Asia Minor in chapters two and three, "He who has an

ear, let him hear what the Spirit says to the churches." The Lord was not speaking of physical ears but of spiritual understanding, and the angel appears to have been doing likewise at this moment. Those with wisdom would understand the explanation.

This verse has long served as the foundation for understanding the intended significance of this harlot as Rome, which has been called "the city of the seven hills."[16] However, most contemporary scholars now dismiss this once popular explanation.[17] Rome, while the epitome of hatred and violence towards Christians of the first and second centuries, now seems hardly a fitting solution for what is said about the "great city" in this chapter and the next. Furthermore, regardless of differing attempts to identify the woman, many commentators reject arguments which view these as actual, physical mountains.[18] Some believe these mountains are representative of kingdoms similar to imagery used in the Old Testament, especially in light of further explanation provided in verse ten.[19] *(Isaiah 2.2, 40.3; Jeremiah 51.25; and Daniel 2.35)* That the angel prefaced the interpretation by urging a mind of wisdom does perhaps suggest that there is more to understanding the interpretation than what may appear as obvious.

Verse 10- "There are also seven kings. Five have fallen, one is, and the other has not yet come. And when he comes, he must continue a short time.

The angel, despite promising to reveal "the mystery of the woman and of the beast," seems to speak in riddles. The beast's seven heads just depicted as seven mountains are now further explained as seven kings. Though there are many interpretations regarding the identity of these leaders, within the context of this passage it seems that we are to understand this as a succession of kings and not necessarily as kings ruling along with the antichrist. Another difficulty often addressed is whether these kings should be understood as actual individual rulers or as kingdoms. Further analysis of this passage may shed some light on this dispute.

Of these seven kings, we are told that "five have fallen," which means that they no longer existed in the time period represented in this passage. The point over which many scholars find disagreement is the obscurity of the time period in which these fallen leaders existed or would exist. Were they already "fallen" at the time of John's actual writing of the book or were they "fallen" in that future time period after the final wrath of God upon mankind? Some expositors have argued that these leaders were actual Roman emperors who had reigned before John's isolation on Patmos, and the sixth king ruled during John's exile.[20] While several solutions have been offered to count these emperors and determine the identity of the seventh king, each of them is admittedly problematic and cannot be argued convincingly.[21]

A better case is made by those who contend that these seven kings are actually the seven major kingdoms spanning the world's history.[22] Accordingly, then, at the time of John's exile on the island of Patmos, the five fallen would denote the Egyptian, Assyrian, Babylonian, Medo-Persian, and Greco-Macedonian kingdoms, and the "one [that] is" would refer to the Roman Empire, which was in power during John's lifetime. The seventh kingdom would be that future one in which the antichrist would ultimately rise to power.[23] This verse goes on to say that when this seventh one comes, it must have power for a short while. The word *must* used here reveals that the Lord would not simply allow this "king" to come to power but that this kingdom *must* emerge according to God's ultimate and perfect plan. Fortunately, the appointed duration of this seventh "king" would be limited by the sovereign hand of Almighty God for only "a short time."

Though many answers have been applied to these seven kings or kingdoms, each is prone to certain objections due to the ambiguity and uncertainty of the angel's explanation. Perhaps too much significance has been placed upon this verse altogether, considering the relevance of the passage seems to lie most heavily not in the seven kings but in the eighth king introduced in the next verse.

Verse 11- "And the beast that was, and is not, is himself also the eighth, and is of the seven, and is going to perdition.

Interpretive difficulties arise from the perceived inconsistency that the beast is described as having seven heads and yet is now specifically associated with only one of them. It should be concluded that this is done to emphasize its symbolic merit. Enough details are given to render the identity of the beast as virtually uncontestable, yet the relationship between "the eighth" and "of the seven" remains unclear. First of all, to suppose that "the eighth" is necessarily identical in symbolic implication as the seven kings before it is speculative. The beast has only seven heads, so the mention of "the eighth" puts forth new, supplementary detail which needs not be treated with identical symbolic import as the seven kings.[24] As explained in verse eight, this chapter seems to refer not only to the ultimate incarnation of an antichrist figure but also to the entire antichristian empire which in the last days will have its capital in this city depicted as Babylon.[25] Therefore, this beast can accurately be described both as the one that "was, and is not" (indicating the antichrist figure) and as being "of the seven" (presumably the seventh, indicating the antichristian empire).

That the beast "is going to perdition" restates the message of verse eight, which encompasses both the beast's nature and his fate—destruction. He would cause destruction upon the earth, and he would be the recipient of destruction both by the wrath of God upon the earth and throughout his eternal destiny in the lake of fire:

> *[19]And I saw the beast, the kings of the earth, and their armies, gathered together to make war against Him who sat on the horse and against His army. [20]Then the beast was captured, and with him the false prophet who worked signs in his presence, by which he deceived those who received the mark of the beast and those who worshiped his image. These two were cast alive into the lake of fire burning with brimstone. (Revelation 19.19–20) The devil, who deceived them, was cast into the lake of fire and brimstone where the beast and the false prophet are. And they will be tormented day and night forever and ever. (Revelation 20.10)*

Notes/Applications

The world in which we live seems to be turning more hostile by the day. Such violent disturbances are Satan's pressing efforts to create mass confusion and capitalize on it by offering what appears to be a solution. *"¹⁴But if you have bitter envy and self-seeking in your hearts, do not boast and lie against the truth. ¹⁵This wisdom does not descend from above, but is earthly, sensual, demonic. ¹⁶For where envy and self-seeking exist, confusion and every evil thing are there." (James 3.14–16)* At one point, Satan will empower a world leader to offer seemingly logical and peaceful solutions to the chaos, but although this world leader's lips will drip with promises of prosperity, his heart will be black with evil intents.

Even now, an evil spirit is preparing the way for the emergence of this world leader who will embody the spirit of antichrist, so believers need to be careful not to be deceived by those who pose influential arguments, great power, and miraculous ways and who are being used as vessels for the spirit of evil. *"¹⁸Little children, it is the last hour; and as you have heard that the Antichrist is coming, even now many antichrists have come, by which we know that it is the last hour...²²Who is a liar but he who denies that Jesus is the Christ? He is antichrist who denies the Father and the Son." (1 John 2.18, 22) "And every spirit that does not confess that Jesus Christ has come in the flesh is not of God. And this is the spirit of the Antichrist, which you have heard was coming, and is now already in the world." (1 John 4.3)*

Rather, we must seek wisdom from the Lord, and He will grant us the ability to discern truth and sincere lovers of truth. We should live in a manner that upholds truth in even the smallest matters so that when greater temptations are upon us we can recall our experiences as assurance that God will carry us through even the most difficult and uncertain times. *"⁴You are of God, little children, and have overcome them, because He who is in you is greater than he who is in the world. ⁵They are of the world. Therefore they speak as of the world, and the world hears them. ⁶We are of God. He who knows God hears us; he who is not of God does not hear us. By this we know the spirit of truth and the spirit of error." (1 John 4.4–6)*

Revelation 17.12–18

Verse 12- *"The ten horns which you saw are ten kings who have received no kingdom as yet, but they receive authority for one hour as kings with the beast."*

The angel further explained that the ten horns were also ten kings who had "received no kingdom as yet," which clearly alludes to a future occasion from the time of John's writing. Moreover, a differentiation is made in this verse between kings and kingdoms, so we are led to conclude that these kings would be actual persons to whom authority will be given. Their ascension to power will occur simultaneously with the rise of the antichrist, who will enlist them as his allies. *"The ten horns are ten kings who shall arise from this kingdom. And another shall rise after them; he shall be different from the first ones, and shall subdue three kings."* *(Daniel 7.24)* Some commentators view the number ten as symbolic but agree that the horns represent the totality of all leaders who would reign over the nations of the earth in allegiance with and under submission to the antichrist.[26] Again, God in His sovereignty will only allow these evil rulers to reign with the antichrist for a short time *(verse 10),* depicted in this verse as "one hour."

Verse 13- *"These are of one mind, and they will give their power and authority to the beast.*

These ten kings would rule with "one mind," meaning that they would be united in their goals and in their alliance. They would be single-mindedly hostile toward the things of the true God, and they would merge their forces to rise up against Him on a global basis. They would rule their corresponding kingdoms as unto the cause of the antichrist, and they would pledge all of the power and strength of their armies unto the beast to fulfill his purposes.

Verse 14- *"These will make war with the Lamb, and the Lamb will overcome them, for He is Lord of lords and King of kings; and those who are with Him are called, chosen, and faithful."*

This verse reveals the intent of the kings' unified mission—to make war with the Lamb, the Lord Jesus Christ. This gives further support for identifying these ten kings as the same mentioned in chapter sixteen. *"For they are spirits of demons, performing signs, which go out to the kings of the earth and of the whole world, to gather them to the battle of that great day of God Almighty." (Revelation 16.14)* These armies would gather for war at Armageddon *(Revelation 16.16)*, though it would be no contest. There is no description of any great struggle or immense battle, only of the result, which would be final, swift, and severe. The Lamb would decisively conquer them all, and the reason given for this victory is not because the Lord's army was larger or more powerful or because He used better tactics or technology. The reason is simple yet powerful—because "He is Lord of lords and King of kings." The Lord Jesus Christ will be the Victor simply because of Who He is!

An emphasis is also placed upon saints who were with the Lamb. They were singled out from the opposing armies as those who "are called, chosen, and faithful." Such a distinction is given only to believers as a corporate whole, those who are His elect. *"Moreover whom He predestined, these He also called; whom He called, these He also justified; and whom He justified, these He also glorified." (Romans 8.30)* An account of their presence is recorded here only to illustrate that they were now in the Lord's presence and that they had accompanied Him when He returned to the earth, as will be detailed in later chapters. In no sense does this imply that their accompanying the Lord was a necessary element in Jesus' magnificent triumph. Rather, it is more likely that they will be present to celebrate the great victory of the Lord when He alone will prevail over Satan and evil.

DIG DEEPER: *LORD OF LORDS*

Although this title for Jesus Christ is used twice in the Book of Revelation, its roots go back to the Law. *(Deuteronomy 10.17)* Paul, in his letter to Timothy, spoke of the appearance of Jesus Christ, "which He will manifest in His own time, He who is the blessed and only Potentate, the King of kings, and Lord of Lords, who alone has immortality, dwelling in unapproachable light, whom no man has seen or can see, to whom be honor and everlasting power." *(1 Timothy 6.15–16)* All the nations of the earth cannot hope to vanquish this mighty Warrior and King.

Verse 15- Then he said to me, "The waters which you saw, where the harlot sits, are peoples, multitudes, nations, and tongues.

The angel continued explaining to John what had been witnessed. As studied in verse one, the "waters" upon which the woman sat represented people of all nationalities, races, and languages—a vast, seemingly countless number of people. The implication is that this group comprised all the people upon the earth who had committed fornication with the harlot. Several commentators view the fourfold presentation of the description as being symbolic of the encompassing the whole world.[27] However, the scriptural basis itself surely provides sufficient evidence that this group would include all the earth's inhabitants who were harvested for the great winepress of God's wrath. *"¹⁸And another angel came out from the altar, who had power over fire, and he cried with a loud cry to him who had the sharp sickle, saying, 'Thrust in your sharp sickle and gather the clusters of the vine of the earth, for her grapes are fully ripe.' ¹⁹So the angel thrust his sickle into the earth and gathered the vine of the earth, and threw it into the great winepress of the wrath of God." (Revelation 14.18–19)*

Verse 16- "And the ten horns which you saw on the beast, these will hate the harlot, make her desolate and naked, eat her flesh and burn her with fire.

The ten kings, represented by the ten horns of the beast, would rebel in their hatred toward the harlot. The description of their actions is shocking if not somewhat confusing since they worked on behalf of the beast. *(verse 13)* The fierce actions described herein depict a systematic, part-by-part destruction of the city that had once served the kings so well, and this destruction would be both thorough and irreversible. More than simply do away with her, they utterly annihilated her so that she would never be revived. This parallels an Old Testament account of a prophecy in the Book of Ezekiel:

²²'Therefore, Oholibah, thus says the Lord GOD: "Behold, I will stir up your lovers against you, from whom you have alienated yourself, and I will bring them against you from every side. ²⁵I will set My jealousy against you, and they shall deal furiously with you;

they shall remove your nose and your ears, and your remnant shall
fall by the sword; they shall take your sons and your daughters,
and your remnant shall be devoured by fire. ²⁶They shall also strip
you of your clothes and take away your beautiful jewelry. ²⁷Thus I
will make you cease your lewdness and your harlotry brought from
the land of Egypt, so that you will not lift your eyes to them, nor
remember Egypt anymore." ²⁸For thus says the Lord GOD: "Surely I
will deliver you into the hand of those you hate, into the hand of
those from whom you alienated yourself. ²⁹They will deal hatefully
with you, take away all you have worked for, and leave you naked
and bare. The nakedness of your harlotry shall be uncovered, both
your lewdness and your harlotry."' (Ezekiel 23.22,25–29)

In an ironic sequence of events, the kings of the earth who had
gathered to ally themselves with the beast would completely
destroy the great city, the pinnacle of pagan idolatry. Such are
Satan's self-destructive ways, all doomed to failure. The greatest
forces he could amass against Almighty God would ultimately turn
against the very empire that had once been the center of their
strength. However, the critical reason for this is clearly stated in the
following verse.

**Verse 17- "For God has put it into their hearts to fulfill His pur-
pose, to be of one mind, and to give their kingdom to the beast,
until the words of God are fulfilled.**

What an paradoxical assurance is presented here! These ten
kings fully believed that they were fulfilling the cause of their
leader, the antichrist. Their desire to align themselves with God's
enemy, however, was put into their hearts by God Himself. By obey-
ing the antichrist, they would unwittingly fulfill the sovereign will of
Almighty God. *"The Lord has made all for Himself, yes, even the wicked for
the day of doom." (Proverbs 16.4)* While seeking to "give their kingdom
to the beast," they unsuspectingly fulfilled the words and will of the
very God that they believed their actions opposed. *"¹¹And for this reason God will send them strong delusion, that they should believe the lie,
¹²that they all may be condemned who did not believe the truth but had
pleasure in unrighteousness." (2 Thessalonians 2.11–12)*

Verse 18- "And the woman whom you saw is that great city which reigns over the kings of the earth."

As already discussed at some length, the woman that John saw represents the great city called Babylon, the capital of idolatry and apostasy which has existed as various cities at various times throughout history but whose ultimate identity will one day be revealed. In that period during the ultimate incarnation of antichrist, this city would appear to offer everything. She would entice the world's inhabitants with her beauty, wealth, and opportunities, but her destiny is unreserved doom. This core of the antichristian empire would be utterly decimated upon the pouring out of the seventh bowl of God's wrath *(Revelation 16.19)*, and the true extent of God's fierce and meticulous wrath against this woman can be better understood in the account of her destruction, as detailed in the next chapter.

Notes/Applications

As portrayed by the outwardly beautifully attired harlot in this chapter, evil works very hard to disguise itself by incorporating tenets of truth in order to appear as an alternative path to God when, in fact, it is a blasphemy to the one, true God and Jesus Christ, His Son.

With her deceptive, smiling lips, the harlot curses all who follow her. Like an animal savagely dining upon her own offspring, this great harlot will trap the inner beings of even her own and ravage them, proving her source to be the devil, the evil one who seeks to kill and destroy. Nevertheless, these two will not act alone. They may prey upon man's vulnerabilities, but each individual remains essentially responsible for succumbing to the harlot's wiles. Such evil manifests itself where it finds a home in a spirit of disobedience, so it is ultimately man's rebellion, his refusal to adhere to the precepts of a righteous God, which allows him to be swept into the harlot's clutches. *"The foolishness of a man twists his way, and his heart frets against the Lord." (Proverbs 19.3)*

Ultimately, the harlot and the beast upon which she rides are intertwined elements of Satan's scheme to condemn mankind. It is the antichrist's rise in power and growing popularity that will eventually seduce the majority of people into embracing a false christ that will ultimately condemn them to the wrath of God and eternal damnation. *"13'Enter by the narrow gate; for wide is the gate and broad is the way that leads to destruction, and there are many who go in by it. 14Because narrow is the gate and difficult is the way which leads to life, and there are few who find it.'"* (Matthew 7.13–14) The harlot's kiss will lead to the death and destruction of many.

Chapter Eighteen

Revelation 18.1–8

Verse 1- After these things I saw another angel coming down from heaven, having great authority, and the earth was illuminated with his glory.

This chapter details what some have referred to as the "death song for Babylon."[1] John saw the seventh bowl of judgment being poured out and how the great city referred to as Babylon received the fierceness of God's wrath. *(Revelation 16.19)* Afterward, in a separate yet related vision, an angel showed John why Babylon deserved the wrath she would experience at God's hands—she had made the nations drunk with her fornications, and she herself was drunk with the blood of the saints and martyrs. *(Revelation 17.1–4)* Now, in what appears to be a continuation of that vision, John would be given a better understanding of the effects that the destruction of the great city would have on the world's inhabitants.

After one of the seven angels who had poured out God's wrath had finished interpreting the vision of the harlot and the beast, another angel, more prominent than that which preceded him, descended from Heaven. Unlike other passages where convincing evidence suggests that the Lord appeared as an angel *(Revelation 10 and 11)*, the description of this angel's glory is insufficient reason to draw conclusions that this might be an appearance of Christ.[2] Why this angel had been given "great authority" is not disclosed, but the magnificence of his presence filled the entire earth. All those throughout the world would immediately become aware of his presence.

Verse 2- And he cried mightily with a loud voice, saying, "Babylon the great is fallen, is fallen, and has become a dwelling place of demons, a prison for every foul spirit, and a cage for every unclean and hated bird!

This angel's voice was strong, and he was heard from a great distance as he loudly proclaimed, *"Babylon the great is fallen!" "Then he answered and said, 'Babylon is fallen, is fallen! And all the carved images of her gods He has broken to the ground.'" (Isaiah 21.9b)* The great system that had served as the capital of the antichristian empire would face its judgment. The angel called the city a habitation for devils and evil spirits—a place where evil freely reigned and had many agents through which to accomplish its work. There would also be an abundance of "unclean and hated" birds, detestable, aggressive animals that subsisted on carrion. *"21'But wild beasts of the desert will lie there, and their houses will be full of owls; ostriches will dwell there, and wild goats will caper there. 22The hyenas will howl in their citadels, and jackals in their pleasant palaces. Her time is near to come, and her days will not be prolonged.'" (Isaiah 13.21–22)*

Verse 3- "For all the nations have drunk of the wine of the wrath of her fornication, the kings of the earth have committed fornication with her, and the merchants of the earth have become rich through the abundance of her luxury."

This verse reiterates the reason that Babylon faced God's wrath—all nations had shared in this city's unfaithfulness as described in the previous chapter. Even those who lived outside the city were under her control. In a sense, the world's leaders who had pledged their loyalties to the antichrist had participated in her harlotry and, therefore, had "committed fornication with her." Likewise, all the world's merchants, those who were allowed to trade and sell since they had received the mark of the beast, were also guilty because of their relationship with her. Apparently, this category denotes groups that were not necessarily religious or political in nature but had still reaped the benefits of prosperity and luxury by receiving the mark of the beast and submitting themselves to the antichristian powers. *"And that no man might buy or sell, save he that had the mark, or the name of the beast, or the number of his name." (Revelation 13.17)*

Verse 4- And I heard another voice from heaven saying, "Come out of her, my people, lest you share in her sins, and lest you receive of her plagues.

Another voice called from Heaven. The personal, familial content of the message might suggest that this was the voice of the Lord God Himself. However, there is no designation of the voice as coming from the throne *(Revelation 16.17)*, and the following verse refers to God in a third-person viewpoint, so it may serve best to consider this not necessarily as the voice of God but as a voice that speaks for God.

The next sixteen verses compose the remainder of this message from the Lord. They explain the consequences that would come upon Babylon and upon those who had partaken in her fornication. The first two consequences are revealed at the end of this verse. God's faithful were to leave Babylon so that they would not participate in her sin and so that they would not receive the plagues of God's wrath that would befall her. *"Flee from the midst of Babylon, and every one save his life! Do not be cut off in her iniquity, for this is the time of the LORD'S vengeance; He shall recompense her." (Jeremiah 51.6)* In addition to describing the seventh plague of God's wrath, this passage seems also to expound upon the separation of God's people from those who would be thrown into the winepress of God's wrath:

> *⁸And another angel followed, saying, 'Babylon is fallen, is fallen, that great city, because she has made all nations drink of the wine of*

the wrath of her fornication.' ⁹Then a third angel followed them, saying with a loud voice, 'If anyone worships the beast and his image, and receives his mark on his forehead or on his hand,¹⁰he himself shall also drink of the wine of the wrath of God, which is poured out full strength into the cup of His indignation. He shall be tormented with fire and brimstone in the presence of the holy angels and in the presence of the Lamb...' ¹⁴Then I looked, and behold, a white cloud, and on the cloud sat One like the Son of Man, having on His head a golden crown, and in His hand a sharp sickle. ¹⁵And another angel came out of the temple, crying with a loud voice to Him who sat on the cloud, 'Thrust in Your sickle and reap, for the time has come for You to reap, for the harvest of the earth is ripe.' ¹⁶So He who sat on the cloud thrust in His sickle on the earth, and the earth was reaped. (Revelation 14.8–10, 14–16)

Whether or not this verse depicts the physical removal of God's elect from the earth as depicted in chapter fourteen, it is the same message that the Lord has given to His faithful throughout the ages—that we are not to conform to the ways of the world in which we live but are to be set apart from the clutch of sin in which the world indulges itself. *"And do not be conformed to this world, but be transformed by the renewing of your mind, that you may prove what is that good and acceptable and perfect will of God." (Romans 12.2) "Therefore 'Come out from among them and be separate,' says the Lord. 'Do not touch what is unclean, and I will receive you.'" (2 Corinthians 6.17)*

Verse 5- "For her sins have reached to heaven, and God has remembered her iniquities.

In a manner clearly illustrating the extent of Babylon's wickedness, John was told that the accumulation of the city's sins piled high enough to reach Heaven. *"We would have healed Babylon, but she is not healed. Forsake her, and let us go everyone to his own country; for her judgment reaches to heaven and is lifted up to the skies." (Jeremiah 51.9)* The mention of "[remembering] her iniquities" reveals that Almighty God had not turned a blind eye to Babylon's extensive wickedness but was merely reserving judgment according to His timing and purposes; and according to His timing and purposes, that judgment had now come due. *"And great Babylon was remembered before God, to give her the cup of the wine of the fierceness of His wrath." (Revelation 16.19b)*

Verse 6- "Render to her just as she rendered to you, and repay her double according to her works; in the cup which she has mixed, mix double for her.

Upon a cursory reading, it may appear that those who departed Babylon were offered an opportunity to participate in the wrath and plagues being poured out upon her, as if they are told to treat Babylon just as they had been treated under the reign of the antichristian authorities and were to "repay her double" for the persecution she had heaped upon God's faithful. *"O daughter of Babylon, who are to be destroyed, happy the one who repays you as you have served us!" (Psalm 137.8)* However, despite a lack of transition, it should not be thought this command was addressed to God's people, who were instructed "to come out of her." *(verse 4)* God alone could inflict such extensive ruin in so a brief a moment as would come upon this city. *(verse 8)* It seems best, then, to understand these statements as unto God Himself or, possibly, those agents through which His destruction would be appointed.[3] *(Revelation 16.17 and 17.16)*

The Lord would pour out His wrath against Babylon not only for her sins against Him but also as some measure of vengeance for the suffering of His faithful. Just as Babylon had poured out unreserved wrath and affliction upon those refusing to bear the mark of the beast, so, too, would she receive double the consequences for her actions against God's chosen. *(Isaiah 40.2; Jeremiah 16.18; and 50.15, 29)*

Some commentators insist that God would not commit such an injustice as to punish Babylon with double the torment that she had issued, and they instead argue that the meaning of this verse indicates only that she would receive her just due.[4] This, however, would not be a matter of mere justice but one of wrath, and that God would for so long defer judgment against such a depraved core of evil only further expresses the great extent of His mercy.

Verse 7- "In the measure that she glorified herself and lived luxuriously, in the same measure give her torment and sorrow; for

she says in her heart, 'I sit as queen, and am no widow, and will not see sorrow.'

To the same excess that Babylon had "lived luxuriously" or prospered materially under the reign of the antichristian empire, she would experience the same excess of suffering under the wrath of God. Not only would the city have all such opulence stripped away, but she would experience excessive anguish and affliction to the same measures.

Despite her blatant fornications, she fancied herself not as a harlot but as a queen. Obviously, after being depicted not only as a woman but also for what she truly was, a seductress of sin, she would hardly be thought of as a king. The gender distinction of the authoritative position of queen instead of king might even signify yet another perversion of God's will that Christ Jesus shall rule as King. She is also described as "no widow" as if to express a belief that she would not experience such sorrow as was prepared for her:

> [8]*'Therefore hear this now, you who are given to pleasures, who dwell securely, who say in your heart, "I am, and there is no one else besides me; I shall not sit as a widow, nor shall I know the loss of children";* [9]*but these two things shall come to you in a moment, in one day: the loss of children, and widowhood. They shall come upon you in their fullness because of the multitude of your sorceries, for the great abundance of your enchantments.'* (Isaiah 47.8–9)

The overwhelming pride of Babylon would culminate in her total destruction.

Verse 8- "Therefore her plagues will come in one day—death and mourning and famine. And she will be utterly burned with fire, for strong is the Lord God who judges her.

The Lord promised the swift destruction of Babylon. In one day, which should be interpreted as a literal twenty-four hour period since no evidence exists to suggest otherwise, she would be accursed with plagues, famine, mourning, and death. *"'Behold, I will engrave its inscription,' says the Lord of hosts, 'And I will remove the iniquity of that land in one day.'" (Zechariah 3.9b)* This would be the complete and inescapable collapse of this great city.

Babylon would be burned, according to this passage, by an actual all-consuming fire. *(Revelation 17.16)* This city would be extremely powerful and influential but would also fall under the hand of Almighty God, Who would be her Judge. Her sentence would be severe and comprehensive.

Notes/Applications

It has been stated that "Babylon is a counterfeit church," whose mission is to "[attack] with seduction…to destroy the purity of the saints."[5] In fact, some scholars consider the harlot, Babylon, to be a direct antithesis to the Bride of Christ, the Church.[6]

The harlot, Babylon, will live in a lewd, perverted relationship with the devil, whom she worships. She will seek to seduce the world from eternal truth. Corruption will characterize the heart of her home as manifested in the waywardness of her children. She will "buy" her followers with economic benefits and worldly opulence. She will arrogantly exalt herself to be a queen when in fact she will be a slave to sin, living in the clutches of and serving the master of spiritual bondage.

The Bride of Christ, the Church, is characterized by her purity, the righteousness of Christ that shrouds her as fine linen. She continuously lives in blessed assurance according to the faithful covenant made by Jesus Christ, her Bridegroom. She worships the only true God, and she possesses eternal wealth incomparable to the harlot's fleeting offerings. Such heavenly treasure can only be found in a sacred union sealed by the Spirit of the Living God. Her Bridegroom has given His life for her and purchased her with His own blood. Nothing will sever this bonded love. Eternal love is powerful, sustaining love. *"As the bridegroom rejoices over the bride, so shall your God rejoice over you." (Isaiah 62.5b)*

During such troubling times, the rewards for following the harlot will present themselves in the form of material lavishness, whereas the cost of obedience to God will be utter persecution and even death. Although the harlot will seek to lure the church from the Bridegroom, her evil attempts will be to no avail. Believers may desire the comforts enjoyed by those they see partaking of the harlot's prosperity, but the price of such temporal gratification will be too great. The Holy Spirit will empower true Christ followers to keep worldly goods in perspective as they recognize the wrath that will befall the harlot and her followers. *"For the love of money is a root of all kinds of evil, for which some have strayed from the faith in their greediness, and pierced themselves through with many sorrows." (1 Timothy 6.10)*

Let us rejoice in the secure union that we have in our Lord Jesus Christ, the true Bridegroom, Who has bought us with His own blood and Who will return to gather us unto Himself:

'Then the kingdom of heaven shall be likened to ten virgins who took their lamps and went out to meet the bridegroom. ²Now five of them were wise, and five were foolish. ³Those who were foolish took their lamps and took no oil with them, ⁴but the wise took oil in their vessels with their lamps. ⁵But while the bridegroom was delayed, they all slumbered and slept. ⁶And at midnight a cry was heard: "Behold, the bridegroom is coming; go out to meet him!" ⁷Then all those virgins arose and trimmed their lamps. ⁸And the foolish said to the wise, "Give us some of your oil, for our lamps are going out." ⁹But the wise answered, saying, "No, lest there should not be enough for us and you; but go rather to those who sell, and buy for yourselves." ¹⁰And while they went to buy, the bridegroom came, and those who were ready went in with him to the wedding; and the door was shut.' (Matthew 25.1–10)

Revelation 18.9–19

Verses 9, 10- "⁹The kings of the earth who committed fornication and lived luxuriously with her will weep and lament for her, when they see the smoke of her burning, ¹⁰standing at a distance for fear of her torment, saying, 'Alas, alas, that great city Babylon, that mighty city! For in one hour your judgment has come.'

The kings, one of three groups of Babylon loyalists mentioned within this passage, were addressed first. The kings that had committed their allegiance to Babylon, had contributed to her success, and had prospered along with her would grievously mourn her downfall. They would watch her destruction and the smoke from the fire in which she burned, and they would wail and cry out for her. At one time, these kings thought their futures were solely dependent on her success and longevity, but she would be instantly destroyed, which would produce immeasurable anguish to these rulers. *"And it shall be, in the day of the Lord's sacrifice, that I will punish the princes and the king's children, and all such as are clothed with foreign apparel." (Zephaniah 1.8)*

It is also noted that these kings who had supported the success of Babylon watched her destruction from a distance. They were not standing by her side, assisting her until all efforts became obviously useless. Rather, they were watching her destruction from far away as if, it seems, to avoid the fate that befell her. There was no loyalty demonstrated because deception lay at the heart of their devotion. They had participated and prospered in her success, but they also tried to separate themselves from her and would have nothing to do with her when she was under the direct wrath of God.

From their positions far away from the rising smoke of Babylon's devastation, they exclaimed, "Alas, alas, that great city Babylon, that mighty city! For in one hour your judgment has come." This was, at the very least, an acknowledgment that Babylon was not merely being destroyed but was under the very judgment of Almighty God.

Verse 11- "And the merchants of the earth will weep and mourn over her, for no one buys their merchandise anymore:

The merchants, the second of three groups of Babylon loyalists mentioned within this passage, were addressed next. These merchants, as previously studied, had directly prospered from their allegiance to this great city and the antichristian authorities that empowered it and, concurrently, the economic system operating within her global structure. *"And the merchants of the earth have become rich through the abundance of her luxury." (Revelation 18.3b)* Like the kings previously mentioned, the merchants mourned for her, though by the phrasing of this verse, it seems they were grieved not so much for the loss of the city as for the loss of their own prosperity. Nobody would be able to buy or sell anything, including food, clothing, medical supplies, or any other vital provisions, which indicates a total collapse of the global economy. The merchants, therefore, mourned the ruin of their financial security as well as the threat of their physical well-being. *"Neither their silver nor their gold shall be able to deliver them in the day of the Lord's wrath; but the whole land shall be devoured by the fire of His jealousy, for He will make speedy riddance of all those who dwell in the land." (Zephaniah 1.18)*

Verses 12, 13- "¹²merchandise of gold and silver, precious stones and pearls, fine linen and purple, silk and scarlet, every kind of citron wood, every kind of object of ivory, every kind of object of most precious wood, bronze, iron, and marble; ¹³and cinnamon and incense, fragrant oil and frankincense, wine and oil, fine flour and wheat, cattle and sheep, horses and chariots, and bodies and souls of men.

This verse specifies certain material luxuries whose marketing had been halted because of the Babylon's destruction. This merchandise includes fine metals, precious gems, fine textiles, exquisite fabrics, luxurious building materials, the finest metal compounds, and spices and fragrances. This list included the finest merchandise the world had to offer. More importantly, however, this list also included things that were necessary for life and well-being, such as ointments for medicinal purposes, drinking and baking products, and livestock used for farming, transportation, and food. This verse shows that not only would the wealthy be affected but also the poor. Regardless of stature or wealth of an individual or family, all would mourn Babylon's fall because of the impact that it would have on the world. Those who partook in her fornication, all those who received the mark of the beast so that they could buy and sell, would experience the direct and immediate consequences of her demise. *"Riches do not profit in the day of wrath."* *(Proverbs 11.4a)*

Along with all of these material assets, we are told that another commodity no longer able to be bought or sold was the "souls of men." Some commentators point to this description to signify that life would be the most notable item sacrificed during the antichrist's reign, yet its placement at the end of this list seems to hint at the low value that would be placed on life itself.[7] Others view this as a reference to slavery and prostitution.[8] On the other hand, it may simply refer to persons whose labor services were viewed as commodities. The Greek word translated as *soul* is ψυχάζ (psuche), which in several usages of the word refers more to the desires or appetites of a person's soul.[9] *(Psalm 107.9; Isaiah 29.8)* As such, it might be interpreted that this extensive list is concluded by saying, in a sense, *and anything else that a person might desire.* We should not suppose that any of these interpretations are not equally plausible in light of the antichrist's nature, which would value life so little as to lead the entirety of his followers into perdition. *(Revelation 20.12–15)*

Verse 14- *"The fruit that your soul longed for has gone from you, and all the things which are rich and splendid have gone from you, and you shall find them no more at all.*

The "fruit that your soul longed for" refers to all other worldly goods that mankind sought to own. This verse basically states that any and all things of a material nature that the world would desire to own during this final period of tribulation would be taken away. Not only would people be unable to acquire these things, but the items themselves would not even be available. *"Behold, the Lord makes the earth empty and makes it waste, distorts its surface and scatters abroad its inhabitants."* *(Isaiah 24.1)*

Verses 15, 16- *"¹⁵The merchants of these things, who became rich by her, will stand at a distance for fear of her torment, weeping and wailing, ¹⁶and saying, 'Alas, alas, that great city that was clothed in fine linen, purple, and scarlet, and adorned with gold and precious stones and pearls!*

Like the kings in earlier verses, the merchants that had gained prosperity because of Babylon's success would not stand near her during her destruction as a demonstration of their gallant allegiance, but they would watch her destruction from far away. Again, no measure of loyalty would cause them to run to her aid at the risk of being accidentally swept away in the terrible fate that befell her. They had participated in her economic prosperity but separated themselves from her when God's judgment came.

At their positions far away from the rising smoke of Babylon's devastation, they loudly voiced their despair. This exclamation, completed in the verse that follows, demonstrated the reason for their weeping and wailing. It is clear that the only consequences that these merchants bemoaned were from the loss of the material possessions they had enjoyed during her more affluent days.

Verses 17, 18- *"'¹⁷For in one hour such great riches came to nothing.' Every shipmaster, all who travel by ship, sailors, and as many as trade on the sea, stood at a distance ¹⁸and cried out when they saw the smoke of her burning, saying, 'What is like this great city?'"*

This verse completes the merchants' outcry as they stood in the distance. After describing Babylon in the previous verses as a great city adorned in only the finest luxuries, they cried, "For in one hour such great riches came to nothing." It was an acknowledgment that all of the world's riches, which certainly Babylon possessed, could not stop or alter the wrath of God. The man who trusted in his wealth would soon learn the error of his ways. *"Here is the man who did not make God his strength, but trusted in the abundance of his riches, and strengthened himself in his wickedness." (Psalm 52.7)*

Also introduced in this verse is the third of three groups mentioned in this chapter that specifically mourned the destruction of the city. This group consisted of the shipmasters or captains of the sea-going vessels that transported all of the merchandise to all other ports around the world, revealing again the scope of the influence that this antichristian regime would have over the global economy. Also included in this group were sailors, dockhands, and every other type of person who might have benefited from her commercial trade system. They, too, stood in the distance, as far removed as possible from God's wrath being poured out upon this city that once flourished.

These shipmasters and sailors, like the merchants and the kings before them, grieved aloud from their position far in the distance as they watched their jobs and security go up in the smoke that arose from the all-consuming flames, crying, "What is like this great city?'" They acknowledged that there was no greater city in the world yet realized that the prosperity they had experienced under her opulence was now past. They would certainly also realize how much more powerful Almighty God is than the supposed might and affluence of this great city they had once served.

Notes/Applications

Like throwing a stone into a pond of water and watching the ripples of that one action flow all the way to the pond's far shores, Almighty God's judgment will penetrate the entire world at this point in history. In one hour, the world's structure of material wealth will fall.

Material wealth such as gold, silver, monetary markets, and possessions may offer some level of collateral in this life, but it is not lasting. We are eternal beings in need of eternal riches that enrich our souls. Therefore, the love of earthly wealth will never satisfy in the long-run and the fervent pursuit of such will leave us empty, lonely, and afraid. *"15Do not love the world or the things in the world. If anyone loves the world, the love of the Father is not in him. 16For all that is in the world—the lust of the flesh, the lust of the eyes, and the pride of life— is not of the Father but is of the world. 17And the world is passing away, and the lust of it; but he who does the will of God abides forever." (1 John 2.15–17)* Security is not a place; it is a state. Security then is only found by building our lives upon a sure foundation, which is Jesus Christ, the Cornerstone. *"Therefore thus says the Lord God: 'Behold, I lay in Zion a stone for a foundation, a tried stone, a precious cornerstone, a sure foundation; whoever believes will not act hastily.'"* (Isaiah 28.16)

Living in this world requires the use of the world's resources, but we are not to trust in them. We are to manage them in a manner that glorifies Jehovah-Jireh, our Provider.

Revelation 18.19–24

Verse 19- *"They threw dust on their heads and cried out, weeping and wailing, and saying, 'Alas, alas, that great city, in which all who had ships on the sea became rich by her wealth! For in one hour she is made desolate.'*

The shipmasters cast dust on their heads as a public display of their grief and anguish. In the midst of their weeping and grief, they called out much like the kings and the merchants before them. In a moment's time, the great system in which they had prospered and to which they had devoted their allegiance was wiped out.

Three times in this chapter we are told that this judgment occurred in only one hour's time, and there is no reason to suggest this means any more than a literal sixty minutes. It marks the outpouring of God's wrath, and it can and will occur in a mere moment. His judgment would pass swiftly, obliterating man's continuing confidence in his ability to have another tomorrow. *"¹³Come now, you who say, 'Today or tomorrow we will go to such and such a city, spend a year there, buy and sell, and make a profit'; ¹⁴whereas you do not know what will happen tomorrow. For what is your life? It is even a vapor that appears for a little time and then vanishes away." (James 4.13–14)*

Verse 20- *"Rejoice over her, O heaven, and you holy apostles and prophets, for God has avenged you on her!"*

This verse concludes the proclamation of judgment against Babylon that began in verse six. The redeemed of Heaven were instructed to rejoice. This group likely included all believers throughout the ages. They were instructed to rejoice because of the devastation that had taken place. In addition, this verse further supports that it would be God Almighty Who poured out this destruction and not His faithful mentioned in verses four and five. *"I have trodden the winepress alone, and from the peoples no one was with Me. For I have trodden them in My anger, and trampled them in My fury; their blood is sprinkled upon My garments, and I have stained all My robes.'" (Isaiah 63.3)*

While mankind mourned the loss of Babylon, Heaven celebrated the significance of her destruction. God had at last avenged the blood and persecution of the saints, which had been anxiously anticipated by those who sought Babylon's ruin. *"And they cried with a loud voice, saying, 'How long, O Lord, holy and true, until You judge and avenge our blood on those who dwell on the earth?'" (Revelation 6.10)*

Verse 21- Then a mighty angel took up a stone like a great millstone and threw it into the sea, saying, "Thus with violence the great city Babylon shall be thrown down, and shall not be found anymore.

John saw a powerful angel heave what looked like an enormous boulder into the depths of the sea. The mighty angel then spoke, comparing what he had done with the destruction of the city, saying that Babylon would be "thrown down" in the same manner, meaning that it would have a tremendous, far-reaching impact and it would occur instantaneously. *"'Then you shall say, 'Thus Babylon shall sink and not rise from the catastrophe that I will bring upon her.'" (Jeremiah 51.64)* Like a great stone dropped into the ocean, Babylon would be gone, never again to be found on the face of the earth, and the effects of her destruction would ripple out and reach every corner of the world. Babylon—the great city, the globally-influential core of paganism, idolatry, and sinfulness—would be violently and utterly destroyed by the wrath of God Almighty, and it would leave no person on the face of the earth unaffected.

Verse 22- "The sound of harpists, musicians, flutists, and trumpeters shall not be heard in you anymore. No craftsman of any craft shall be found in you anymore, and the sound of a millstone shall not be heard in you anymore.

The mighty angel introduced in the previous verse continued speaking, further describing the utter destruction of Babylon. There would be no more music played or heard throughout the world, nor would any craftsmen of any type be found. The sound of the millstone or any other type of tool used for producing even simple foods would be distinctly absent. The mention of these trades demonstrates the far-reaching impact of Babylon's destruction on even those who would seemingly have little if anything to do with her prosperity. Unpretentious things that might bring simple joy would never again enhance Babylon's streets.

Verse 23- "The light of a lamp shall not shine in you anymore, and the voice of bridegroom and bride shall not be heard in you anymore. For your merchants were the great men of the earth, for by your sorcery all the nations were deceived.

Not even the light of a candle would be present after God's wrath befell this city, for Babylon's ruins would lie in utter darkness. No light of any kind would endure to illuminate what little would remain of the once exalted city.

Again, the extent of the destruction is illustrated with a specific example. The merriment and joviality of such things as weddings and wedding parties would be gone forever. *"'Then I will cause to cease from the cities of Judah and from the streets of Jerusalem the voice of mirth and the voice of gladness, the voice of the bridegroom and the voice of the bride. For the land shall be desolate.'" (Jeremiah 7.34)*

Finally, this verse confirms that all merchants had formerly prospered. However, not only would buyers and sellers flourish within this economy but, more importantly, all mankind would submit to Babylon's authority through manipulation, as indicated by the final part of the verse, which states, "For by your sorcery all the nations were deceived." This removes any doubt that Babylon represented much more than just an illustrious city but also describes her eminence that, through the empowerment of the antichristian administration, would control the entire earth.

DIG DEEPER: *SORCERY*

Sorcery is the practice of influencing or predicting future events through appealing to the spirit world. Those who practice this type of divination seek information from those powers that oppose the only living God, Who with Jesus Christ is Sovereign over all other powers. Resorting to sorcery of any kind for any purpose whatsoever is an offense against the almighty Creator. The entire body of Scripture forbids God's people to be involved in any practice that seeks guidance from any other gods. Paul warned that those who practice such will not inherit the Kingdom of Heaven. *(Galatians 5.19–21)*

Verse 24- "And in her was found the blood of prophets and saints, and of all who were slain on the earth."

Babylon's ascendancy would not come without a price. There would be great bloodshed of those who sought to remain faithful to the true God. Just as the influence of Babylon's wealth would impact lives all over the world, so, too, would her influence impact those who refused to participate in her fornications all over the world. Not only would she be held responsible for the bloodshed within her borders but also for the deaths of any and all of God's faithful throughout the earth.[10] *"For true and righteous are His judgments, because He has judged the great harlot who corrupted the earth with her fornication; and He has avenged on her the blood of His servants shed by her.'" (Revelation 19.2)*

Notes/Applications

Chapters seventeen and eighteen describe Babylon as a "great" city. As a result, many debates center upon the actual identity and location of this city. As already studied, several theorists contend that this city is actually Rome despite the city's present lack of worldly prominence. In response to this problem, other scholars suggest that a revived city of Babylon will be rebuilt to serve as the center of world power from where the antichrist will reign.

In essence, this city's actual location and identity are not nearly as relevant as her fate. Babylon will represent everything contrary to God's will, and dripping from her hands will be the blood of God's saints. Therefore, regardless of the city's actual identity, one thing remains absolutely certain: Babylon will be judged by the Lord God Almighty and will be destroyed by His wrath according to His predetermined measure. *(Revelation 18.6)*

Some may ponder how a loving God could unleash such fury upon His creation. Where is the long-suffering God to Whom the multitudes more easily subscribe?

Our sin nature has convoluted the issue and, therefore, perverted our perception of the Almighty God. The God of longsuffering Who has been ruling for all eternity is also a righteous Warrior of truth, and righteousness requires that there be an accounting for evil. *"The Lord is longsuffering and abundant in mercy, forgiving iniquity and transgression; but He by no means clears the guilty, visiting the iniquity of the fathers on the children to the third and fourth generation.'"* (Numbers 14.18) Therefore, the same Almighty God Who lovingly sacrificed His Son on Calvary's cross and raised Him from the dead as the penalty for our transgressions will, in His righteousness, rightfully avenge the harlot's fornication and her torture of His faithful saints.

Chapter Nineteen

Revelation 19.1–7

Verse 1- After these things I heard a loud voice of a great multitude in heaven, saying, "Alleluia! Salvation and glory and honor and power belong to the Lord our God!

The chapter begins with the phrase, "After these things," which signifies that what is about to be explained chronologically follows that which has just taken place—namely, the judgment of Babylon. After the fall of Babylon, John heard the voices of many people in Heaven. This was likely the entire multitude of Heaven, including the angels, the twenty-four elders, the four beasts, and the countless believers that now constituted a host of glorified saints. They all worshipped the Lord with shouts of praise, saying, "Alleluia! Salvation and glory and honor and power belong to the Lord our God!" Before praising the Lord for what He had done, they praised Him for Who He is.

Interestingly, this chapter is the only passage in the New Testament where the word *Alleluia* appears, and it seems quite appropriate that such distinctive praise and adoration should come upon the heels of Almighty God's thorough destruction of that city which embodied the greatest concentration of evil the world would ever know.

Verse 2- "For true and righteous are His judgments, because He has judged the great harlot who corrupted the earth with her fornication; and He has avenged on her the blood of His servants shed by her."

The heavenly multitude continued to praise God Almighty in unison. After praising Him for Who He is, they praised Him for what He had done in pouring out His wrath against Babylon, and immediately, they acknowledged that these judgments were "true and righteous." In His wrath could be found no fault or sense of unfairness. Fairness is a human design used to determine the appropriateness of a decision, but it is not an attribute of God. Justice, however, is. God did not judge according to anyone else's standards but His own, which are perfect. There may be many standards, but God Almighty has only one, which is eternally true, unchangeable, absolute, and perfect, and all His judgment is meted out according to His ever-present, righteous, consistent standard.

Babylon, the great harlot, received God's wrath for her deception and fornication, and her destruction was well-deserved. For this reason, the heavenly multitude rejoiced. Our great and powerful Lord God Almighty carried out the vengeance of the saints upon Babylon and repaid her for the enormous spilling of the blood of "His servants."

Verse 3- Again they said, "Alleluia! Her smoke rises up forever and ever!"

The heavenly multitude concluded its praise with another heartfelt, "Alleluia!" Another clear indication that this progression occurred chronologically was the vision of smoke rising from the ruins of Babylon, as introduced in the previous chapter. John told us that this smoke rose up forever and ever, meaning either that it was a fire that continually smoldered or that the smoke did not dissipate as it rose toward Heaven and beyond. *"⁸For it is the day of the LORD'S vengeance, the year of recompense for the cause of Zion. ⁹Its streams shall be turned into pitch, and its dust into brimstone; its land shall become burning pitch. ¹⁰It shall not be quenched night or day; its smoke shall ascend forever." (Isaiah 34.8–10a)* Some scholars have theorized that this eternal burning is a poetic metaphor to illustrate the absolute devastation of the city.[1] Whatever the actual meaning of the statement, Babylon's annihilation would forever serve as a reminder of the great significance and eternal consequence of God's judgment.

Verse 4- And the twenty-four elders and the four living creatures fell down and worshiped God who sat on the throne, saying, "Amen! Alleluia!"

John then saw the twenty-four elders and four creatures that were seated around God's throne fall prostrate in adoration and worship. The elders and beasts praised God, again saying, "Amen!" and "Alleluia!" As previously discussed, it seems that the twenty-four elders and four creatures existed solely for the purpose of praising and worshiping God Almighty on the throne. *(Revelation 4.8–11)*

Verse 5- Then a voice came from the throne, saying, "Praise our God, all you His servants and those who fear Him, both small and great!"

A voice emerged from the throne in Heaven commanding all God's servants to praise the Lord. The believers were further addressed as those "that fear him." This mandate to both small and great to praise God indicates that all believers throughout history, regardless of earthly status or importance, were included among this group.

The voice of the one speaking might be that of Almighty God, based upon the source of the voice being "from the throne." However, the use of pronouns, such as "Praise *our* God" and "those who fear *Him*" suggests that this was more likely the voice of one of the twenty-four elders or of the four beasts near the throne. Again, the source of the voice is not as important as the message. This is the third of four identities that offered praise to the Lord in the first seven verses of this chapter.

Verse 6- And I heard, as it were, the voice of a great multitude, as the sound of many waters and as the sound of mighty thunderings, saying, "Alleluia! For the Lord God Omnipotent reigns!

The next two verses express the fourth statement of praise that was given by yet another identity in Heaven. Despite a pronoun use resembling the declaration of praise given in verse five, many scholars contend that the description of this voice suggests that it was the voice of God Almighty Himself. It is described as a voice like that "of a great multitude, and as the sound of many waters, and as the sound of mighty thunderings." Similar descriptions are given throughout Scripture to describe the voice of the Lord. *"The voice of the Lord is over the waters; the God of glory thunders; the Lord is over many waters." (Psalm 29.3) "When He utters His voice, there is a multitude of waters in the heavens." (Jeremiah 10.13a) "His voice was like the sound of many waters." (Ezekiel 43.2b) "And the sound of his words like the voice of a multitude." (Daniel 10.6b)*

Though such arguments are very persuasive, we are led to believe by surrounding verses and the use of a second-person pronoun that this was not the voice of the Lord but the voice of a special being chosen by God to deliver this last and very important message. Most convincing support for this objection is that the angel adamantly rejected John's worship and identified himself as one "of [his] brethren who have the testimony of Jesus." *(verse 10)*

This person further praised the omnipotence of God, which, like *almighty* and *sovereign,* is an attribute exclusive to God. No other being possesses this trait, for it is the very essence of God alone. Like the multitude before him who praised God first for Who He is and then for what He had done *(verses 1 and 2)*, this voice also praises God first for Who He is before praising Him for what was about to take place.

Verse 7- "Let us be glad and rejoice and give Him glory, for the marriage of the Lamb has come, and His wife has made herself ready."

The great cause for rejoicing and celebration was revealed. The marriage of the Lamb had come, and the bride was ready. The

Bride, comprised of God's elect from the dawn of creation, were all present with the Lamb in Heaven. The total sum of those who would live forever in God's presence as His bride were present and accounted for. The word marriage describes the relationship between Christ and His Church to demonstrate an eternal union that is intimate, loving, and faithful. *"For I am jealous for you with godly jealousy. For I have betrothed you to one husband, that I may present you as a chaste virgin to Christ." (2 Corinthians 11.2)*

This correlation is beautifully illustrated in the Book of Hosea, where the loyal husband remained faithful to his adulterous wife until she was eventually restored unto him:

> [16]*'And it shall be, in that day,' says the LORD, 'That you will call Me "My Husband," and no longer call Me "My Master"...* [19]*'I will betroth you to Me forever; yes, I will betroth you to Me in righteousness and justice, in lovingkindness and mercy;* [20]*I will betroth you to Me in faithfulness, and you shall know the LORD.* [21]*It shall come to pass in that day that I will answer,' says the LORD; 'I will answer the heavens, and they shall answer the earth.* [22]*The earth shall answer with grain, with new wine, and with oil; they shall answer Jezreel.* [23]*Then I will sow her for Myself in the earth, and I will have mercy on her who had not obtained mercy; then I will say to those who were not My people, "You are My people!" and they shall say, "You are my God!"'* (Hosea 2.16, 19–23)

Notes/Applications

What distinguishes us as members of the human race from the rest of creation is that the Creator has crafted us in His own image and offered us a unique relationship, one of being saved by His grace and, thereby, joined with Him for all eternity! The above verses compare this intimate relationship to the privately tender yet publicly binding covenant between a groom and his bride. *(John 3.29; Matthew 9.15; Ephesians 5.25–33; and Revelation 21.2)* It is through the Lamb's redemption that we may enter a covenant-relationship with the Lord Jesus Christ the Bridegroom.

According to biblical tradition, the process of finalizing a marriage union consisted of several steps. First, the familial parties had to agree upon the price paid to the potential bride's father for his daughter's hand in marriage. Once the parties reached an agreement, the couple entered the relationship's engagement phase, also known as betrothal. At this time, the young girl was set apart for marriage and was no longer available to participate in a relationship with another man. Essentially, she belonged to the bridegroom, promised to him until their oaths could be consummated on a glorious wedding day filled with feasts and celebration.[2]

Generally speaking, during this engagement period, the bridegroom took great measures to make the necessary arrangements for his maiden to join him in his father's house, and the bride, too, prepared herself for married life. She would diligently fashion herself for the wedding day ceremonies. She would bathe and dress herself in white robes, which were often richly embroidered. She would wrap a bridal girdle around her waist, cover her face with a veil, and place a garland on her head.[3] *"Let us be glad and rejoice and give Him glory, for the marriage of the Lamb has come and His wife has made herself ready." (Revelation 19.7)* After all of her efforts to appear beautiful before her groom and the wedding guests, she must have rejoiced when she espied how her groom gazed lovingly upon her with pride emanating from his eyes, for on this day, the two would be joined in a holy, spiritual union that no man could separate. *"And as the bridegroom rejoices over the bride, so shall your God rejoice over you." (Isaiah 62.5b)*

Have we made ourselves ready for the Bridegroom's return and the consummation of our eternal matrimony with Him? He has been preparing us and our eternal home for His return. *"I will greatly rejoice in the Lord, my soul shall be joyful in my God; for He has clothed me with the garments of salvation, He has covered me with the robe of righteousness, as a bridegroom decks himself with ornaments, and as a bride adorns herself with her jewels." (Isaiah 61.10)* Surely, at the Lord's appearing, we, as His bride, will not eye our garments but our dear Bridegroom's face, and we will not be transfixed by glory itself but upon our King of grace.[4]

Revelation 19.8–14

Verse 8- *"And to her it was granted to be arrayed in fine linen, clean and bright, for the fine linen is the righteous acts of the saints."*

We are told both what the Bride of Christ wore and what her clothing represented. She was dressed in the finest, purest, whitest linen, which signifies, as described, "the righteous acts of the saints." The saints that comprised the Bride had the sins of their human lives washed away and forgiven forever by God at Calvary when the substitutionary Sacrifice became sin for man. *(2 Corinthians 5.21)* They were a pure, sinless body of redeemed that were able to stand before the perfect holiness of the righteous Lamb and God Almighty because of the grace and mercy of God Who had forgiven them. *"Wash me, and I shall be whiter than snow." (Psalm 51.7b) "The next day John saw Jesus coming toward him, and said, 'Behold! The Lamb of God who takes away the sin of the world!'" (John 1.29)*

Verse 9- *Then he said to me, "Write: 'Blessed are those who are called to the marriage supper of the Lamb!'" And he said to me, "These are the true sayings of God."*

The voice told John to write these things down that he saw and heard. More specifically, he was told to record what was told to him: "Blessed are those who are called to the marriage supper of the Lamb." Truly blessed beyond what words can describe are those who have been called by God's sovereign grace to join the Lamb and to worship in His presence forevermore! John was also told that these were the "true sayings of God." The message was directed by Almighty God and was, therefore, perfect and truthful in its merit.

Verse 10- *And I fell at his feet to worship him. But he said to me, "See that you do not do that! I am your fellow servant, and of your brethren who have the testimony of Jesus. Worship God! For the testimony of Jesus is the spirit of prophecy."*

Being overwhelmed with all that he witnessed, John fell prostrate at the feet of the angel who had been revealing these visions.

The being immediately rejected this gesture of worship and insisted that John rise to his feet. Refusing undeserved worship, he declared his status as a "fellow servant." Though he was an angel, he equated his position as being no greater than that of John or of his "brethren who have the testimony of Jesus." *"⁸Now I, John, saw and heard these things. And when I heard and saw, I fell down to worship before the feet of the angel who showed me these things. ⁹Then he said to me, 'See that you do not do that. For I am your fellow servant, and of your brethren the prophets, and of those who keep the words of this book. Worship God.'"* *(Revelation 22.8–9)* They were both servants of God, neither greater than the other and each subject only to the Almighty Lord, to Whom the angel redirected John's worship. Then, he further explained that this testimony of Jesus was "the spirit of prophecy." This statement has received varied interpretation from commentators. Perhaps the most straightforward explanation is to conclude that the angel sought to redirect John's focus upon Jesus Christ, from Whom these visions were given and to Whom all authentic prophecy pertains.[5] The Bride was made ready, and the Bridegroom was about to make His unforgettable entrance.

Verse 11- Now I saw heaven opened, and behold, a white horse. And He who sat on him was called Faithful and True, and in righteousness He judges and makes war.

This verse begins what is arguably one of the most awe-inspiring passages in the entire Bible—the majestic arrival of Jesus Christ as the King of kings, the Victor over sin and death, and the triumphant, majestic Ruler of the world! The heavens parted like great curtains opening to an enormous stage, and a radiant figure emerged riding upon a white horse. It was the Lord Jesus Christ, called "Faithful and True" not as adjectives but as a title depicting His character. It is mentioned that "He judges and makes war" in righteousness since these would be the very reasons He would appear among the clouds. He had returned to wage a holy war *(verses 19–21)* that would culminate in the judgment of all mankind *(Revelation 20.12–15)*. This would be an unparalleled scene that would certainly be visible from every corner of the world. *"For as the lightning comes from the east and flashes to the west, so also will the coming of the Son of Man be.'" (Matthew 24.27)*

Verse 12- His eyes were like a flame of fire, and on His head were many crowns. He had a name written that no one knew except Himself.

After describing the appearance of the Lord Jesus Christ, John offers a physical description of the glorious Rider seated upon the white horse. His eyes were like flames, seeming to emphasize the Judge's inescapable and penetrating gaze.[6] *(Revelation 1.14)* The many crowns atop His head draw an immediate contrast far superior to the beast's ten crowns. *(Revelation 13.1)* This has been commonly accepted as referring to Christ's endless dominion and unlimited sovereignty.[7]

John also noted that the triumphant Messiah had a name written that could not be understood by anyone other than Himself. Though many commentators have presented certain possibilities to answer this apparent riddle, readers must be satisfied with the unknown on this subject except, perhaps, as it serves to exhibit Christ's transcendence. In fact, seldom can we be more certain that an answer will not be made known than for the text itself to verify the matter so conclusively as to simply say "that no one knew." Therefore, speculation on this matter is pointless. Jesus had already been identified as "Faithful and True" and would be further identified in the verse which follows.

Verse 13- He was clothed with a robe dipped in blood, and His name is called The Word of God.

John describes the returning King as wearing a robe that had been dipped in blood. One possibility is that the blood was Christ's own—that redeeming blood by which the victory over sin and death was accomplished for God's faithful.[8] *"And you shall take some of the blood that is on the altar, and some of the anointing oil, and sprinkle it on Aaron and on his garments, on his sons and on the garments of his sons with him; and he and his garments shall be hallowed, and his sons and his sons' garments with him." (Exodus 29.21)* Another possibility is that the blood on the robe belonged to the Lord's enemies, both those whose judgment had already taken place and those whose judgment was now imminent. *"I have trodden the winepress alone, and from the peoples no one was with Me. For I have trodden them in My anger, and trampled them in My fury; their blood is sprinkled upon My garments, and I have stained all My robes." (Isaiah 63.3)* *"And the winepress was trampled outside the city, and blood came out of the winepress, up to the horses' bridles." (Revelation 14.20)* The blood signifies that Jesus alone had the right to serve as the righteous and holy Judge over mankind.

The name of Him Who sat upon the white horse was the Word of God. This is the One and same Jesus Christ Who formed the earth and later manifested Himself as one of His own creation to purchase its redemption. *"In the beginning was the Word, and the Word was with God, and the Word was God. [14]And the Word became flesh and dwelt among us, and we beheld His glory, the glory as of the only begotten of the Father, full of grace and truth." (John 1.1, 14)* He now reappeared at the conclusion of earth's lifespan as the conquering King to avenge the blood of His servants *(Revelation 19.2)*, to abolish forever His enemy and sin *(Revelation 20.10)*, to judge the reprobate for their unfaithfulness *(Revelation 20.12–15)*, and to establish His eternal kingdom *(Revelation 21.1–3)*.

Verse 14- And the armies in heaven, clothed in fine linen, white and clean, followed Him on white horses.

An army of Heaven followed the Lord as He returned to the earth. They, too, all rode upon white horses and were dressed in fine linen, which represents the righteousness they possessed through their Leader. *(verse 8)* This multitude had assembled to accompany the Lord Jesus Christ at His return to the earth not because the Lord would require their assistance to secure His victory but so that they might participate in the celebration with Him.

Whether this army was comprised of saints or angels or both is uncertain. It seems consistent with other Scriptures to affirm that, at the very least, this group will consist of those whose redemption was purchased by the Messiah's sacrifice at Calvary. *"These will make*

*war with the Lamb, and the Lamb will overcome them, for He is Lord of
lords and King of kings; and those who are with Him are called, chosen, and
faithful.'" (Revelation 17.14)*

Notes/Applications

> *Bride of the Lamb, awake, awake!*
> *Why sleep for sorrow now?*
> *The hope of glory, Christ, is thine,*
> *A child of glory thou.*
>
> *Thy spirit, through the lonely night,*
> *From earthly joy apart,*
> *Hath sighed for One that's far away—*
> *The Bridegroom of thy heart.*
>
> *But see! the night is waning fast,*
> *The breaking morn is near;*
> *And Jesus comes, with voice of love,*
> *Thy drooping heart to cheer.*
>
> *He comes—for oh, His yearning heart*
> *No more can bear delay—*
> *To scenes of full unmingled joy*
> *To call His bride away.*
>
> *Then weep no more; 'tis all thine own*
> *His crown, His joy divine;*
> *And, sweeter far than all beside*
> *He, He Himself is thine!*[9]

The Lord and Savior Jesus Christ, the Son of the Living God, will
one great day return to earth in all of His glory to reconcile all
wrongs. He, as the "Word...the Truth; the Amen, the Faithful Witness
of the mind of God," will descend from His place at the Father's
right hand to judge the archenemy and rule the earth according to
His holy banner of truth and righteousness.[10]

Furthermore, when Christ returns to battle the archenemy, He will not enter upon a lowly colt as He chose to do when He entered Jerusalem during the Passover. He will triumphantly return upon a white stallion, and we, as His bride, will follow on white horses because He has redeemed us from the earth with His precious blood. *(verse 14)*

To be able to ride with the Lord among the armies of Heaven transcends our minds because it will be an experience beyond our loftiest dreams, yet Scripture confirms that this will be an actuality. If we remind ourselves of the gift of God's promises wrapped in these prophetic words, it will help us to endure present tribulations with prayerful anticipation.

Faithful and True, O, Living Word, we anticipate your triumphant return, for then our eyes shall behold as You wage war against the serpent of old. By the sword of Your mouth, You will bring the archenemy to shame, crushing his evil empire and casting him into the brimstone's flame. Lord of lords, King of kings, Faithful Witness of the Father's mind, we await the day when every tongue will proclaim that Jesus Christ is the name above all names.

Revelation 19.15–21

Verse 15- Now out of His mouth goes a sharp sword, that with it He should strike the nations. And He Himself will rule them with a rod of iron. He Himself treads the winepress of the fierceness and wrath of Almighty God.

This verse employs imagery familiar in the Old Testament to depict the Lord's judgment. The Lord, Who returned to the earth with the army of Heaven, would slay the nations with a sharp sword which emerged from His mouth. *"And take the helmet of salvation, and the sword of the Spirit, which is the word of God."* (Ephesians 6.17) It was with truth that their deceptions would be exposed and their sins would be judged. The words of truth spoken by the Lord Jesus Christ would be the only standard necessary to judge and condemn all that opposed Him. *"He shall strike the earth with the rod of His mouth, and with the breath of His lips He shall slay the wicked."* (Isaiah 11.4b)

When Christ returned to earth, He would "rule them with a rod of iron," which typifies the firm, unbending characteristic of His authority.[11] The reign of Christ would be black and white. There would be no room for leniency or tolerance of wickedness. *"'You shall break them with a rod of iron; You shall dash them to pieces like a potter's vessel.'"* (Psalm 2.9) *"'He shall rule them with a rod of iron; they shall be dashed to pieces like the potter's vessels.'"* (Revelation 2.27a)

Finally, the Lord Jesus Christ treaded "the winepress of [His] fierceness and wrath." *"'I have trodden the winepress alone, and from the peoples no one was with Me. For I have trodden them in My anger, and trampled them in My fury; their blood is sprinkled upon My garments, and I have stained all My robes.'"* (Isaiah 63.3) The glorious Messiah upon the white horse would summon the intense fury of God's wrath upon mankind as the consequences of its sinfulness and disobedience.

Verse 16- And He has on His robe and on His thigh a name written: KING OF KINGS AND LORD OF LORDS.

John notes yet another of Jesus' royal titles written on His robe and on His leg: KING OF KINGS AND LORD OF LORDS. Nobody would ever underestimate the absolute sovereignty of this majestic Champion. Though many did not believe that Jesus was the promised Messiah when He came to earth as an unassuming teacher, there would never again be any mistaking His identity when this imposing Warrior returned to the earth for the second time. *"¹⁴That you keep this commandment without spot, blameless until our Lord Jesus Christ's appearing, ¹⁵which He will manifest in His own time, He who is the blessed and only Potentate, the King of kings and Lord of lords." (1 Timothy 6.14–15)*

Verses 17, 18- ¹⁷Then I saw an angel standing in the sun; and he cried with a loud voice, saying to all the birds that fly in the midst of heaven, "Come and gather together for the supper of the great God, ¹⁸that you may eat the flesh of kings, the flesh of captains, the flesh of mighty men, the flesh of horses and of those who sit on them, and the flesh of all people, free and slave, both small and great."

John then saw an angel standing in the midst of the remaining brightness of the sun. He called out with a thunderous, commanding voice to all of the birds that flew among the heavens—a call that could be heard all around the earth. The angel summoned creation, the foul of the air, to come and to perform a specific task, which was to gather for a huge feast he referred to as "the supper of the great God." These were scavenger birds being summoned to feast upon the dead flesh at the great slaughter that was about to take place:

> *¹⁷'And as for you, son of man, thus says the Lord God, "Speak to every sort of bird and to every beast of the field: 'Assemble yourselves and come; gather together from all sides to My sacrificial meal which I am sacrificing for you, a great sacrificial meal on the mountains of Israel, that you may eat flesh and drink blood. ¹⁸You shall eat the flesh of the mighty, drink the blood of the princes of the earth, of rams and lambs, of goats and bulls, all of them fatlings of Bashan.'"' (Ezekiel 39.17–18)*

These verses indicate that none who opposed God would be spared, whether the greatest of leaders (kings, captains, and mighty men) or the most common of men ("all people, both free and slave, both small and great"). It was much more than a great battle that would take place at Armageddon. It would be unreserved carnage.

Verse 19- And I saw the beast, the kings of the earth, and their armies, gathered together to make war against Him who sat on the horse and against His army.

This scene describes the actual "battle" of Armageddon. It is the event to which the Lord Jesus Christ would return from Heaven to earth. *"¹⁴For they are spirits of demons, performing signs, which go out to the kings of the earth and of the whole world, to gather them to the battle of that great day of God Almighty. ¹⁶And they gathered them together to the place called in Hebrew, Armageddon." (Revelation 16.14, 16)* Within this scene, John saw the beast—the antichrist figure through which Satan would mount His campaign—and all of his armies led by the world leaders, the kings of the earth. In a battle where size and strength might have been a decisive factor, the armies of the antichrist would seem to have the advantage. However, this war would be won without the clash of any swords other than the sword of truth and judgment which proceeded from the Lord's mouth. This great multitude had been deceived into gathering to make war against Jesus Christ and His heavenly army, yet they were apparently unaware of their imminent and certain fate upon His arrival. God had afforded the antichrist power to sway the multitudes only for His preordained purposes and His preordained period of time, both of which were now fulfilled.

Verse 20- Then the beast was captured, and with him the false prophet who worked signs in his presence, by which he deceived those who received the mark of the beast and those who worshiped his image. These two were cast alive into the lake of fire burning with brimstone.

The battle would be over before it ever began. The antichrist and the false prophet were immediately overcome. There is no mention of an actual physical conflict taking place because it was entirely unnecessary for the Lord to engage the enemy to secure the victory. In His perfect sovereignty, Almighty God is able to bring anything and everything to pass by the simple force of His will.

These two were the most powerful and influential people, apart from the Lord Himself, that the world would ever know, yet their destruction would come in a moment. They were not killed but were thrown alive into the "lake of fire burning with brimstone." Their bodies, therefore, were being burned as physical specimens that could never be consumed and could never receive relief from the torment and anguish prepared for them.

DIG DEEPER: *LAKE OF FIRE*

This is the first of four times this term appears in Revelation. As the theme develops in the following chapter, we find that the beast and his prophet *(19.19)*, the devil *(20.10)*, Death and Hades *(20.15)*, and all those who are not found in the Book of Life *(20.15)* are cast into this place of everlasting torment. Throughout the gospel narratives, Jesus also uses the imagery of a fiery judgment for those who do not believe in Him. *(Matthew 5.22; 7.19; 13.40–42, 50; 18.8–9; 25.41; Mark 9.43, 48–49; Luke 16.24; and John 15.6)*

Verse 21- *And the rest were killed with the sword which proceeded from the mouth of Him who sat on the horse. And all the birds were filled with their flesh.*

After the antichrist and the false prophet were overcome, the Lord judged the rest of those who had gathered to make war against Him. Their judgment was severe and instantaneous. The countless armies that had gathered to rise against the Lord Jesus Christ were immediately slain. They were not thrown into the lake of fire with the antichrist and false prophet but were destroyed in their earthly bodies by "the sword which proceeded from the mouth of Him who sat on the horse." Again, this is not to signify an actual, physical conflict but, rather, the sovereign act of God's wrath which resulted in the immediate and unreserved deaths of all who had aligned themselves with His enemy, whereupon the birds began to eat their "supper of the great God." *(verse 17)*

Notes/Applications

It should never cease to move us when we consider what a powerful, almighty God we serve. Everything that happens, regardless of how great or how seemingly insignificant, submits to the control of the supreme King of kings and Lord of lords. *"And Jesus came and spoke to them, saying, 'All authority has been given to Me in heaven and on earth.'"* *(Matthew 28.18)* *"For of Him and through Him and to Him are all things, to whom be glory forever. Amen."* *(Romans 11.36)* Even the beast's rise and reign over the earth will occur only at the direction of Almighty God's ordinance, so we must recognize that God's will is not a reactionary, haphazard strategy but a perfect plan of divine wisdom and divine holiness.

When the time of defeat arrives for the antichrist, false prophet, and even Satan, there will be no physical confrontation because these events will be entirely accomplished by God's decree. By nothing more than His command, He will overcome the evil one and his followers with the sword that proceeds out of His Son's mouth, consuming everything anti-God. *"And then the lawless one will be revealed, whom the Lord will consume with the breath of His mouth and destroy with the brightness of His coming."* *(2 Thessalonians 2.8b)*

Perhaps it is difficult for us to meditate upon these verses with hopeful anticipation or even excitement. We can easily become so absorbed in the painful, difficult times that will accompany the earth's last days that we unintentionally lose focus of the glorious outcome.

Could our sense of urgency be the Holy Spirit's beckoning within our hearts to consider what manner of fellowship we have with Jesus Christ, the Lord of lords? Have we responded to His invitation to be partakers in the marriage supper of the Lamb? Truly, children of God, those who have been "called to the marriage supper of the Lamb," can rest in the Father's sovereignty and enjoy a foretaste of His eternal rewards by anticipating with wholehearted enthusiasm the events and promises spoken of in this chapter. Indeed, Jesus Christ will return as King of kings and Lord of lords, and His victory is certain! *"⁹The judgments of the LORD are true and righteous altogether. ¹⁰More to be desired are they than gold, yea, than much fine gold; sweeter also than honey and the honeycomb. ¹¹Moreover by them Your servant is warned, and in keeping them there is great reward."* *(Psalm 19.9b–11)*

Chapter Twenty

Of the many interpretations that are established within the Book of Revelation, one of the most debated is that which finds its roots in this chapter—the Millennium. There are essentially three positions regarding this period of time: 1) Premillennial, which generally views these as one thousand literal years during which time the Lord Jesus Christ will reign following His Second Coming; 2) Postmillennial, which views these one thousand years as depicting the consummation of the Church's history during which time the saints will ultimately accomplish their gospel mission of evangelizing the world through those agents provided them, namely, the Holy Spirit and the Word of God, after which time the Lord will return to the earth, as described in chapter nineteen; and 3) Amillennial, which generally considers this period as referring to the span between the Messiah's first and second advent but views these thousand years as referring only to themes of spiritual significance.[1]

Each position poses certain inherent complexities whose examinations are better reserved for other compositions. However, certain matters deserve mention for the sake of determining a perspective from which to approach this commentary. First, those who view 19.19–21 as depicting the same event as that presented in 20.9–10 encounter an obstacle in the description of Satan being

thrown into the lake of fire "where the beast and the false prophet
are," which appears to refer to different entities experiencing the
same fate at different points in time. Furthermore, the events
depicted in each chapter noticeably portray different events with
different characters and different outcomes.

As such, the presentation of this commentary approaches this
chapter as following those events depicted in the previous chapter,
whereby the thousand years portrayed herein will follow the triumphant return of the Lord Jesus Christ. Whether or not this is a
span of one thousand literal years cannot be positively resolved,
but the identical designation of this period occurring six times in
the first seven verses seems to support a literal reading. These
determinations aside, it is perhaps most important to note that
these interpretive disputes should never undermine the magnitude
of the last four chapters *(19–22),* which entail the marvelous return
of the Lord Jesus Christ; His final wrath, judgment, and punishment
of all sin and evil; the vindication of all who have placed their faith
in the one true God; and the establishment of God's glorious, eternal Kingdom where all His faithful will dwell forevermore in His
presence.[2]

Revelation 20.1–6

Verse 1- *Then I saw an angel coming down from heaven, having the key to the bottomless pit and a great chain in his hand.*

After observing the warrior Messiah overcome the beast, false prophet, and all those who gathered to join them in battle, John saw another angel descend from the heavenly realms. The angel held in his hands a large chain and the keys to the bottomless pit. This may have been the same angel who had earlier released some demons for judgment. *"Then the fifth angel sounded: and I saw a star fallen from heaven to the earth. To him was given the key to the bottomless pit." (Revelation 9.1)*

Whether this bottomless pit depicts a literal or symbolic place is uncertain, but within the context of this verse and similar verses in chapters nine and eleven, it can be assumed that it was a place designated by the Lord to exile certain spiritual beings. *(Revelation 9.1–11 and 11.7)*

Verses 2, 3- *²He laid hold of the dragon, that serpent of old, who is the Devil and Satan, and bound him for a thousand years; ³and he cast him into the bottomless pit, and shut him up, and set a seal on him, so that he should deceive the nations no more till the thousand years were finished. But after these things he must be released for a little while.*

God empowered this angel to bind Satan and cast him into the bottomless pit for one thousand years. If this is to be understood as a literal chain, it would be powerful enough to bind Satan only by the strength supplied it by the Lord God. There can be little doubt regarding the identity of the one being overcome since he is referred to by every name that he is called in the Book of Revelation—the Devil and Satan *(12.9)*, the dragon *(12.3)*, and the "serpent of old" *(12.9)*.

As with the overthrow of the beast and the false prophet in the previous chapter, there is no description of a struggle occurring. The angel was in no danger of being harmed by Satan because he was carrying out Almighty God's will.

In previous chapters, demons were loosed from the bottomless pit to wreak havoc upon the earth for a predetermined time of judgment. *(Revelation 9.2 and 11.7)* This time, the Lord had Satan bound and sent into the bottomless pit by one of His angels so that "he should deceive the nations no more." For one thousand years, escape would be impossible. After this time, as this verse forecasts and later verses detail, Satan would again be loosed upon the earth for a short period.

It can hardly be argued that Satan has been bound as a result of Christ's sacrifice at Calvary as some commentators have suggested, for his being loosed again would then seem to indicate that the sacrifice was ultimately ineffective.[3] Furthermore, such a position denies the weight of other biblical references that clearly portray the devil as actively and aggressively pursuing the destruction of believers in our present age. *(Acts 5.3; 2 Corinthians 4.3–4; Ephesians 2.2; 2 Timothy 2.26; and 1 Peter 5.8)* Finally, there are several Old Testament passages which seem to refer neither to the present age nor to the eternal, heavenly state, and are, therefore, better reconciled with an understanding of a future millennial period absent of Satan's influence.[4] *(Isaiah 11.6–9, 65.20; Zechariah 14.5–17)*

Verse 4- And I saw thrones, and they sat on them, and judgment was committed to them. Then I saw the souls of those who had been beheaded for their witness to Jesus and for the word of God, who had not worshiped the beast or his image, and had not received his mark on their foreheads or on their hands. And they lived and reigned with Christ for a thousand years.

John saw an assembly of thrones and was given the knowledge and discernment to understand that those who sat upon them were given responsibilities of judgment. No clarification is made as to how many thrones he saw or whether these thrones were located in Heaven or upon the earth. Within the context of the following verses, though, it becomes clear that this would be an earthly reign since nations would later be deceived from "the four corners of the earth." *(verse 8)*

John, seeing thrones of judgment, also observed beings—which he ambiguously referred to only as "they" and "them"—sitting on these thrones. Immediately afterward, he observed the souls of those who were killed for their unwavering faith in Christ Jesus and for refusing to bear the mark of the beast. Some commentators argue that this verse actually denotes two groups, encompassing all believers from Christ's first advent through His Second Coming and also those martyred for the sake of Christ.[5] Others view this verse as referring to the redeemed from both Old and New Testament eras.[6] Both positions consider the army returning with Christ to encompass all believers who would reign with Christ during this millennial period. *(Revelation 19.14)* However, these positions are primarily built not upon these verses but other biblical references in which believers are promised to reign with Christ in some manner. *(Daniel 7.21–27; 1 Corinthians 6.2; and 2 Timothy 2.12)*

The question, then, remains. Who are those that will live and reign with Christ for a thousand years? That these tribulation martyrs are the only group specifically identified suggests only two reasonable possibilities. First, some commentators support an interpretation that, although a definitive correlation is not made, the second part of this verse may be the description of those who were awarded the seats of these thrones.[7] In other words, those who "had not worshiped the beast or his image" comprise the same group to whom "judgment was committed." The second interpretation contends that the entire sum of redeemed throughout history were intended to reign with the Lord Jesus Christ, and these martyrs were simply specified from among all others for some unstated reason, even if only to acknowledge the ultimate sacrifice that they had paid. Again, the ambiguity with which John conveyed the identities of "they [who] sat on them" leaves this question effectively unanswered. Fortunately, it suffices to conclude that whether or not we fully understand the scope of Christ Jesus' millennial reign, He alone appoints those who will occupy these thrones, and His will and purposes are perfect and beyond scrutiny.

Verse 5- But the rest of the dead did not live again until the thousand years were finished. This is the first resurrection.

In light of the vast information presented in these few verses, it must be understood that the "rest of the dead" signifies those who

have died in unbelief throughout the ages.[8] This resurrection is not
one of second chance for the reprobate who died in their sins but
one of divine appointment for all God's faithful:

> [35]*'But those who are counted worthy to attain that age, and the res-
> urrection from the dead, neither marry nor are given in marriage;
> [36]nor can they die anymore, for they are equal to the angels and are
> sons of God, being sons of the resurrection.' (Luke 20.35–36)* [20]*But
> now Christ is risen from the dead, and has become the firstfruits of
> those who have fallen asleep.* [21]*For since by man came death, by
> Man also came the resurrection of the dead.* [22]*For as in Adam all
> die, even so in Christ all shall be made alive. (1 Corinthians
> 15.20–22)* [13]*But I do not want you to be ignorant, brethren, con-
> cerning those who have fallen asleep, lest you sorrow as others
> who have no hope.* [14]*For if we believe that Jesus died and rose
> again, even so God will bring with Him those who sleep in Jesus.
> (1 Thessalonians 4.13–14) 'Most assuredly, I say to you, the hour is
> coming, and now is, when the dead will hear the voice of the Son
> of God; and those who hear will live.' (John 5.25)*

It can hardly be disputed in light of the entirety of Scripture
that this event will include all of God's redeemed. However, it
should further be noted that the verses in this chapter do not necessarily describe this resurrection so much as make reference to it.
Though it is very difficult to delineate chronologically the scope of
events described in the Book of Revelation since they span such a
relatively brief period of time, it is generally agreed that the Bible
depicts this resurrection as occurring in conjunction with the
Second Coming of the Lord Jesus Christ:

> [51]*Behold, I tell you a mystery: We shall not all sleep, but we shall all
> be changed—[52]in a moment, in the twinkling of an eye, at the last
> trumpet. For the trumpet will sound, and the dead will be raised
> incorruptible, and we shall be changed.* [53]*For this corruptible must
> put on incorruption, and this mortal must put on immortality. (1
> Thessalonians 15.51–53)* [15]*For this we say to you by the word of
> the Lord, that we who are alive and remain until the coming of the
> Lord will by no means precede those who are asleep.* [16]*For the Lord
> Himself will descend from heaven with a shout, with the voice of*

an archangel, and with the trumpet of God. And the dead in Christ will rise first. (1 Thessalonians 4.15–16)

Because scriptural evidence confirms that the resurrection of the redeemed will coincide with Christ's return, the event would appear to have already occurred by this point. *(Revelation 14.14–16; and 19.11–13)* As such, it is important to note that this resurrection would be unto ultimate immortality and incorruption, and it should not be presumed that it would be accomplished solely for the purpose of this millennial reign. Consequently, those who died without salvation through Christ would remain in the grave until the millennial period was completed, at which time they would be raised unto judgment and then eternally condemned. *(verses 12–15)*

Verse 6- Blessed and holy is he who has part in the first resurrection. Over such the second death has no power, but they shall be priests of God and of Christ, and shall reign with Him a thousand years.

Those to whom this first resurrection pertains are considered "blessed and holy." It can hardly be thought that such a distinction should ever be made of an unbeliever. As such, while these verses do not clearly identify those seated on the thrones of judgment, this is the verse by which many contend that the honor of judgment is bestowed upon all of God's faithful. The case is made by the evident link within the statement, "He who has part in the first resurrection...shall reign with Him a thousand years." They would also have no part in "the second death," which will be remarked upon in verse fourteen. Further, it is reiterated that this resurrected group would reign for one thousand years as "priests of God and of Christ," indicating, it seems, their unhindered access to the Lord God Almighty and the Lamb. Indeed, what a blessing this title and responsibility would be for those who rule upon thrones with the King of kings and Lord of lords!

It must be observed at this point that another quandary arises when attempting to determine the identity of those over whom those seated on thrones of judgment would reign. The most biblically defensible position argues that, despite the apparent enormity of the armies assembled by the beast and the false prophet to make war with the Lamb, this group did not consist of the entire sum of the earth's population but only those who actively engaged in the beast's battle against the returning Son of God.[9] Accordingly, there would be many throughout the earth both of young and old and men and women who, while under the wide-reaching influence of Babylon and the antichristian empire, had not actively participated in the beast's campaign nor in the destruction of his armies, and these would remain on earth to be ruled by those God appointed to seats of judgment.

Notes/Applications

These verses give us a glimpse of how the end of man's days on this earth will come to pass. As we are reminded of Christ's sovereign authority and of His definitive victory, the eyes of our hearts peer upward, becoming set on the reality that eternity belongs to Almighty God. All of these events ranging from tribulation to triumph will usher us into a kingdom ruled by our Lord Jesus Christ when He will bind the dragon's limited power.

For believers, the dawning of this day is what our hearts long to see. This will be the dawning of righteousness, justice, and peace prevailing throughout the earth when evil will be called into account. This will be the day when the end of the serpent which has tormented all of creation with his lies and evil designs will be in our sights. Therefore, we pray:

Thy Kingdom come, O God,
Thy rule, O Christ, begin;
Break with Thine iron rod
the tyrannies of sin.

Where is Thy reign of peace,
and purity, and love?
When shall all hatred cease,
as in the realms above?

When comes the promised time
that war shall be no more—
Oppression, lust, and crime,
shall flee Thy face before?

We pray Thee, Lord, arise,
and come in Thy great might;
Revive our longing eyes,
which languish for Thy sight.

Men scorn Thy sacred Name,
and wolves devour Thy fold;
By many deeds of shame
we learn that love grows cold.

O'er heathen lands afar
thick darkness broodeth yet:
Arise, O morning Star,
arise, and never set![10]

Revelation 20.7–15

Verses 7, 8- ⁷Now when the thousand years have expired, Satan will be released from his prison, ⁸and will go out to deceive the nations which are in the four corners of the earth, Gog and Magog, to gather them together to battle, whose number is as the sand of the sea.

We are never given to understand fully God's purposes for establishing a millennial kingdom after He obliterates the beast, the false prophet, the kings, and the armies that had risen to make war against Him. *(Revelation 19.19–21)* Final judgment would seem a fitting conclusion at this point in time, yet God would choose to merely bind Satan rather than destroy him while allowing another thousand years to transpire on earth, during which time He would rule the nations with those He resurrected. In yet another humanly inconceivable act of His perfect will, God would release Satan from his captivity in the bottomless pit when the thousand years are finished so that he could resume his objective to deceive mankind. He would be given one last chance, a short-lived opportunity, to do everything within his power to deceive and persuade mankind into believing his lies. Obviously, the devil would be unable to draw away any of those belonging to Christ. *"And I give them eternal life, and they shall never perish; neither shall anyone snatch them out of My hand."* *(John 10.28)*

The mention of "Gog and Magog" should be considered as a general symbolic reference. In Ezekiel 38 and 39, Gog is described as the chief prince over the land of Magog, which also represents the people that followed Gog and his rebellion against the Israelites and against Almighty God. Similarly, Satan would be loosed to deceive the people and to cause them to rise up against God. This would not be an assembly of the world's greatest military might, such as was amassed by the beast and the false prophet. *(Revelation 16.13–14; 19.19)* Rather, this would be a gathering of "the nations," the people over which God's resurrected had reigned and ruled for these thousand years. It is apparent that they would comprise a seemingly countless number of the world's inhabitants since they are described as gathering from "the four corners of the earth" and as having a number as vast "as the sand of the sea."

Furthermore, this verse substantiates that man rebels against his Creator because wickedness is at the core of the human heart. *(Genesis 6.5, 8.21; Proverbs 19.3; Luke 6.45; and Acts 8.21–22)* Despite experiencing a thousand years of God's perfect rule over the earth without Satan's influence, the nations would continue to despise God inwardly and would flock to Satan the moment of his release, as demonstrated in the following verses.

Verse 9- They went up on the breadth of the earth and surrounded the camp of the saints and the beloved city. And fire came down from God out of heaven and devoured them.

The nations joined Satan in his doomed effort to defeat Christ and those who reigned with Him. People came from throughout the earth and surrounded "the beloved city," where the "camp of the saints" was evidently located. Many identify this city as Jerusalem, such that the city would be re-established as the world's capital city under Christ just as Babylon served under the antichrist.[11] *"Now it shall come to pass in the latter days that the mountain of the Lord's house shall be established on the top of the mountains, and shall be exalted above the hills; and all nations shall flow to it." (Isaiah 2.2)* However, the "camp of the saints" and "the beloved city" may simply be a double reference to the saints scattered throughout the world, such as they were surrounded wherever they lived across "the breadth of the earth."[12] In contrast to that sizeable army which gathered with the beast and false prophet at Armageddon, this battlefield would know no boundaries.

Despite Satan's long-awaited and well-attended scheme to overcome Christ and His faithful, his greatest efforts would meet immediate destruction. As with those gathered for battle at Armageddon, those who followed Satan in seeking hostility against God and His faithful would be destroyed without any physical confrontation. Rather, the Lord's unconditional victory would be secured in a mere moment when God Almighty would send an all-consuming fire down from Heaven, instantly and utterly consuming Satan's vast armies.

Verse 10- The devil, who deceived them, was cast into the lake of fire and brimstone where the beast and the false prophet are. And they will be tormented day and night forever and ever.

This was Almighty God's final act of judgment against Satan, the final elimination of sin and evil. The devil was thrown into the lake of fire and brimstone to join the beast and false prophet, who had been permanently cast there by the Lord upon His Second Coming. *(Revelation 19.20)* Now, the instigator of all evil, the devil himself, would at last join his two chief agents.

These three—Satan, the beast, and the false prophet, which formed the unholy trilogy—would live in eternal anguish in the lake of fire. We often entertain mental images of Satan as the ruler of Hell, the place where those who die in unbelief descend to its depths and become slaves or servants of this cruel and commanding taskmaster who has horns and wields a trident. This verse should obliterate all such notions about Hell and the lake of fire. This lake of fire has been created and controlled by God Almighty for the sole purpose of eternal condemnation. It is not a place where Satan will govern as ringleader but the location where he will serve out his punishment. Some commentators prefer a view of annihilationism, wherein they believe this lake of fire refers to where Satan will be consumed by fire and utterly obliterated.[13] However, this verse clearly portrays a place of eternal conscious torment prepared for Satan as just condemnation for his persistent ruthless campaign against the Lord God Almighty and His elect.[14]

Verse 11- Then I saw a great white throne and Him who sat on it, from whose face the earth and the heaven fled away. And there was found no place for them.

John observed a great white throne upon which sat One Whose identity was described only as He "from whose face the earth and the heaven fled away." Even though other Revelation passages place God the Father on the throne *(Revelation 4.2–11, 7.9–10, and 12.5)*, this and other scriptural references suggest that this would be a particular throne of judgment appointed for and occupied by the Lord Jesus Christ:

*But why do you judge your brother? Or why do you show con-
tempt for your brother? For we shall all stand before the judgment
seat of Christ. (Romans 14.10) For we must all appear before the
judgment seat of Christ, that each one may receive the things done
in the body, according to what he has done, whether good or bad.
(2 Corinthians 5.10) I charge you therefore before God and the
Lord Jesus Christ, who will judge the living and the dead at His
appearing and His kingdom. (2 Timothy 4.1) Because He has
appointed a day on which He will judge the world in righteousness
by the Man whom He has ordained. He has given assurance of this
to all by raising Him from the dead. (Acts 17.31)*

From this great throne, Jesus Christ would judge all mankind,
past and present. The eternal destiny of all men would there and
then be determined.[15]

Scriptural evidence demands a literal interpretation of the
earth and heaven fleeing away:

*Lift up your eyes to the heavens, and look on the earth beneath. For
the heavens will vanish away like smoke, the earth will grow old
like a garment, and those who dwell in it will die in like manner;
but My salvation will be forever, and My righteousness will not be
abolished. (Isaiah 51.6) 'Heaven and earth will pass away, but My
words will by no means pass away.' (Matthew 24.35) But the day
of the Lord will come as a thief in the night, in which the heavens
will pass away with a great noise, and the elements will melt with
fervent heat; both the earth and the works that are in it will be
burned up. (2 Peter 3.10)*

Though such was not testified to by John, it could be debated
whether the heavens and earth passed away with the "fire [that]
came down from God out of heaven and devoured them." *(verse
9)* Whatever the case, these elements had already "passed away"
and "no place was found for them" by the time the next scene
opens. *"Now I saw a new heaven and a new earth, for the first heaven
and the first earth had passed away. Also there was no more sea."
(Revelation 21.1)*

**Verse 12- And I saw the dead, small and great, standing before
God, and books were opened. And another book was opened,**

which is the Book of Life. And the dead were judged according to their works, by the things which were written in the books.

John noted only "small and great" standing before God, which indicates the inclusion of all people regardless of earthly importance. Some commentators place the whole of mankind, both believers and unbelievers, standing before this throne of judgment.[16] *(Matthew 25.31–33; John 5.28–29; Romans 14.10; and 1 Peter 4.5)* Others view this as a resurrection only of unbelievers unto condemnation.[17] *(John 3.18, 5.24)* Whether or not all mankind is intended, John paid special attention hereafter to chronicle the fate of those who died in unbelief.

The dead were judged according to books that were opened before the Lord, including the Book of Life, which will be addressed in verse fifteen. Specifically, they were judged "according to their works." Unbelievers can be judged *only* according to their works because they have never received Christ's sacrifice on their behalf. Therefore, they will be judged by the law, the Word of God. The redeemed, too, are guilty of transgressing the Law of God, but their sins have been washed by the sacrifice of Christ's blood. Therefore, they will not be judged according to their works, which would otherwise condemn them also, but by the righteousness of Christ, Who willingly accepted the penalty for their sins. *"And this is the condemnation, that the light has come into the world, and men loved darkness rather than light, because their deeds were evil." (John 3.19)*

Verse 13- *The sea gave up the dead who were in it, and Death and Hades delivered up the dead who were in them. And they were judged, each one according to his works.*

To further emphasize that this judgment included the entire realm of the dead, it is revealed that even "the sea gave up [its] dead," and "death and Hades delivered up [its] dead."[18] Despite many errant ideas that Hades is the eternal destination of those who die in unbelief, this verse clearly establishes Hades as a place for the unbelievers between the time of their death and this final judgment.[19] *(Luke 16.19–28)* Again, it is stated that all were raised from the dead to face the judgment of God according to their works, which only serve to testify against them.

Verse 14- Then Death and Hades were cast into the lake of fire. This is the second death.

Death and Hades, which contains the souls of all of those who died apart from faith in the Lord Jesus Christ, were cast into the lake of fire with Satan, the beast, and the false prophet. This was called "the second death." *"Blessed and holy is he who has part in the first resurrection. Over such the second death has no power." (Revelation 20.6a)* All unbelievers throughout history will experience this condemnation of eternal torment.

Hades was instituted for keeping the souls of God's unrepentant creation, and now this domain, including all its occupants, was thrown into the eternal lake of fire. Death, too, was finally eradicated. *"The last enemy that will be destroyed is death." (1 Corinthians 15.26)* Their purposes no longer existed, but the continued and eternal consequence of the unbelievers was still required.

DIG DEEPER: *THE SECOND DEATH*

This term appears only in Revelation. The first occurrence is found in Revelation chapter two as Jesus addresses the church of Smyrna. *(Revelation 2.11)* Since Death and Hades will be cast into the lake of fire, we should understand that there will be no second chances. Those decisions made during one's physical existence will determine his eternal destination. This second death is final from which there is no reprieve.

Verse 15- And anyone not found written in the Book of Life was cast into the lake of fire.

This verse plainly states that those whose names were not written in the Book of Life were "cast into the lake of fire" for eternal condemnation with Satan and his demons. They would exist in eternal, indestructible bodies that would forever suffer the consequences of their sins.[20] Conversely, believers in the Lord Jesus Christ and His finished work at Calvary have their names written in the Book of Life and will live eternally in the presence of Almighty God. With all evil finally wiped out, only the establishment of God's eternal kingdom remains unsettled, and this blessed event, serving as the pinnacle of this extraordinary book, is revealed in the final two chapters.

Notes/Applications

When Satan is bound for the thousand years that the Lord Jesus Christ rules the earth, people will not be able to blame the devil, justly or unjustly, for their sins. During Christ's millennial reign, this world will be cloaked in a perfect environment because of the Lord of lords' presiding rule according to His Father's commandments. However, there will be many who will still internally rebel against righteousness, proving how innately evil man truly is even when his environment offers the best of circumstances. Consequently, those who refuse to submit to Christ will face judgment, but this holds true whether such rebellion occurs during Christ's millennial reign or any other period in history. The one who has not totally emptied himself of self and yielded to Christ's loving yet absolute authority over his life will be judged, resulting in that individual's eternal condemnation:

> *I dreamed that the great judgment morning*
> *had dawned and the trumpet had blown;*
> *I dreamed that the nations had gathered*
> *to judgment before the white throne;*
> *From the throne came a bright shining angel,*
> *and he stood on the land and the sea,*
> *and he swore with his hand raised to Heaven,*
> *that time was no longer to be.*
>
> *And O, what a weeping and wailing,*
> *as the lost were told of their fate;*
> *They cried for the rocks and the mountains,*
> *they prayed, but their prayer was too late.*

The moral man came to the judgement,
but self righteous rags would not do;
The men who had crucified Jesus
had passed off as moral men, too;
The soul that had put off salvation,
'Not tonight; I'll get saved by and by,
No time now to think of religion!'
At last they had found time to die.[21]

We must be honest with ourselves. Our station in life matters little in eternity's eyes. What truly matters is the condition in which we will appear before Christ's heavenly courtroom where our eternity will be pronounced. Let us not wait until it is too late before we bow ourselves to His sovereign rule over our lives. *"[8]If we say that we have no sin, we deceive ourselves, and the truth is not in us. [9]If we confess our sins, He is faithful and just to forgive us our sins and to cleanse us from all unrighteousness. [10]If we say that we have not sinned, we make Him a liar, and His word is not in us." (1 John 1.8–10)*

Chapter Twenty-one

So much of Revelation seems to raise more questions than offer answers. Which things are to be taken literally and which are to be taken metaphorically? What does this city refer to, and what does that character depict? When will this event take place, and who will be affected? Readers of all ages find themselves asking these and other questions time and again throughout the book.

One pattern that becomes evident in the description of the new heaven and new earth in this chapter is the recurring use of numbers with multiples of twelve. Much has been made of the symbolic relevance of this number, primarily that it indicates completeness.[1] At the very least, it seems that when God decided to lead His faithful on earth, He did so in the pattern of twelve, such as with the twelve tribes of Israel and the twelve disciples. Beyond that, the varied explanations ascribed to the symbolic implication of the number twelve appear unpersuasive and, as such, should not import more significance than necessary to the interpretation of the vision.

One thing, however, is certain. Though debates still arise concerning certain details of these last two chapters, the relevance of these disparities is relatively inconsequential when compared to the indisputable majesty and splendor contained within these passages. Most commentators agree that the significance of chapters twenty-one and twenty-two rests in the blessed assurance that believers will one day enjoy an eternal inheritance in the glorious presence of the Almighty Father and the Lamb of God.

Revelation 21.1–7

Verse 1- *Now I saw a new heaven and a new earth, for the first heaven and the first earth had passed away. Also there was no more sea.*

After Satan and evil were forever banished, John saw a new heaven and new earth. *"For behold, I create new heavens and a new earth; and the former shall not be remembered or come to mind.'" (Isaiah 65.17)* The old earth upon which mankind lived for thousands of years "passed away." It was a temporal dwelling for a temporal creation, so fittingly, the new heaven and new earth would be an eternal dwelling for an eternal creation. Disputes surface over whether the old earth will be transformed into the new earth or whether the old earth will be completely destroyed to make way for an entirely new creation. Neither position can be argued irrefutably, especially if based solely within the framework of this simple description "passed away." Therefore, it is perhaps best to conclude that whatever the case may be, experiencing the reality of the new heaven and earth one day will render all earthly debate over the subject as sheer foolishness.

Again, there is no explanation for the passing of the original heaven and earth in the Book of Revelation, but external sources reveal more detail on the subject:

[10]But the day of the Lord will come as a thief in the night, in which the heavens will pass away with a great noise, and the elements will melt with fervent heat; both the earth and the works that are in it will be burned up. [11]Therefore, since all these things will be dissolved, what manner of persons ought you to be in holy conduct and godliness, [12]looking for and hastening the coming of the day of God, because of which the heavens will be dissolved, being on fire, and the elements will melt with fervent heat? (2 Peter 3.10–12) 'Lift up your eyes to the heavens, and look on the earth beneath. For the heavens will vanish away like smoke, the earth will grow old like a garment, and those who dwell in it will die in like manner; but My salvation will be forever, and My righteousness will not be abolished.' (Isaiah 51.6)

One can only speculate as to why a specific mention is made that there would be "no more sea" in the new heaven and new earth except to say that it must bear some significance considering what little else we are told. This does not necessarily designate that there will be no bodies of water at all, for we learn differently in later verses. *"And he showed me a pure river of water of life, clear as crystal, proceeding from the throne of God and of the Lamb." (Revelation 22.1)*

Verse 2- Then I, John, saw the holy city, New Jerusalem, coming down out of heaven from God, prepared as a bride adorned for her husband.

John then saw a new Jerusalem descend from Heaven. Some commentators prefer to consider this a depiction of the universal Church, especially in that it is described as "a bride adorned for her husband" such as the saints were earlier portrayed.[2] *(Revelation 19.7)* In this view, the believers would be delivered unto their eternal reward in a manner similar to the reprobate that were delivered unto their eternal condemnation. *(Revelation 20.14)* However, John clearly viewed a city, "the holy city," and in light of the extensive detail provided in the final eighteen verses of this chapter, it seems most sensible to view this as a literal city.[3]

John's statement about this wonderful new city appearing as a "bride adorned for her husband" should not be considered a pertinent to the description of the Lamb's bride. He was likely describing the beauty of the city as that of an exquisitely decorated bride.

Verse 3- And I heard a loud voice from heaven saying, "Behold, the tabernacle of God is with men, and He will dwell with them, and they shall be His people. God Himself will be with them and be their God.

John heard a loud voice coming from Heaven revealing incredible insight about this new heaven and new earth. There would be no more "tabernacle," or more specifically, no more designated gathering place for worship, for God Himself would be the tabernacle and would dwell among His redeemed creation. No longer would man's relationship with the Creator be hindered by sin. *"Then I will*

*give them a heart to know Me, that I am the Lord; and they shall be My peo-
ple, and I will be their God, for they shall return to Me with their whole
heart.'" (Jeremiah 24.7)* In this new earth and new heaven, God's elect
would finally be restored unto Him as righteous vessels through the
atonement of Jesus Christ's shed blood. *"For as by one man's disobedience many were made sinners, so also by one Man's obedience many will
be made righteous." (Romans 5.19)*

**Verse 4- "And God will wipe away every tear from their eyes;
there shall be no more death, nor sorrow, nor crying. There shall
be no more pain, for the former things have passed away."**

The voice from Heaven continued to declare the joys of the new
heaven and new earth. In contrast to the unbelievers condemned to
an eternity of torment, the redeemed would live forevermore in
indescribable bliss in God's presence. The pain, distress, and grief
which accompanied their physical lives would never again be experienced in this new and perfect world created by God Almighty for
his faithful servants. No occasion would exist that would cause any
misery or discontent, and this life would never end.

**Verse 5- Then He who sat on the throne said, "Behold, I make all
things new." And He said to me, "Write, for these words are true
and faithful."**

Almighty God, seated majestically upon His throne, declared,
"Behold, I make all things new." Those things that were corrupted by
the sin of man were given new life. In Christ, all things would be
made new and flawless. The Lord also instructed John to write
down that the words that He spoke were "true and faithful" seemingly to reiterate that these visions, though they may have seemed
beyond belief, were trustworthy.

**Verses 6, 7- ⁶And He said to me, "It is done! I am the Alpha and
the Omega, the Beginning and the End. I will give of the fountain of the water of life freely to him who thirsts. ⁷He who overcomes shall inherit all things, and I will be his God and he shall
be My son."**

Without a doubt, the Lord was still speaking to John words that God alone is worthy to utter. Just as He would say this at the close of the tribulation when the pouring out of His wrath was completed, God again declared, "It is done!" This time, it seems, the intent was to indicate that the ultimate consummation of the Lord Jesus Christ's redemption was complete. This was reiterated by His assertion, "I am the Alpha and the Omega, the Beginning and the End." Within this statement, many of His other attributes can be identified, for only the one true God that knows no limits or boundaries in His existence could be almighty, all-powerful, and sovereign. These are all attributes that eternally coexist. *"I am the Alpha and the Omega, the Beginning and the End," says the Lord, 'who is and who was and who is to come, the Almighty.'" (Revelation 1.8)*

God also exclaimed that to those who thirst He would give freely from "the fountain of the water of life." This is evidently not referring to a physical thirst but a spiritual one. The spiritual thirst that could never be fully satisfied while upon the earth would be completely fulfilled in the everlasting presence of Almighty God in the new heaven and new earth. We will never be in want or be unable to quench our desire for communion with God because He will dwell among us and we with Him.

The Lord God promised that those who had persevered through the influences of the world and had remained faithful to Him would inherit all of these things that He had prepared for them. In effect, He proclaimed that the eternal relationship He would have with His own would be the fulfillment of that which He had sought with His people, under varying circumstances, while they were on earth. *"They shall be My people, and I will be their God.'" (Jeremiah 32.38) "'That they may walk in My statutes and keep My judgments and do them; and they shall be My people, and I will be their God.'" (Ezekiel 11.20) "'I will bring them back, and they shall dwell in the midst of Jerusalem. They shall be My people and I will be their God, in truth and righteousness.'" (Zechariah 8.8)*

Notes/Applications

James Shirley (1596–1666), an Elizabethan dramatist, posed thoughts on Heaven when he surmised that it is "the perfection of all that can be said or thought—riches, delight, harmony, health, beauty; and all these not subject to the waste of time, but in their height eternal."[4] Truly, we struggle to imagine the splendor of this eternal dwelling place, for our most adept imaginings are still flawed human renderings of divine beauty and perfection. *"But as it is written: 'Eye has not seen, nor ear heard, nor have entered into the heart of man the things which God has prepared for those who love Him.'"* (1 Corinthians 2.9)

This paradise will be a perfect, sinless world, created by God to be inhabited by Him, His redeemed ones, and His heavenly beings. It will be a place of unimaginable grandeur and indescribable glory, and yet it will also be a place of intimate fellowship where we will forever enjoy God without interruptions. As Alexander MacLaren (1858–1903), one of Great Britain's most noted preachers, once stated: "The joys of heaven are not the joys of passive contemplation, of dreamy remembrance, of perfect repose; but they are described thus, 'They rest not day or night.' 'His servants serve him and see his face.'"[5]

With the presentation of the new heaven, new earth, and new Jerusalem, time, as we have always perceived it, will cease to exist. *"But, beloved, do not forget this one thing, that with the Lord one day is as a thousand years, and a thousand years as one day."* (2 Peter 3.8) The new heaven and new earth will remain for eternity, incapable of being measured in increments such as months, years, or centuries. In that place, there will no longer be the differentiation of day and night, for the glory of the Lord will illuminate His eternal kingdom at all times. We will live forevermore in the existence of our glorified bodies and eternally worship God in His very presence.

Praise the Lord for this great reward that He has promised to those who believe in Him and obey His Holy Word, for they have "in heaven a better and an enduring substance." *(Hebrews 10.34, KJV)*

Revelation 21.8–13

Verse 8- "But the cowardly, unbelieving, abominable, murderers, sexually immoral, sorcerers, idolaters, and all liars shall have their part in the lake which burns with fire and brimstone, which is the second death."

The Lord finished His statement by contrasting the rewards given to His faithful with the fate of those who experienced the second death, the judgment and condemnation of those who had died in their sin apart from the saving grace of the Lord Jesus Christ. *"¹³The sea gave up the dead who were in it, and Death and Hades delivered up the dead who were in them. And they were judged, each one according to his works. ¹⁴Then Death and Hades were cast into the lake of fire. This is the second death." (Revelation 20.13–14)* This list included a sample cross-section of those who would "have their part" in the eternal lake of fire. These included the "abominable, murderers, sexually immoral, sorcerers, idolaters, and all liars." This was not a list of specific sins that condemned a soul to hell but, rather, was indicative of the nature of those controlled by selfish desires and by the world and not by the Spirit of the Living God:

> *⁸But we know that the law is good if one uses it lawfully, ⁹knowing this: that the law is not made for a righteous person, but for the lawless and insubordinate, for the ungodly and for sinners, for the unholy and profane, for murderers of fathers and murderers of mothers, for manslayers, ¹⁰for fornicators, for sodomites, for kidnappers, for liars, for perjurers, and if there is any other thing that is contrary to sound doctrine. (1 Timothy 1.8–10)*

All mankind has sinned, including each and every believer, but it would be those judged by their actions alone because they did not possess the faith and saving grace of Jesus Christ that would be condemned to the lake of fire. This list of sins and sinners would not be comprehensive if not for the one word encompassing the rest of this list and any imaginable omissions—the *unbelieving*. Disbelief would be the only criterion by which God would judge from His great white throne and sentence souls to their eternal consequence in the lake of fire. Unbelief is the only sin that will forever condemn. *"He who believes in Him is not condemned; but he who does not believe is condemned already, because he has not believed in the name of the only begotten Son of God."* (John 3.18) *"Then they said to Him, "²⁸What shall we do, that we may work the works of God?' Jesus answered and said to them, "²⁹This is the work of God, that you believe in Him whom He sent."* (John 6.28–29)

Verse 9- Then one of the seven angels who had the seven bowls filled with the seven last plagues came to me and talked with me, saying, "Come, I will show you the bride, the Lamb's wife."

John was approached by one of the seven angels responsible for carrying out a portion of the bowl judgments of God's wrath. It is not specified which of these angels came and spoke with John, so his exact identity is of no apparent significance. However, John did recognize this angel as one of the seven he had previously observed.

The angel told John to follow him so that he could show John "the bride, the Lamb's wife." This bride of the Lamb would be a stark contrast to the unbelievers listed in the previous verse. As we have studied in chapter nineteen, the bride included all believers, those who had obtained righteousness through God's grace and atonement of their sins by the blood of the Lord Jesus Christ at Calvary. However, this portrayal of the Lamb's wife and the eternal and glorious accommodations that had been prepared for her by God Almighty would be much more detailed and magnificent, as we will read throughout the remaining verses of this chapter.

Verses 10, 11- ¹⁰And he carried me away in the Spirit to a great and high mountain, and showed me the great city, the holy Jerusalem, descending out of heaven from God, ¹¹having the glory of God. Her light was like a most precious stone, like a jasper stone, clear as crystal.

This condition was nothing new to John but is merely stated for reiteration. John had been experiencing this entire revelation from the very beginning "in the spirit." It was only in this spiritual condition that John could be taken from place to place, moving seamlessly between a future heaven and a future earth and witnessing the medley of prophetic visions that had been divulged to him. In this state, it is possible that his physical body never left its position of isolation on the island of Patmos, yet his soul and spirit could be taken up and given this entire revelation of God in every actual sense.

The angel took John up to a "great and high mountain" to get a better perspective from which to view God's great and eternal city, the new Jerusalem. It appears that this angel was showing John greater detail about the presentation of this great city made by the Lord's hands for His faithful. *"Then I, John, saw the holy city, New Jerusalem, coming down out of heaven from God, prepared as a bride adorned for her husband." (Revelation 21.2)* This would be the eternal dwelling place of God and His bride, the righteous in Christ.

The new Jerusalem shone brightly with God's glory. John described the light as that of a precious gem, specifically "like a jasper stone, clear as crystal." This was not necessarily to illustrate a city that was comprised of precious stones or even to suggest that it resembled the construction of such. More likely, this was John's most adequate description of the beautiful city that he beheld. He could only compare the magnificence of the city to the finest things in the world that he had seen. John attempted to convey in mere words a city of otherwise indescribable and unimaginable brilliance, grandeur, and beauty.

Verses 12, 13- ¹²Also she had a great and high wall with twelve gates, and twelve angels at the gates, and names written on them, which are the names of the twelve tribes of the children of Israel: ¹³three gates on the east, three gates on the north, three gates on the south, and three gates on the west.

An enormous wall surrounded the city. John observed that this lofty wall had twelve gates, with three gates facing each direction and an angel at each gate. It is unclear from the text's wording whether the names of all twelve tribes would be inscribed at each gate or if one tribe name would be inscribed at each gate. Regardless, every tribe would be fully and equally represented on the wall of the magnificent city. Another question emerges when one attempts to determine which tribe names would be represented in the new Jerusalem—the original sons of Israel *(Genesis 35.22–26)* or the tribes as listed earlier in the Book of Revelation *(Revelation 7.5–8)*. Common among these lists are the names of Reuben, Simeon, Judah, Levi, Issachar, Joseph, Benjamin, Naphtali, Zebulun, Gad, and Asher. Various reasons have been suggested why Dan *(Genesis 35.25)* would be replaced by Manasseh *(Revelation 7.6)*, but suffice it to say that God's list is complete and His purpose for its presence is unchanged no matter what name is affixed to the gate of the eternal city.

Notes/Applications

In the context of the entire body of Scripture, we can affirm that salvation is a free gift of grace and not based upon works. *"⁸For by grace you have been saved through faith, and that not of yourselves; it is the gift of God, ⁹not of works, lest anyone should boast." (Ephesians 2.8–9)* Why then would verse eight of this chapter seem to imply that such acts would lead to hell's eternal flames? Certainly, all of us at one time or another has committed at least one of the evil acts listed. So, what is the difference between the sinner condemned to Hell and the redeemed? The surface answer lies in the fact that the blood of Christ covers the sins of those who follow Him, but the deeper answer takes into consideration the heart of the matter. Who empowers a person's being? As St. John Chrysostom (AD 344–407), who served as archbishop of Constantinople, surmised, "For to sin, indeed is human: but to persevere in sin is not human but altogether satanic."⁶

Essentially, the sin that condemns the soul is rebellion against the true God. True, this rebellion is often manifested through "abominable" actions such as murder, sexual immorality, sorcery, and idolatry, but so, too, is it manifested in the simple tongue which twists the truth in any manner. *(verse 8)* Indeed, an act is not determined to be sinful according to the measure of its wickedness, for even the simple act of lying is counted among that list of atrocious sins. Rather, an act is determined to be sinful when it falls short by any measure of full obedience to our absolute and holy God. Renowned eighteenth-century preacher and commentator Jonathan Edwards once observed that any sin against the infinitely excellent God is an infinitely heinous deed.[7] Therefore, we must conclude that it is not merely one's actions which make him wicked. Rather, a person's actions reveal the state of that person's heart:

[43]*'For a good tree does not bear bad fruit, nor does a bad tree bear good fruit.* [44]*For every tree is known by its own fruit. For men do not gather figs from thorns, nor do they gather grapes from a bramble bush.* [45]*A good man out of the good treasure of his heart brings forth good; and an evil man out of the evil treasure of his heart brings forth evil. For out of the abundance of the heart his mouth speaks.' (Luke 6.43–45)*

Revelation 21.14–20

Verse 14- Now the wall of the city had twelve foundations, and on them were the names of the twelve apostles of the Lamb.

The massive wall surrounding the new Jerusalem consisted of twelve foundations. This is probably best understood as twelve foundation stones, as some translations have rendered the description.[8] It can only be speculated where and how these individual foundations were situated among one another. Nevertheless, the entire city being laid upon only twelve stones speaks most noticeably to the extraordinary size of these foundations. *"For he waited for the city which has foundations, whose builder and maker is God." (Hebrews 11.10b)* Again, it is unclear whether each of the twelve foundation stones bore the names all the "twelve apostles of the Lamb" or if one name was inscribed per foundation. Regardless, these undoubtedly were the Twelve who had walked with the Messiah, witnessed His miracles, learned from Him, taught others about Him, and beheld His ascension. Just as it was these upon whom the Church of the Lord Jesus Christ was built on earth, so, too, would their names grace the foundations of this eternal dwelling for God's chosen. *"Having been built on the foundation of the apostles and prophets, Jesus Christ Himself being the chief cornerstone." (Ephesians 2.20)* What a humbling honor this scene must have been for John, one counted among these distinguished Twelve!

Verse 15- And he who talked with me had a gold reed to measure the city, its gates, and its wall.

The angel that showed John this vision of the new Jerusalem possessed a golden reed, with which he was able to measure the city, the wall, and the twelve gates. The reed apparently represented some standard of measure, and it was constructed of gold, as were so many of the heavenly vessels recorded throughout the Book of Revelation. *(Revelation 1.12, 4.4, 5.8, 8.3, and 15.7)* This vision corresponds with a vision recorded by the prophet Ezekiel. *"He took me there, and behold, there was a man whose appearance was like the appearance of bronze. He had a line of flax and a measuring rod in his hand, and he stood in the gateway." (Ezekiel 40.3)*

This angel measured God's own creation by God's own standards. The dimensions documented in the verses which follow appear to complicate any interpretations that suggest this new Jerusalem is not a literal city.

Verse 16- The city is laid out as a square; its length is as great as its breadth. And he measured the city with the reed: twelve thousand furlongs. Its length, breadth, and height are equal.

The results of the angel's calculations reveal a city of astonishing scale. The new Jerusalem was perfectly square, having equal length, width, and height. Each side of the city measured twelve thousand furlongs. One furlong equals slightly less than one eighth of a common mile, so the city was approximately fifteen hundred miles long and wide or 2.25 million square miles.

The actual shape of the city was not given. Some commentators suggest the city might be the shape of a pyramid.[9] Most, however, prefer to view the city as a cube, serving as the pattern of perfection for the inner sanctuary of the earthly temple.[10] *"The inner sanctuary was twenty cubits long, twenty cubits wide, and twenty cubits high. He overlaid it with pure gold, and overlaid the altar of cedar." (1 Kings 6.20)* Both theories must take into account some assumptions that are not specified. Nevertheless, in no way whatsoever should such unknowns diminish our amazement from those things that we do know. This would be a city unlike any other, virtually unimaginable in both its size and glory. It is this reason alone—the unbelievable size of the city—that some scholars insist that such a description cannot be taken literally.[11] But why should the Almighty Creator of the Universe establish an eternal dwelling of lesser magnitude and glory just to be more readily comprehensible to our mortal minds? God forbid the splendor of the new heaven and new earth be restricted to our mundane, rational human expectations! Indeed, the indiscriminate efforts of some to lessen the impact of these verses as mere symbolic imagery are far more implausible than simply trusting in the Almighty's capable hands to craft such an astounding city!

Verse 17- Then he measured its wall: one hundred and forty-four cubits, according to the measure of a man, that is, of an angel.

John watched the angel measure the wall of the city, which measured 144 cubits. A cubit equals approximately eighteen inches.[12] This wall, then, measured either in height or in depth—and very possibly both, considering similar patterns found in the dimensions of the city—equaled 216 feet. The height of the wall, while of imposing elevation in and of itself, would not in any manner hinder the view of the splendid city that it encircled. The phrase "according to the measure of a man" appears to signify that they were also being calculated in human modes for the sake of John's understanding and ultimately for the understanding of all of his readers.[13]

Verse 18- The construction of its wall was of jasper; and the city was pure gold, like clear glass.

John's description of jasper may either be a literal description of the wall's physical composition or a figurative description of some heavenly element whose beauty John could only liken to the most beautiful, brilliant stone with which he was familiar. The latter seems more likely the case since John also described the city as being made of pure gold yet at the same time as being "like clear glass." It seems quite fitting that God would compose all things in His eternal creation with material whose magnificence far exceeds anything we can now comprehend. Despite specific descriptions that classify the twelve foundations and gates as distinct precious stones, the same assertion might be considered in the following verses, though such is not proposed with dogmatic certainty so much as reasonable plausibility.

Verses 19, 20- [19]The foundations of the wall of the city were adorned with all kinds of precious stones: the first foundation was jasper, the second sapphire, the third chalcedony, the fourth emerald. [20]The fifth sardonyx, the sixth sardius, the seventh chrysolite, the eighth beryl, the ninth topaz, the tenth chrysoprase, the eleventh jacinth, and the twelfth amethyst.

The foundations of the wall, each of which contained one of the names of the twelve disciples, were garnished with a variety of precious stones. This does not imply that the many foundations would be made of these stones but that they "were adorned with" them. This indicates that their presence was not for structural purposes but solely for decorative reasons, such as to exhibit the God's glory throughout every fragment of His new creation.

In the order they were named, the foundations were garnished with jasper, sapphire, chalcedony, emerald, sardonyx, sardius, chrysolite, beryl, topaz, chrysoprase, jacinth, and amethyst. These twelve stones represent the vast array of all colors of the spectrum and would truly make a breathtaking contribution to the magnificence of God's perfect city. Many commentators suggest this list resembles the Old Testament description of the high priest's breastplate. *"¹⁷And you shall put settings of stones in it, four rows of stones: the first row shall be a sardius, a topaz, and an emerald; this shall be the first row; ¹⁸the second row shall be a turquoise, a sapphire, and a diamond; ¹⁹the third row, a jacinth, an agate, and an amethyst; ²⁰and the fourth row, a beryl, an onyx, and a jasper. They shall be set in gold settings." (Exodus 28.17–20)*

Notes/Applications

Such a magnificent promise of the heavenly city equips us as believers with an eternal perspective much like Abraham's when he traveled the arduous journey of this life:

> *⁸By faith Abraham obeyed when he was called to go out to the place which he would receive as an inheritance. And he went out, not knowing where he was going. ⁹By faith he dwelt in the land of promise as in a foreign country, dwelling in tents with Isaac and Jacob, the heirs with him of the same promise; ¹⁰for he waited for the city which has foundations, whose builder and maker is God. (Hebrews 11.8–10)*

Abraham continually dwelt in the "land of promise," looking beyond the constraints of his humanity to the Builder and Maker of the glorious, eternal city. Abraham trusted in the Builder and Maker's promises. Moreover, he rested in them.

The present world in which we dwell leaves much to be desired, for we live in this earthly realm struggling under the curse of sin and the heartache it brings. We may even ponder why the Lord tarries in His coming or whether He will come at all and if such conjectures are truth or fiction. However, we can trust that the Lord will be true to His Word. Both the history of creation and our individual journeys of faith with Him prove that He is faithful. The promises that we read in His Word about a blessed future are eternal securities of which we are now living off of the interest.

When we feel the burden of this life's yolk, let us not question God's faithfulness. Rather, as Abraham did, let us rest in God's promises. May we look toward the day when Jesus Christ, Who reigns victoriously, will crush the evil that permeates this world and will escort His Bride into a heavenly home of incomparable beauty and majesty:

If God hath made this world so fair
Where sin and death abound,
How beautiful beyond compare
Will paradise be found.[14]

Revelation 21.21–27

Verse 21- The twelve gates were twelve pearls: each individual gate was of one pearl. And the street of the city was pure gold, like transparent glass.

John explained that the twelve gates were made of twelve pearls. Then, as if to accentuate what he had just recorded, he described each gate as being constructed of one solid pearl shining with iridescent splendor. Like all elements of God's new creation, these gates would be beautiful beyond human imagination. John identically described the streets of the city as he had the city itself in that they were made of "pure gold, like transparent glass."

Verse 22- But I saw no temple in it, for the Lord God Almighty and the Lamb are its temple.

No temple existed within the city called the new Jerusalem, and the reason given for this suggests also that no temple existed throughout the new heaven and new earth. There was no structure where God's faithful would gather to worship because the Lord God and the Lamb would continually be in their presence. *"And I heard a loud voice from heaven saying, 'Behold, the tabernacle of God is with men, and He will dwell with them, and they shall be His people. God Himself will be with them and be their God.'" (Revelation 21.3)* There would never again be a need for temples, tabernacles, churches, or any other organized places of worship since worship would take place daily and continually in the very presence of God. Unity would finally be restored between God and His people.

Verse 23- The city had no need of the sun or of the moon to shine in it, for the glory of God illuminated it. The Lamb is its light.

Throughout eternity in the new heaven and new earth, there would never be the need for the sun or the moon. God created the sun and the moon for our benefit and for His glory. These celestial bodies will have served their purposes throughout the temporal duration of the earth for its inhabitants, but their luminosity would be unnecessary in the new Jerusalem. In their place, the radiant glory of God Almighty and the Lamb would serve to illuminate the new earth and new heaven. *"The sun shall no longer be your light by day, nor for brightness shall the moon give light to you; but the Lord will be to you an everlasting light, and your God your glory." (Isaiah 60.19)*

Verse 24- And the nations of those who are saved shall walk in its light, and the kings of the earth bring their glory and honor into it.

All of those who were saved by the redemptive work of Christ Jesus would walk in the light of His glory. John further illustrated the vast number of the redeemed by describing them as *nations*.[15] The use of the word *nations* in this verse should not be understood in the same sense as its use in other passages where the reference indicates multitudes of unbelievers. *(Revelation 11.18, 14.8, 18.23, 19.15, and 20.7–8)* The purpose of the word is to emphasize the enormity of the multitudes and not to insinuate their spiritual condition. The group depicted in this verse is plainly described as "nations of those who are saved." *"Who shall not fear You, O Lord, and glorify Your name? For You alone are holy. For all nations shall come and worship before You, for Your judgments have been manifested." (Revelation 15.4)*

The mention of "the kings of the earth" likewise should not be mistaken as being unbelievers who had escaped the judgment of condemnation and brought their wealth unto the glory of the Almighty. We are distinctly told in the previous chapter that all whose names were "not found written in the Book of Life [were] cast into the lake of fire." *(Revelation 20.15)* Therefore, this should be understood, in part, as the ultimate fulfillment of Isaiah's prophecy, which pertained to Jerusalem and, by its correlation with this vision, even more so to the new Jerusalem. *"The Gentiles shall come to your light, and kings to the brightness of your rising." (Isaiah 60.3)* Moreover, that some of God's elect would be comprised of rich and magnificent kings of the earth only serves to stress the dynamic scope of His selection from among "all nations, tribes, peoples, and tongues." *(Revelation 7.9)* Even these great men would walk in the presence of God's splendid light in equality with all other believers, except these kings would yield their earthly glory unto the divine glory of God in Heaven.[16]

Verse 25- Its gates shall not be shut at all by day (there shall be no night there).

No gate of the city wall would ever be closed, which reiterates that there would not be any enemies from which the city would need protection. *"'Therefore your gates shall be open continually; they shall not be shut day or night, that men may bring to you the wealth of the Gentiles, and their kings in procession.'" (Isaiah 60.11)* All the more, this description portrays the epitome of peace and security through its openness. All enemies of Christ would have already been condemned to their own eternal destinies in the lake of fire. These gates served only for purposes of adornment and beauty *(verse 21)* and to represent of the twelve tribes of Israel, even if we do not yet fully understand the significance of such symbolism.

Another point reiterated in this verse is that the glory of the Lord is eternal, and the brilliance of His glory will never diminish. As already noted, God Himself would be the light that illuminated the new heaven and new earth, and His glory is such that there would exist no more night and no more darkness. *"'Your sun shall no longer go down, nor shall your moon withdraw itself; for the Lord will be your everlasting light, and the days of your mourning shall be ended.'" (Isaiah 60.20) "There shall be no night there: they need no lamp nor light of the sun, for the Lord God gives them light. And they shall reign forever and ever." (Revelation 22.5)*

Verse 26- And they shall bring the glory and the honor of the nations into it.

Again, the word *nations* here simply denotes a vast assembly of people. Matthew Henry aptly described this multitude as "whole nations of saved souls; some out of all nations, and many out of some nations. All those multitudes who were sealed on earth are saved in Heaven."[17] This would be the entire sum of God's elect which completed the population of the new Jerusalem.

As if to accentuate the implication of the previous verse, this statement confirms that it would not only be kings of the earth who would bring glory and honor unto the throne of the Lamb and of God Almighty. The inhabitants of God's new creation were not surrendering things of a material nature but something that was intangible and far more precious to God—they offered their fullest expressions of praise, honor, and worship.

Verse 27- But there shall by no means enter it anything that defiles, or causes an abomination or a lie, but only those who are written in the Lamb's Book of Life.

As we have already read, the gates would never be closed because there would be no threat from which the city needed protection. This verse does not suggest that defilement and abominations would be kept from entering into God's eternal kingdom but that such things would not even exist in the new heaven and new earth.[18] No shred of corruption or wickedness could possibly exist within the perfect destiny that God had created for our eternal habitation or in His holy presence. It will be a city characterized by holiness.

The joy and benefits of this glorious and unimaginable city would be inhabitable only by the servants of the Lord God, those whose names "are written in the Lamb's Book of Life." They were restored unto the very God in Whom they placed their faith while they were on earth, and they now shared in the eternal reward that He had prepared for them in Heaven.

DIG DEEPER: *BOOK OF LIFE*

The Book of Life is referred to seven times in the Book of Revelation, but this is the only occurrence where ownership of that book is defined. This book is owned by the "Lamb slain before the foundation of the world." *(Revelation 13.8; Philippians 4.3)* Again, the focus of Revelation turns our attention back to Jesus Christ, the only One to Whom all praise and honor, glory and power is due, and Who owns the Book of Life and preserves the names of His saints by the power of His blood. *(Acts 20.28)*

Notes/Applications

Renowned commentator Matthew Henry observed: "There is nothing magnificent enough in this world fully to set forth the glory of heaven. Could we, in the glass of a strong imagination, contemplate such a city as is here described, even as to the exterior part of it, such a wall, and such gates, how amazing, how glorious would the prospect be! And yet this is a faint and dim representation of what heaven is in itself."[19]

Interestingly, after such a vivid technical description of that "great city," we are reminded of the essence of the gospel message. Jesus said, "I am the Alpha and the Omega, the Beginning and the End. I will give of the fountain of the water of life freely to him who thirsts. He who overcomes shall inherit all things, and I will be his God and he shall be My son." Jesus' words explain the criterion upon which one may enter the holy city. This eternal place is only for those who possess eternal life.

While ministering upon the earth, Jesus spoke of the time when some would approach Him and claim to be His children and rightful heirs to eternal life. Nevertheless, the Lord said that in that day, He would command them to depart from His presence, for He would not know them as His own. *"21'Not everyone who says to Me, "Lord, Lord," shall enter the kingdom of heaven, but he who does the will of My Father in heaven. 22Many will say to Me in that day, "Lord, Lord, have we not prophesied in Your name, cast out demons in Your name, and done many wonders in Your name?" 23And then I will declare to them, "I never knew you; depart from Me, you who practice lawlessness!"'" (Matthew 7.21–23)* Due to a lack of surrender to the Light of the world, many will be guilty of rejecting Christ as Lord and Savior, which is the sin that condemns, the sin that truly defiles man's soul and forfeits a heavenly home worshipping the Light of Heaven.

The Lamb knows those who belong to Him. He has called them, and He knows them by name. *"2'But he who enters by the door is the shepherd of the sheep. 3To him the doorkeeper opens, and the sheep hear his voice; and he calls his own sheep by name and leads them out. 4And when he brings out his own sheep, he goes before them; and the sheep follow him, for they know his voice.'" (John 10.2–4)* Since nothing that defiles will be present in that holy city, only those whose names are written in His book will be given a permanent address in God's sacred, eternal tabernacle. Figuratively speaking, our names must be written in the Lamb's blood for us to be ushered into His glorious presence forevermore. *"26'But you do not believe, because you are not of My sheep, as I said to you. 27My sheep hear My voice, and I know them, and they follow Me. 28And I give them eternal life, and they shall never perish; neither shall anyone snatch them out of My hand.'" (John 10.26–28)*

Chapter Twenty-two

Revelation 22.1–6

Verse 1- And he showed me a pure river of water of life, clear as crystal, proceeding from the throne of God and of the Lamb.

Since there is no transitional phrasing, we can assume that the angel introduced in 19.9 was still revealing to John certain essentials of the new Jerusalem. We now find ourselves with John inside the walls of God's eternal city, and what we observe through his writings appears to be a restoration of God's perfect creation before the fall. With the curse of sin removed, redeemed mankind would once again enjoy an unhindered fellowship with God in an unspoiled dwelling, as personified in the Garden of Eden.[1]

After witnessing the glorious city with its magnificent foundations and gates, John was shown "a pure river of water of life" that flowed from God's throne. Many writers have devised various explanations for the metaphorical significance of the river of life. It seems, though, that the most obvious imagery emphasizes life forevermore in God's presence since the river is characterized as being *of life,* and it flows from the eternal throne of the Father and the Lamb.[2]

Verse 2- In the middle of its street, and on either side of the river, was the tree of life, which bore twelve fruits, each tree yielding its fruit every month. The leaves of the tree were for the healing of the nations.

This verse arouses many diverse remarks because the reader is presented with what appears to be an elusive description where a street and a river in some manner converge at a point also occupied by the tree of life. It is possible, as some writers have interpreted this depiction, that the tree of life stood at a fork in the river, as if on its own island.[3] As such, the river would pass around the tree, and the description of the tree being on "either side of the river" would still be accurate. Other arguments are made by those who suggest that this tree, though singular in description, referred to many trees of life which would line the banks along both sides of the river.[4] Further complicating our understanding is that this river(s) and tree(s) converged in "the middle of its street." Again, this description seems illogical. It could have been a road that passed around each side of the tree and also over the river. Some writers suggest that the river and street would run side by side with the tree(s) of life standing in between.[5] Whatever the logistics of this interesting configuration, it is clear that there was a main intersection, probably near the center of the city, where the river of life and the main street of the city crossed over the same area occupied by the tree of life. Surely, the throne of God and of the Lamb would not be very far from this spectacular location.

This tree bore twelve different types of fruit and produced a ripe crop of these fruits every month. We do *not* know if the use of the word *month* in this context had any literal relation to time or if it was merely an attempt by John to convey a timely and consistent repetition. We *do* know that time will have no bearing on the eternality of the new heaven and new earth. *"And this is the promise that He has promised us—eternal life." (1 John 2.25) "In hope of eternal life which God, who cannot lie, promised before time began." (Titus 1.2)*

Again, we note the symbolic use of the number twelve to explain the fruit on the tree. Whether this bears some outward significance or whether God Almighty simply decided to pattern much of His creation after this number for His own reasons, we do not know and are only prone to speculate.

Ultimately, the leaves of this tree would be used for the healing of the nations, which again indicated the "nations of those who are saved." *(Revelation 21.24)* We know that there will be no sickness or dying or suffering in the new heaven and new earth *(Revelation 21.4)*, so any interpretations insisting that the leaves of this tree would be the means by which actual, physical healing would occur seem unfounded.[6] Nonetheless, the entire setting brings to mind the sacred river depicted in the Book of Ezekiel. *"Along the bank of the river, on this side and that, will grow all kinds of trees used for food; their leaves will not wither, and their fruit will not fail. They will bear fruit every month, because their water flows from the sanctuary. Their fruit will be for food, and their leaves for medicine." (Ezekiel 47.12)*

DIG DEEPER: *TREE OF LIFE*

The tree of life was first introduced in the Book of Genesis as the means by which one could live forever. *(Genesis 2.8–3.24)* Adam and Eve were invited to partake of its fruit but were forbidden from eating of the Tree of the Knowledge of Good and Evil. They disobeyed God, sin entered the world, and so did the consequence of sin—death. *(Romans 6.23)* When the curse of death is lifted, all of God's redeemed will once again be permitted to partake of the tree of life, the privilege forfeited at the dawn of creation and restored at the end of it. *(Revelation 22)*

Verse 3- And there shall be no more curse, but the throne of God and of the Lamb shall be in it, and His servants shall serve Him.

John was not only shown things pertaining to the new Jerusalem but was also made to understand the meaning of certain other unseen and unspoken things. Such appears to be the case when he stated that there would be "no more curse," which man brought upon himself through his sin in the Garden of Eden:

[17]Then to Adam He said, 'because you have heeded the voice of your wife, and have eaten from the tree of which I commanded

you, saying, "You shall not eat of it": cursed is the ground for your
sake; in toil you shall eat of it all the days of your life. ¹⁸Both thorns
and thistles it shall bring forth for you, and you shall eat the herb of
the field. ¹⁹In the sweat of your face you shall eat bread till you
return to the ground, for out of it you were taken; for dust you are,
and to dust you shall return.' (Genesis 3.17–19)

The throne of God and the Lamb would be ever present in the
new Jerusalem, and the Lord would no longer prevent the inhabitants from eating of the tree unto eternal life. Rather, the redeemed
would live forevermore in the glorious service of Almighty God and
the Lord Jesus Christ and would worship and praise Him Who
saved them unto this magnificent eternity.

Verse 4- They shall see His face, and His name shall be on their foreheads.

John noted that God's followers would see His face just as
promised in Scripture. *"For now we see in a mirror, dimly, but then face to*
face. Now I know in part, but then I shall know just as I also am known." (1
Corinthians 13.12) "Beloved, now we are children of God; and it has not yet
been revealed what we shall be, but we know that when He is revealed, we
shall be like Him, for we shall see Him as He is." (1 John 3.2) The
redeemed would be able to look upon their Creator and Redeemer
as He appears. What an incredible joy to see the Lord as a personal,
loving, and ever-present God, and how much more grateful and
amazed His elect would be to stand in awe of His glorious presence as Moses did! *"So the LORD spoke to Moses face to face, as a man*
speaks to his friend." (Exodus 33.11a)

Furthermore, God's name would be upon the foreheads of all
the inhabitants of the new heaven and new earth. Just as the
144,000 who were sealed for preservation through the tribulation
(Revelation 7.3) and the countless multitudes who bore the mark of
the beast and allied themselves with him by doing so *(Revelation*
13.16–17), this would be a mark of ownership placed on the foreheads of God's servants by the very One who purchased their
redemption through His grace with His blood and secured their
eternity in His presence through His sovereign will.

Verse 5- There shall be no night there: They need no lamp nor light of the sun, for the Lord God gives them light. And they shall reign forever and ever.

This description has been addressed in earlier verses. *"²³The city had no need of the sun or of the moon to shine in it, for the glory of God illuminated it. The Lamb is its light. ²⁵Its gates shall not be shut at all by day (there shall be no night there)." (Revelation 21.23, 25)* That there would "be no night there" should be understood both literally, in that God's glory would make obsolete the need for any objects of illumination, and spiritually, in that no trace of sin or evil would ever exist within the new heaven and new earth.

"They" who would reign is obviously the same group as that to whom God would give light—His redeemed. However, the identity of those over whom the redeemed will reign has often been speculated but is essentially irrelevant. *(1 Corinthians 6.3)* The new heaven and new earth are under Christ's reign alone, and we shall all serve under Him as "fellow servants" of His royal court. *(verse 9)* This is the most straightforward sense with which we can understand how we "shall reign forever and ever." *"But the saints of the Most High shall receive the kingdom, and possess the kingdom forever, even forever and ever." (Daniel 7.18)*

Verse 6- Then he said to me, "These words are faithful and true." And the Lord God of the holy prophets sent His angel to show His servants the things which must shortly take place.

As the Lord Himself had already done, the angel spoke to John and told him that these visions witnessed were "faithful and true." *"Then He who sat on the throne said, 'Behold, I make all things new.' And He said to me, 'Write, for these words are true and faithful.'" (Revelation 21.5)* John was assured that all he had seen and learned since he was taken up in the spirit, no matter how unbelievable it may have all seemed, would surely come to pass. The angel hereby established and affirmed the authenticity of the prophecies contained within the book. The Greek words translated as *shortly* are ἐν τάχει (en tachai), which carry the idea of occurring swiftly but are not necessarily intended to indicate a sense of occurring in the near future.[7]

All of these visions that John had witnessed had been preordained, and precisely at their appointed times, these events would occur swiftly. When these events that will turn the world upside down begin to occur, they will do so suddenly and rapidly without opportunity for reflection or repentance.

Though the scene is not described as such, it appears that this verse signifies the moment at which John's spirit was returned to his physical body and the visions of the revelation were concluded. These remaining verses are often referred to as the Epilogue or as John's closing remarks.[8] They summarize the things John had seen and the things which had been revealed unto him through the "Lord God of the holy prophets." Surely considered one of these esteemed prophets from this point forward, John recorded the entire revelation for the sake of other believers who would read the book.

Notes/Applications

In Exodus 33.18–23, God told Moses that no man could look upon the face of Almighty God and live. Nevertheless, God allowed Moses to behold His back, but He hid His awesome face from the servant so that he might not be struck dead.

Verse four in this passage, which states, "They shall see His face, and His name shall be on their foreheads," enlightens us to the reality that in God's holy city we will no longer be subject to human limitations. *"Beloved, now we are children of God; and it has not yet been revealed what we shall be, but we know that when He is revealed, we shall be like Him, for we shall see Him as He is." (1 John 3.2b)* It is interesting how verse four in Revelation twenty-two affirms verse three of chapter twenty-one, which states, "Behold, the tabernacle of God is with men, and He will dwell with them, and they shall be His people. God Himself will be with them and be their God." Both verses seem to depict the certain destiny awaiting the redeemed beyond eternity's threshold. First, Heaven will be the everlasting tabernacle of God, and second, His children will see Him face to face and will be sealed with His name forevermore.

In Heaven, there will be no more curse, no more physical or spiritual barriers between us and God, and there will also no longer be the need for symbols because we will abide in what the symbols sought to commemorate—God's eternal tabernacle. As Moses, we cannot behold Almighty God in our human frames, but in that glorious city, those adorned with His seal of ownership will partake in the birthright given to every child of His family. His presence will envelop us, and yet we will gaze upon Him face to face in all of His majesty.

Only by Christ's righteousness which drops the scales of sin from our eyes and cleanses us can we, once members of a fallen race, behold the glory of the Holy God. Only by the blood of the sacrificial Lamb can we, once the world's reprobate, become sanctified vessels who are holy as He is holy. Only by His extended grace, incomprehensible mercy, and immeasurable love will we, those marked with His name in our foreheads, enter the eternal tabernacle of God and worship Him unhindered and undivided. *"¹⁶The Spirit Himself bears witness with our spirit that we are children of God, ¹⁷and if children, then heirs—heirs of God and joint heirs with Christ, if indeed we suffer with Him, that we may also be glorified together." (Romans 8.16–17)*

Revelation 22.7–14

Verse 7- "Behold, I am coming quickly! Blessed is he who keeps the words of the prophecy of this book."

John heard what appears to be the words of Jesus Christ in which the Lord spoke of His return. *"For as the lightning comes from the east and flashes to the west, so also will the coming of the Son of Man be." (Matthew 24.27)* Added to His opening statement is a promise that anyone who reads and "keeps the words of the prophecy of this book" would be blessed. This is a book of judgment and of promise, a book of terrifying truths for the unbeliever and splendid truths for the believer.

Verse 8- Now I, John, saw and heard these things. And when I heard and saw, I fell down to worship before the feet of the angel who showed me these things.

After the visions of revelation were finished, John was so overwhelmed by the incredible things that he had seen, heard, and understood that he fell down prostrate before the angel that showed him these things that would come to pass. John was completely awestruck, and after observing all of these coming events, he instinctively fell to the ground in a gesture of humility and worship. Earlier in the revelation, he had reacted similarly to the angel who had shown him the vision of Christ's return, and the response of the angel then was the same as it was now.

Verse 9- Then he said to me, "See that you do not do that. For I am your fellow servant, and of your brethren the prophets, and of those who keep the words of this book. Worship God."

As on that earlier occasion, the angel urged John not to worship him because he was a "fellow servant." The angel considered himself John's equal, not God's. In the eternal presence of God, the angels are no different than the prophets and every other believer who has read, learned, and committed themselves to the writings of this book. Accordingly, the angel gently reminded John to focus all of his worship upon God, the only One truly worthy of all glory and praise. *"And I fell at his feet to worship him. But he said to me, 'See that you do not do that! I am your fellow servant, and of your brethren who have the testimony of Jesus. Worship God! For the testimony of Jesus is the spirit of prophecy.'"* *(Revelation 19.10)*

Verse 10- And he said to me, "Do not seal the words of the prophecy of this book, for the time is at hand.

The angel directed John to record all that he had witnessed and not to seal up the prophecies revealed unto him. This is the opposite of what the prophet Daniel was told to do after receiving similar end times visions. *"And he said, 'Go your way, Daniel, for the words are closed up and sealed till the time of the end.'"* *(Daniel 12.9)* The difference between the two prophecies was the timing of the revelations. Daniel's visions and prophecies were given hundreds of years before the birth of the long-awaited Messiah. John, on the other hand, was told that the "time is at hand." This statement needs not be understood that Christ's return is imminent, though such anticipation is to be expected by Christians of all eras. *(Matthew 24.42–44; Revelation 3.3)* Rather, it means only that the time for John to reveal these prophecies was immediate. Regardless of the timing of the Lord's return, the call for response is always pressing. Since these visions were undoubtedly true *(verse 6)*, those who continue in rebellion against God must understand the urgency of their dilemma.

Verse 11- "He who is unjust, let him be unjust still; he who is filthy, let him be filthy still; he who is righteous, let him be righteous still; he who is holy, let him be holy still."

This verse must be understood in context with the following verse. If read by itself, it seems that the wicked have been urged to continue in their wickedness just as the righteous have been directed to remain righteous. *"'Many shall be purified, made white, and refined, but the wicked shall do wickedly; and none of the wicked shall understand, but the wise shall understand.'"* *(Daniel 12.10)*

This is not necessarily the callous statement it first appears, wherein the opportunity for salvation is removed from the unjust. Truly, that day will come when all mankind's fate will be fixed and the opportunity for repentance will be no more, which will be at Christ's Second Coming. Until that time, though, as verse seventeen affirms, all are welcome to repent and turn to the Lord God. *"And the Spirit and the bride say, 'Come!' And let him who hears say, 'Come!' And let him who thirsts come. Whoever desires, let him take the water of life freely." (Revelation 22.17)*

Verse 12- "And behold, I am coming quickly, and My reward is with Me, to give to every one according to his work.

For the second of three times since the conclusion of the visions, John was told, "Behold, I am coming quickly." When the Lord comes again to the earth, He will come to judge. *"Now I saw heaven opened, and behold, a white horse. And He who sat on him was called Faithful and True, and in righteousness He judges and makes war." (Revelation 19.11)* This time, Christ Jesus reiterated His role as Judge by declaring, "My reward is with me," and His recompense to each is based "according to his work":

> *'28Do not marvel at this; for the hour is coming in which all who are in the graves will hear His voice 29and come forth—those who have done good, to the resurrection of life, and those who have done evil, to the resurrection of condemnation.' (John 5.28–29) 'The sea gave up the dead who were in it, and Death and Hades delivered up the dead who were in them. And they were judged, each one according to his works.' (Revelation 20.13)*

Verse 13- "I am the Alpha and the Omega, the Beginning and the End, the First and the Last."

There can be little doubt that these were the very words of the Lamb of God, Who again emphasized that He is the one true eternal God. He is Creator, not the created. There was never a moment that He began or came into existence because there was never a moment in time or eternity when He did not already exist. It is a concept that is inconceivable to the human mind, but one that is consistent with God's eternal essence. He has always been and will always be. *"LORD, You have been our dwelling place in all generations. 2Before the mountains were brought forth, or ever You had formed the earth and the world, even from everlasting to everlasting, You are God." (Psalm 90.1–2)*

Verse 14- Blessed are those who do His commandments, that they may have the right to the tree of life, and may enter through the gates into the city.

Like those who keep the words of this prophecy *(verse 7)*, those who keep God's commandments are considered blessed because they will have unimpeded access to the tree of life in the new Jerusalem. "Those who do His commandments" is intended to describe those that receive the forgiveness of their sins through the atonement provided by Jesus Christ and not simply those who randomly, even inadvertently, obey God's laws. Only those who receive the salvation of the Lord Jesus Christ will be granted the reward of eternal life and all of the glorious things that God has prepared for the righteous. *"Jesus said to him, 'I am the way, the truth, and the life. No one comes to the Father except through Me.'" (John 14.6)*

Notes/Applications

In verse seven of this chapter, the Lord told John for the first of three times after the conclusion of the visions, "Behold, I come quickly." Again, these words did not necessarily denote an imminent arrival, but rather, one that would be unexpected. *"⁴²'Watch therefore, for you do not know what hour your Lord is coming. ⁴³But know this, that if the master of the house had known what hour the thief would come, he would have watched and not allowed his house to be broken into. ⁴⁴Therefore you also be ready, for the Son of Man is coming at an hour you do not expect.'" (Matthew 24.42–44)*

Whereas the Lord's return to earth could conceivably occur at any time, the significance of His proclamation exists for the Christian and not for Christ. *"'But of that day and hour no one knows, not even the angels of heaven, but My Father only.'" (Matthew 24.36)* Therefore, this declaration should promote an attitude of expectation and urgency in the life of every Christian. Perhaps only with such anticipation will we passionately and compassionately share the gospel message with our respective Judea, Samaria, and uttermost parts of the earth. *(Acts 1.8)*

Our blessed Lord and Savior Jesus Christ will return to earth one day. As His children, we need to be comforted that the reality of His second advent is as sure as that of His first one. Only by continually revisiting this truth will we gain the eternal perspective and heavenly focus needed to rise above our present circumstances as divine joy flows from the throne of Heaven into our earthbound lives.

Truly, the very moment of our Lord's return has been appointed by Almighty God before the foundation of the world. Regardless of when that moment might be, are we ready? May we be among those presented with crowns of righteousness because they loved the promise of His return. *"Finally, there is laid up for me the crown of righteousness, which the Lord, the righteous Judge, will give to me on that Day, and not to me only but also to all who have loved His appearing."* (2 Timothy 4.8)

Revelation 22.15–21

Verse 15- But outside are dogs and sorcerers and sexually immoral and murderers and idolaters, and whoever loves and practices a lie.

This verse resembles one in the previous chapter in which was listed a representative cross section of those who would not have any part in the glorious eternity God had prepared for His faithful servants. *"But the cowardly, unbelieving, abominable, murderers, sexually immoral, sorcerers, idolaters, and all liars shall have their part in the lake which burns with fire and brimstone, which is the second death.'"* *(Revelation 21.8)* Again, this is not a list of sins that are unforgivable by God but of actions and attitudes that are prevalent in the lives of the unbelievers, here even depicted as dogs.

Verse 16- "I, Jesus, have sent My angel to testify to you these things in the churches. I am the Root and the Offspring of David, the Bright and Morning Star."

Jesus verified that He Himself was the source of this revelation and that He had sent the angels that escorted John throughout these visions. The purpose of the visions was not a private matter intended solely for John's benefit but for all churches and believers throughout history.[9]

Jesus then confirmed His identity by calling Himself the "Root and the Offspring of David." *"There shall come forth a Rod from the stem of Jesse, and a Branch shall grow out of his roots." (Isaiah 11.1) "But one of the elders said to me, 'Do not weep. Behold, the Lion of the tribe of Judah, the Root of David, has prevailed to open the scroll and to loose its seven seals.'" (Revelation 5.5)* Jesus was both the spiritual foundation Who eternally preexisted David and also the physical descendant of the line of David. Jesus has always existed, even before the creation of the world. *"In the beginning was the Word, and the Word was with God, and the Word was God. ²He was in the beginning with God." (John 1.1–2)* Jesus also referred to Himself as "the Bright and Morning Star." *"And I will give him the morning star.'" (Revelation 2.28)* It is this same bright glory of God the Father and of Jesus Christ that will illuminate the new heaven and new earth throughout eternity.

Verse 17- And the Spirit and the bride say, "Come!" And let him who hears say, "Come!" And let him who thirsts come. Whoever desires, let him take the water of life freely.

Some commentators argue that this call to "come" is from the Bride to her Bridegroom, such that the redeemed are beckoning Christ's return as promised in these visions.[10] *"Behold, I am coming quickly! Blessed is he who keeps the words of the prophecy of this book." (Revelation 22.7)* However, in consideration of the verse as presented in its entirety, it appears that the Spirit and the Bride of the Lamb, the multitude of believers that have received this unmerited reward of God's grace, are offering an awesome invitation to come and drink of the water of life. All who are thirsty, all who long for the spiritual restoration that only the Lord Jesus Christ can offer as the Savior of the world, are invited to receive forgiveness of their sins.[11] The Spirit is the agent of conviction Who works through the evangelistic efforts of the redeemed.

The truth of the end times—the judgment of the wicked and the promise of the glorious reward for the believer—has been laid open for all mankind to read. Those who observe the warnings to the unjust are invited to drink of the water of life, which is the Lord Jesus Christ. *"Jesus answered and said to her, 'If you knew the gift of God, and who it is who says to you, "Give Me a drink," you would have asked Him, and He would have given you living water.'" (John 4.10) "And He said to me, 'It is done! I am the Alpha and the Omega, the Beginning and the End. I will give of the fountain of the water of life freely to him who thirsts.'" (Revelation 21.6)* Those who hear and respond may come and partake of this living water. Whosoever is spiritually thirsty can come and drink unto life everlasting. The invitation is open to all, for the price has already been paid by the Lord Jesus Christ at Calvary's cross.

Verse 18- For I testify to everyone who hears the words of the prophecy of this book: If anyone adds to these things, God will add to him the plagues that are written in this book;

John warned all who read the prophecies of God Almighty revealed in this book of a grave responsibility. Anyone who reads or hears the words of the Revelation are subject to the warning of condemnation upon any person that adds anything in word or thought to these infallible and inspired writings of God's Word. Anyone who does so would subject himself to the plagues described in the book. Because the same admonishment was given in the Old Testament, we should not believe that anyone who does not heed this warning will receive only the plagues described in Revelation but also all of the plagues listed throughout the Bible.

Verse 19- And if anyone takes away from the words of the book of this prophecy, God shall take away his part from the Book of Life, from the holy city, and from the things which are written in this book.

The warning continues. Those who diminish the prophecies of Revelation (and arguably the entire Bible) are subject to condemnation in the lake of fire since their names would not be found in the Book of Life. They will have no part in the glorious new heaven and new earth that God has prepared for His faithful followers.

Just as nothing is to be added, nothing is to be deleted or denied. The Word of God must be conveyed in its entirety. The plagues are every bit as real and significant as the promises, and the curses are as certain as the blessings. The message of an eternal destiny of anguish and torment in the lake of fire for every unbeliever is every bit as certain as that of an eternal Heaven in the presence of God for every believer.

> **DIG DEEPER:** *THE BOOK*
>
> Readers are admonished in verses eighteen and nineteen not to add to or take from any part of "this book," referring to the Book of Revelation, which is called "this prophecy." The same warning holds true for the entire Bible. *(Deuteronomy 4.2; Proverbs 30.6)* God's Word is complete as intended and inerrant as presented.

Verse 20- He who testifies to these things says, "Surely I am coming quickly." Amen. Even so, come, Lord Jesus!

This verse marks the third and final time that the Lord declared, "I am coming quickly." This phrase could be considered a theme for this final chapter of Revelation. Though the significance of this repeated message has already been studied, John added his own commentary to this particular passage: "Amen. Even so, come, Lord Jesus." This should be the attitude of every believer until the Lord returns.

There are many positions regarding the return of the Lord Jesus Christ, and each has been adamantly defended with Scripture. However, regardless of any believer's particular position, there should be nothing that keeps us from anticipating the Lord's glorious return. The promise of the magnificent eternity that God Almighty has prepared for His elect should far outshine even the most ominous and terrifying events that must also come to pass. This glorious hope we have in Jesus Christ should focus our hearts and attitudes to ever be *Even so, come, Lord Jesus!*

Verse 21- *The grace of our Lord Jesus Christ be with you all. Amen.*

John concluded his writings with a simple benediction. In it, John expressed his wishful desire for the grace of the Lord Jesus Christ to rest upon all who read this book. *"But grace and truth came through Jesus Christ." (John 1.17b)* Truly, the reward to all of God's redeemed as revealed and promised in the Book of Revelation is far greater than can be imagined and is far beyond what even the most righteous among mankind deserves. *"But as it is written: Eye has not seen, nor ear heard, nor have entered into the heart of man the things which God has prepared for those who love Him." (1 Corinthians 2.9)*

Among the many insights revealed in this book, perhaps the greatest is the assurance that God has a perfect plan, and He will carry it through to its completion according to His timing and according to His precise and unchallengeable will. All that will and must come to pass rests in His sovereign hands. *"Let us hold fast the confession of our hope without wavering, for He who promised is faithful." (Hebrews 10.23)*

Notes/Applications

How does one summarize what is one of the most sobering books of the Holy Bible? There is probably no other biblical book that so vividly reveals that there is indeed a Hell to be shunned and a Heaven to be gained. Every individual that has ever lived is subject to an eternity either in the tormenting lake of fire or in the glorious presence of God Almighty and the Lord Jesus Christ.

What appear to be mysteries in this book are perhaps the stones that God uses to build our faith and to keep us trusting Him and studying His Word. The warning He gives in verses eighteen and nineteen is unmistakable: Anyone who changes any portion of the Holy Word of God, no matter how large or small it may seem, brings judgment and damnation upon himself. Certainly, each of us must take this admonishment seriously. Are we conveying the truth of the Holy Word of God in its entirety? Are we conveying it at all?

As Christians, our commitment to conveying truth in its entirety charges us to accept God's sovereign plan as depicted in His Word. Whether tribulation, triumph, or triumph through tribulation, righteous and just is the Lord's plan for His creation and His children. *"Shall not the Judge of all the earth do right?"* *(Genesis 18.25b)* If we are to discern truth properly, we must also prepare ourselves and the body of Christ for suffering that has been anointed and blessed by God's righteous hand.

How tragic it would be to delve into such a concerted study of the Book of Revelation, glimpse the Lord Jesus Christ in His glory, and yet not be infused all the more with the truth of the Revelation: Jesus Christ, King of kings and Lord of lords, is the blessed hope to Whom we must cling. May we never diminish this revelation by supposing that we will escape all aspects of persecution or even martyrdom. However, we can know without fear or doubt that God sustains His children. As depicted in a German hymn from the nineteenth century, no matter what may happen in the physical realm of this life, our souls are protected by Him and preserved in Him:

Whate'er my God ordains is right:
He is my Friend and Father;
He suffers naught to do me harm,
though many storms may gather,
Now I may know both joy and woe,
some day I shall see clearly
that He hath loved me dearly.

Whate'er my God ordains is right:
though now this cup, in drinking,
may bitter seem to my faint heart,
I take it, all unshrinking.
My God is true; each morn new
sweet comfort yet shall fill my heart,
and pain and sorrow shall depart.

Whate'er my God ordains is right:
here shall my stand be taken;
Though sorrow, need, or death be mine,
yet I am not forsaken.
My Father's care is round me there;
He holds me that I shall not fall:
and so to Him I leave it all.[12]

Even so, come, Lord Jesus!

Text Notes

INTRODUCTION

1. J.D. Douglas, ed., *New Bible Dictionary*, 2nd ed. (Wheaton, IL: Tyndale House Publishers, 1962), 1024.
2. Merrill C. Tenney, *Interpreting Revelation: A Reasonable Guide to Understanding the Last Book in the Bible* (1957; reprint, Peabody, Massachusetts: Hendrickson Publishers, 2001), 135–146.
3. R.C. Sproul, *The Last Days According to Jesus* (Grand Rapids: Baker Books, 1998), 153–159.
4. Bruce B. Barton et al., *Life Application Bible Commentary: Revelation* (Wheaton: Tyndale House Publishers, 2000), xi–xii.
5. Steve Gregg, ed., *Revelation: Four Views, A Parallel Commentary* (Nashville: Thomas Nelson Publishers, 1997), 13.
6. Barton et al., *Life Application Bible Commentary: Revelation*, xiii.
7. Albert Barnes, *Revelation*, of *Barnes' Notes on the New Testament* (1884; reprint, Grand Rapids: Baker Books, 2001), xlvi–xlix.
8. Robert H. Mounce, *The Book of Revelation*, of *The New International Commentary on the New Testament*, 2nd ed. (Grand Rapids: Eerdmans Publishing Company, 1998), 19.

9. Vern S. Poythress, *The Returning King: A Guide to the Book of Revelation* (Phillipsburg, New Jersey: P & R Publishing, 2000), 11–13.

CHAPTER ONE

1. George Ricker Berry, *Greek to English Interlinear New Testament (KJV)* (Grand Rapids: World Publishing, 1981), 623.
2. John Gill, *Exposition of the Old and New Testaments*, vol. 9 (1810; reprint, Paris, Arkansas: The Baptist Standard Bearer, 1989), 683–684.
3. Kenneth L. Barker and John R. Kohlenberger III, ed., *Zondervan NIV Bible Commentary*, vol. 2 (Grand Rapids: Zondervan Publishing House, 1994), 1132.
4. Barker and Kohlenberger, *Zondervan NIV Bible Commentary*, 1132.
5. Joseph A. Seiss, *The Apocalypse – Exposition of the Book of Revelation* (Grand Rapids: Kregel Publications, 1987), 31.
6. Seiss, *The Apocalypse*, 31.
7. Gill, *Exposition of the Old and New Testaments*, vol. 9, 686.
8. Barker and Kohlenberger, *Zondervan NIV Bible Commentary*, 1135.
9. Gill, *Exposition of the Old and New Testaments*, vol. 9, 688.
10. William MacDonald, *Believer's Bible Commentary*, ed. Art Farstad (Nashville: Thomas Nelson Publishers, 1995), 2353.
11. W. E. Vine, *Vine's Expository Dictionary of Old and New Testament Words* (Nashville: Thomas Nelson Publishers, 1997), 75–76.
12. Excerpt from "O Christ, the Heavens' Eternal King," author unknown (ca 6th century).
13. Matthew Henry, *Matthew Henry's Commentary on the Whole Bible* (Peabody, Massachusetts: Hendrickson Publishers, 1991), 2465.
14. Charles F. Pfeiffer and Everett F. Harrison, *The Wycliffe Bible Commentary* (Chicago: Moody Press, 1962), 1502.
15. George Eldon Ladd, *A Commentary on the Revelation of John* (Grand Rapids: Eerdmans Publishing Company, 1972), 33.

CHAPTER TWO

1. J.B. Jackson, *A Dictionary of Scripture Proper Names* (Neptune, New Jersey: Loizeaux Brothers, 1909), 30.
2. Robert H. Mounce, *The Book of Revelation,* of *The New International Commentary on the New Testament,* 2nd ed. (Grand Rapids: Eerdmans Publishing Company, 1998), 66–67.
3. Kenneth L. Barker and John R. Kohlenberger III, ed., *Zondervan NIV Bible Commentary,* vol. 2 (Grand Rapids: Zondervan Publishing House, 1994), 1140.
4. Mounce, *The Book of Revelation,* 67.
5. Matthew Henry, *Matthew Henry's Commentary on the Whole Bible* (Peabody, Massachusetts: Hendrickson Publishers, 1991), 2465.
6. W. E. Vine, *Vine's Expository Dictionary of Old and New Testament Words* (Nashville: Thomas Nelson Publishers, 1997), 951–952.
7. Barker and Kohlenberger, *Zondervan NIV Bible Commentary,* 1142.
8. John Gill, *Exposition of the Old and New Testaments,* vol. 9 (1810; reprint, Paris, Arkansas: The Baptist Standard Bearer, 1989), 697.
9. Frank S. Mead, ed., *12,000 Religious Quotations* (1965; reprint, Grand Rapids: Baker Book House, 1989), 258.
10. Mead, *12,000 Religious Quotations,* 259.
11. Barker and Kohlenberger, *Zondervan NIV Bible Commentary,* 1142.
12. Mounce, *The Book of Revelation,* 73.
13. Gill, *Exposition of the Old and New Testaments,* vol. 9, 697.
14. Joseph A. Seiss, *The Apocalypse – Exposition of the Book of Revelation* (Grand Rapids: Kregel Publications, 1987), 70.
15. William MacDonald, *Believer's Bible Commentary,* ed. Art Farstad (Nashville: Thomas Nelson Publishers, 1995), 2356.
16. Gill, *Exposition of the Old and New Testaments,* vol. 9, 698.
17. Henry, *Matthew Henry's Commentary on the Whole Bible,* 2466.
18. Jackson, *A Dictionary of Scripture Proper Names,* 74.
19. G. R. Beasley-Murray, *The Book of Revelation,* of *The New Century Bible Commentary* (Grand Rapids: Eerdmans Publishing Company, 1974), 84.

20. Barker and Kohlenberger, *Zondervan NIV Bible Commentary,* 1144.
21. Mounce, *The Book of Revelation,* 78.
22. John R. W. Stott, *What Christ Thinks of the Church, Expository Addresses on the First Three Chapters of the Book of Revelation* (Grand Rapids: Eerdmans Publishing Company, 1958), 54.
23. Henry, *Matthew Henry's Commentary on the Whole Bible,* 2466–2467.
24. Gill, *Exposition of the Old and New Testaments,* vol. 9, 699.
25. J. Vernon McGee, *Thru the Bible,* vol. 5 (Nashville: Thomas Nelson Publishers, 1982), 906.
26. Seiss, *The Apocalypse,* 71.
27. Mounce, *The Book of Revelation,* 81; Barker and Kohlenberger, Zondervan NIV Bible Commentary, 1144.
28. Jackson, *A Dictionary of Scripture Proper Names,* 15, 70.
29. Stott, *What Christ Thinks of the Church,* 66.
30. Thomas A. Kempis, *The Imitation of Christ, trans. Harold Bolton and Aloysius Croft* (Milwaukee, Wisconsin: Bruce Publishing Company, 1940), 106.
31. Jackson, *A Dictionary of Scripture Proper Names,* 93.
32. Barker and Kohlenberger, *Zondervan NIV Bible Commentary,* 1145.
33. Cleon L. Rogers, Jr. and Cleon L. Rogers III, *The New Linguistic and Exegetical Key to the Greek New Testament* (Grand Rapids: Zondervan Publishing House, 1998), 618.
34. *Antiquities of the Jews,* in *The Complete Works of Flavius Josephus,* trans. William Whiston (Grand Rapids: Kregel Publications, 1960), 245.
35. Mounce, *The Book of Revelation,* 84–85.
36. Gill, *Exposition of the Old and New Testaments,* vol. 9, 703.
37. *New Geneva Study Bible,* ed. R.C. Sproul (Nashville: Thomas Nelson Publishers, 1995), 502.
38. Barker and Kohlenberger, *Zondervan NIV Bible Commentary,* 1145.
39. Mounce, *The Book of Revelation,* 86–87.
40. Barker and Kohlenberger, *Zondervan NIV Bible Commentary,* 1146.

41. Mounce, *The Book of Revelation,* 88.
42. Henry, *Matthew Henry's Commentary on the Whole Bible,* 2467.
43. James Moffatt, *The Revelation of St. John the Divine,* vol. 5 of *The Expositor's Greek Testament* (Grand Rapids: Eerdmans Publishing Company, 1951), 361.
44. Mounce, *The Book of Revelation,* 90.
45. Henry, *Matthew Henry's Commentary on the Whole Bible,* 2469.

CHAPTER THREE

1. J.B. Jackson, *A Dictionary of Scripture Proper Names* (Neptune, New Jersey: Loizeaux Brothers, 1909), 81.
2. Kenneth L. Barker and John R. Kohlenberger III, ed., *Zondervan NIV Bible Commentary,* vol. 2 (Grand Rapids: Zondervan Publishing House, 1994), 1147.
3. John Gill, *Exposition of the Old and New Testaments,* vol. 9 (1810; reprint, Paris, Arkansas: The Baptist Standard Bearer, 1989), 706.
4. J.D. Douglas, ed., *New Bible Dictionary,* 2nd ed. (Wheaton, IL: Tyndale House Publishers, 1962), 88.
5. Robert H. Mounce, *The Book of Revelation,* of *The New International Commentary on the New Testament,* 2nd ed. (Grand Rapids: Eerdmans Publishing Company, 1998), 91–92.
6. Barker and Kohlenberger, *Zondervan NIV Bible Commentary,* 1148.
7. Gill, *Exposition of the Old and New Testaments,* vol. 9, 707.
8. William MacDonald, *Believer's Bible Commentary,* ed. Art Farstad (Nashville: Thomas Nelson Publishers, 1995), 2358.
9. Jackson, *A Dictionary of Scripture Proper Names,* 75.
10. Mounce, *The Book of Revelation,* 98–99.
11. Steve Gregg, ed., *Revelation: Four Views, A Parallel Commentary* (Nashville: Thomas Nelson Publishers, 1997), 75.
12. G. R. Beasley-Murray, *The Book of Revelation,* of *The New Century Bible Commentary* (Grand Rapids: Eerdmans Publishing Company, 1974), 100.
13. George Eldon Ladd, *A Commentary on the Revelation of John* (Grand Rapids: Eerdmans Publishing Company, 1972), 59.

14. Beasley-Murray, *The Book of Revelation,* 100–101.
15. Simon J. Kistemaker, *Revelation,* of *New Testament Commentary* (Grand Rapids: Baker Books, 2001), 162–163.
16. Cleon L. Rogers, Jr. and Cleon L. Rogers III, *The New Linguistic and Exegetical Key to the Greek New Testament* (Grand Rapids: Zondervan Publishing House, 1998), 621.
17. Matthew Henry, *Matthew Henry's Commentary on the Whole Bible* (Peabody, Massachusetts: Hendrickson Publishers, 1991), 2469.
18. Excerpt from "Thus Saith the Holy One, and True," words by John Newton, in *Olney Hymns,* Book 1, 1779. Public Domain.
19. Jackson, *A Dictionary of Scripture Proper Names,* 58.
20. Bruce B. Barton et al., *Life Application Bible Commentary: Revelation* (Wheaton: Tyndale House Publishers, 2000), 46.
21. M.G. Easton, *Illustrated Bible Dictionary* (New York: Harper and Brothers, 1897), 415.
22. Gregg, *Revelation: Four Views,* 78.
23. Mounce, *The Book of Revelation,* 107.
24. Ladd, *A Commentary on the Revelation of John,* 64.
25. Barton et al., *Life Application Bible Commentary: Revelation,* 48.
26. MacDonald, *Believer's Bible Commentary,* 2360.
27. Robert Jamieson, Andrew R. Fausset, and David Brown, *Jamieson, Fausset, and Brown's Commentary* (Grand Rapids: Zondervan Publishing House, 1961), 1540.
28. Mounce, *The Book of Revelation,* 113.
29. Henry, *Matthew Henry's Commentary,* 2469.
30. Henry, *Matthew Henry's Commentary,* 2470.
31. Henry, *Matthew Henry's Commentary,* 2469.

CHAPTER FOUR
1. John Gill, *Exposition of the Old and New Testaments,* vol. 9 (1810; reprint, Paris, Arkansas: The Baptist Standard Bearer, 1989), 716; Bruce B. Barton et al., *Life Application Bible Commentary: Revelation* (Wheaton: Tyndale House Publishers, 2000), 53; William MacDonald, *Believer's Bible Commentary,* ed. Art Farstad (Nashville: Thomas Nelson Publishers, 1995), 2361.

2. Joseph A. Seiss, *The Apocalypse – Exposition of the Book of Revelation* (Grand Rapids: Kregel Publications, 1987), 95–97; Steve Gregg, ed., *Revelation: Four Views, A Parallel Commentary* (Nashville: Thomas Nelson Publishers, 1997), 85.

3. Merrill C. Tenney, *Interpreting Revelation: A Reasonable Guide to Understanding the Last Book in the Bible* (1957; reprint, Peabody, Massachusetts: Hendrickson Publishers, 2001), 141.

4. Seiss, *The Apocalypse*, 99.

5. Robert H. Mounce, *The Book of Revelation*, of *The New International Commentary on the New Testament*, 2nd ed. (Grand Rapids: Eerdmans Publishing Company, 1998), 119.

6. Vern S. Poythress, *The Returning King: A Guide to the Book of Revelation* (Phillipsburg, New Jersey: P & R Publishing, 2000), 99.

7. Gregg, *Revelation: Four Views*, 87–89.

8. Mounce, *The Book of Revelation*, 121–122.

9. J. Vernon McGee, *Thru the Bible*, vol. 5 (Nashville: Thomas Nelson Publishers, 1982), 930–931.

10. Pfeiffer and Harrison, *The Wycliffe Bible Commentary*, 1505.

11. Seiss, *The Apocalypse*, 102.

12. Matthew Henry, *Matthew Henry's Commentary on the Whole Bible* (Peabody, Massachusetts: Hendrickson Publishers, 1991), 2470.

13. *Natural Bridge of Virginia*, http://www.naturalbridgeva.com, (25 June 2001).

14. George Ricker Berry, *Greek to English Interlinear New Testament (KJV)* (Grand Rapids: World Publishing, 1981), 631.

15. Kenneth L. Barker and John R. Kohlenberger III, ed., *Zondervan NIV Bible Commentary*, vol. 2 (Grand Rapids: Zondervan Publishing House, 1994), 1156.

16. MacDonald, *Believer's Bible Commentary*, 2362.

17. Henry, *Matthew Henry's Commentary on the Whole Bible*, 2470–2471.

CHAPTER FIVE

1. W. A. Criswell, *Expository Sermons on Revelation* (Grand Rapids: Zondervan Publishing House, 1962), 56.

2. Merrill C. Tenney, *Interpreting Revelation: A Reasonable Guide to Understanding the Last Book in the Bible* (1957; reprint, Peabody, Massachusetts: Hendrickson Publishers, 2001), 126.
3. Kenneth L. Barker and John R. Kohlenberger III, ed., *Zondervan NIV Bible Commentary,* vol. 2 (Grand Rapids: Zondervan Publishing House, 1994), 1157.
4. Bruce B. Barton et al., *Life Application Bible Commentary: Revelation* (Wheaton: Tyndale House Publishers, 2000), 59; Robert H. Mounce, *The Book of Revelation,* of *The New International Commentary on the New Testament,* 2nd ed. (Grand Rapids: Eerdmans Publishing Company, 1998), 129.
5. John Gill, *Exposition of the Old and New Testaments,* vol. 9 (1810; reprint, Paris, Arkansas: The Baptist Standard Bearer, 1989), 723.
6. Matthew Henry, *Matthew Henry's Commentary on the Whole Bible* (Peabody, Massachusetts: Hendrickson Publishers, 1991), 2471; Barker and Kohlenberger, *Zondervan NIV Bible Commentary,* 1158.
7. Joseph A. Seiss, *The Apocalypse – Exposition of the Book of Revelation* (Grand Rapids: Kregel Publications, 1987), 114.
8. Mounce, *The Book of Revelation,* 131.
9. Barton et al., *Life Application Bible Commentary: Revelation,* 60; Mounce, *The Book of Revelation,* 144; Henry, *Matthew Henry's Commentary on the Whole Bible,* 2471.
10. R. C. H. Lenski, *The Interpretation of St. John's Revelation,* of *Commentary on the New Testament* (Columbus: Wartburg Press, 1943), 200.
11. Gill, *Exposition of the Old and New Testaments,* vol. 9, 727–728.
12. Barton et al., *Life Application Bible Commentary: Revelation,* 66.
13. Isaac Watts, "What Equal Honors Shall We Bring," in *Hymns and Spiritual Songs,* 1707–1709. Public Domain.

CHAPTER SIX

1. Bruce B. Barton et al., *Life Application Bible Commentary: Revelation* (Wheaton: Tyndale House Publishers, 2000), 71.
2. Joseph A. Seiss, *The Apocalypse – Exposition of the Book of Revelation* (Grand Rapids: Kregel Publications, 1987), 125.

3. Matthew Henry, *Matthew Henry's Commentary on the Whole Bible* (Peabody, Massachusetts: Hendrickson Publishers, 1991), 2472.
4. Kenneth L. Barker and John R. Kohlenberger III, ed., *Zondervan NIV Bible Commentary*, vol. 2 (Grand Rapids: Zondervan Publishing House, 1994), 1160–1161.
5. Barker and Kohlenberger, *Zondervan NIV Bible Commentary*, 1161.
6. Robert H. Mounce, *The Book of Revelation*, of *The New International Commentary on the New Testament*, 2nd ed. (Grand Rapids: Eerdmans Publishing Company, 1998), 144.
7. Steve Gregg, ed., *Revelation: Four Views, A Parallel Commentary* (Nashville: Thomas Nelson Publishers, 1997), 111.
8. M. Eugene Boring, *Revelation* (Louisville: John Knox Publishers, 1989), 122.
9. R. C. H. Lenski, *The Interpretation of St. John's Revelation*, of *Commentary on the New Testament* (Columbus: Wartburg Press, 1943), 228.
10. George Eldon Ladd, *A Commentary on the Revelation of John* (Grand Rapids: Eerdmans Publishing Company, 1972), 103.
11. William MacDonald, *Believer's Bible Commentary*, ed. Art Farstad (Nashville: Thomas Nelson Publishers, 1995), 2364.
12. W. E. Vine, *Vine's Expository Dictionary of Old and New Testament Words* (Nashville: Thomas Nelson Publishers, 1997), 984.
13. Barton et al., *Life Application Bible Commentary: Revelation*, 78.

CHAPTER SEVEN
1. Gleason L. Archer, *Encyclopedia of Bible Difficulties* (Grand Rapids: Zondervan Publishing House, 1982), 432–444; Michael Wilcock, *The Message of Revelation* (Downers Grove: Inter-Varsity Press, 1975), 80.
2. Joseph A. Seiss, *The Apocalypse – Exposition of the Book of Revelation* (Grand Rapids: Kregel Publications, 1987), 162.
3. Kenneth L. Barker and John R. Kohlenberger III, ed., *Zondervan NIV Bible Commentary*, vol. 2 (Grand Rapids: Zondervan Publishing House, 1994), 1165.

4. J.B. Jackson, *A Dictionary of Scripture Proper Names* (Neptune, New Jersey: Loizeaux Brothers, 1909), 55.
5. Jackson, 79, 32.
6. Jackson, 11, 68.
7. Jackson, 62.
8. Jackson, 89.
9. Jackson, 58.
10. Jackson, 46.
11. Jackson, 97, 54, 17.
12. Seiss, *The Apocalypse,* 172.
13. Albert Barnes, *Revelation,* of *Barnes' Notes on the New Testament* (1884; reprint, Grand Rapids: Baker Books, 2001), 182.
14. William MacDonald, *Believer's Bible Commentary,* ed. Art Farstad (Nashville: Thomas Nelson Publishers, 1995), 2364.
15. Robert H. Mounce, *The Book of Revelation,* of *The New International Commentary on the New Testament,* 2nd ed. (Grand Rapids: Eerdmans Publishing Company, 1998), 163.
16. Robert W. Wall, *Revelation,* of *New International Biblical Commentary* (Peabody, Massachusetts: Hendrickson Publishers, 1991), 120.
17. Mounce, *The Book of Revelation,* 164–165.
18. Bruce B. Barton et al., *Life Application Bible Commentary: Revelation* (Wheaton: Tyndale House Publishers, 2000), 89–90.
19. Frank S. Mead, ed., *12,000 Religious Quotations* (1965; reprint, Grand Rapids: Baker Book House, 1989), 214.
20. Soli Deo Gloria Ministries, "Meet the Puritans: Ezekiel Hopkins," 21 January 2003, http://www.sdgbooks.com/SDG books/hall 7_hopkins.html (21 January 2003).
21. Excerpt from "There is a Land of Pure Delight," words by Isaac Watts, in *Hymns and Spiritual Songs,* 1707. Public Domain.

CHAPTER EIGHT
1. Steve Gregg, ed., *Revelation: Four Views, A Parallel Commentary* (Nashville: Thomas Nelson Publishers, 1997), 139.
2. George T. Montague, *The Apocalypse* (Ann Arbor: Servant Publications, 1992), 116–117.

3. Bruce B. Barton et al., *Life Application Bible Commentary: Revelation* (Wheaton: Tyndale House Publishers, 2000), 89–90.
4. Robert H. Mounce, *The Book of Revelation,* of *The New International Commentary on the New Testament,* 2nd ed. (Grand Rapids: Eerdmans Publishing Company, 1998), 174–175.
5. Joseph A. Seiss, *The Apocalypse – Exposition of the Book of Revelation* (Grand Rapids: Kregel Publications, 1987), 190–192.
6. Albert Barnes, *Revelation,* of *Barnes' Notes on the New Testament* (1884; reprint, Grand Rapids: Baker Books, 2001), 199–200.
7. Barton et al., *Life Application Bible Commentary: Revelation,* 96.
8. W. E. Vine, *Vine's Expository Dictionary of Old and New Testament Words* (Nashville: Thomas Nelson Publishers, 1997), 1246.
9. Mounce, *The Book of Revelation,* 181.
10. Cleon L. Rogers, Jr. and Cleon L. Rogers III, *The New Linguistic and Exegetical Key to the Greek New Testament* (Grand Rapids: Zondervan Publishing House, 1998), 630.
11. R. C. H. Lenski, *The Interpretation of St. John's Revelation,* of *Commentary on the New Testament* (Columbus: Wartburg Press, 1943), 283.

CHAPTER NINE

1. Joseph A. Seiss, *The Apocalypse – Exposition of the Book of Revelation* (Grand Rapids: Kregel Publications, 1987), 204; William MacDonald, *Believer's Bible Commentary,* ed. Art Farstad (Nashville: Thomas Nelson Publishers, 1995), 2366.
2. Albert Barnes, *Revelation,* of *Barnes' Notes on the New Testament* (1884; reprint, Grand Rapids: Baker Books, 2001), 210.
3. Robert H. Mounce, *The Book of Revelation,* of *The New International Commentary on the New Testament,* 2nd ed. (Grand Rapids: Eerdmans Publishing Company, 1998), 187.
4. J.B. Jackson, *A Dictionary of Scripture Proper Names* (Neptune, New Jersey: Loizeaux Brothers, 1909), 1, 9.
5. Barnes, *Revelation,* 226.
6. Steve Gregg, ed., *Revelation: Four Views, A Parallel Commentary* (Nashville: Thomas Nelson Publishers, 1997), 186.

7. R. C. H. Lenski, *The Interpretation of St. John's Revelation,* of *Commentary on the New Testament* (Columbus: Wartburg Press, 1943), 301.
8. Barnes, *Revelation,* 227.
9. Robert Jamieson, Andrew R. Fausset, and David Brown, *Jamieson, Fausset, and Brown's Commentary* (Grand Rapids: Zondervan Publishing House, 1961), 1553.
10. Simon J. Kistemaker, *Revelation,* of *New Testament Commentary* (Grand Rapids: Baker Books, 2001), 298; Mounce, *The Book of Revelation,* 196.
11. Barnes, *Revelation,* 229–230.
12. Frank S. Mead, ed., *12,000 Religious Quotations* (1965; reprint, Grand Rapids: Baker Book House, 1989), 481.

CHAPTER TEN
1. R. H. Charles, *The Revelation of St. John,* vol. 1, of *The International Critical Commentary* (Edinburgh: T & T Clark, 1920), 258–259.
2. R. C. H. Lenski, *The Interpretation of St. John's Revelation,* of *Commentary on the New Testament* (Columbus: Wartburg Press, 1943), 311.
3. Donald W. Richardson, *The Revelation of Jesus Christ* (Louisville: John Knox Publishers, 1964), 101; Matthew Henry, *Matthew Henry's Commentary on the Whole Bible* (Peabody, Massachusetts: Hendrickson Publishers, 1991), 2475.
4. Robert H. Mounce, *The Book of Revelation,* of *The New International Commentary on the New Testament,* 2nd ed. (Grand Rapids: Eerdmans Publishing Company, 1998), 201.
5. Joseph A. Seiss, *The Apocalypse – Exposition of the Book of Revelation* (Grand Rapids: Kregel Publications, 1987), 223–224.
6. Bruce B. Barton et al., *Life Application Bible Commentary: Revelation* (Wheaton: Tyndale House Publishers, 2000), 111.
7. Mounce, *The Book of Revelation,* 204.
8. George T. Montague, *The Apocalypse* (Ann Arbor: Servant Publications, 1992), 128.
9. Mounce, *The Book of Revelation,* 208.

10. William MacDonald, *Believer's Bible Commentary,* ed. Art Farstad (Nashville: Thomas Nelson Publishers, 1995), 2367.

11. William Hendrickson, *More Than Conquerors* (Grand Rapids: Baker Books, 1944), 151; Kenneth L. Barker and John R. Kohlenberger III, ed., *Zondervan NIV Bible Commentary,* vol. 2 (Grand Rapids: Zondervan Publishing House, 1994), 1174; Lenski, *The Interpretation of St. John's Revelation,* 323–324.

12. Mounce, *The Book of Revelation,* 209.

13. Simon J. Kistemaker, *Revelation,* of *New Testament Commentary* (Grand Rapids: Baker Books, 2001), 317.

14. "Come, Divine Interpreter," words by Charles Wesley, in *Short Hymns on Select Passages of Holy Scripture,* 1762. Public Domain.

CHAPTER ELEVEN

1. Gerhard A. Krodel, *Revelation,* of *The Augsburg Commentary on the New Testament* (Minneapolis: Augsburg Publishing House, 1989), 221.

2. Cleon L. Rogers, Jr. and Cleon L. Rogers III, *The New Linguistic and Exegetical Key to the Greek New Testament* (Grand Rapids: Zondervan Publishing House, 1998), 633.

3. Bruce B. Barton et al., *Life Application Bible Commentary: Revelation* (Wheaton: Tyndale House Publishers, 2000), 116.

4. Steve Gregg, ed., *Revelation: Four Views, A Parallel Commentary* (Nashville: Thomas Nelson Publishers, 1997), 222.

5. Albert Barnes, *Revelation,* of *Barnes' Notes on the New Testament* (1884; reprint, Grand Rapids: Baker Books, 2001), 268.

6. Gregg, *Revelation: Four Views,* 220.

7. R. C. H. Lenski, *The Interpretation of St. John's Revelation,* of *Commentary on the New Testament* (Columbus: Wartburg Press, 1943), 328; M. Eugene Boring, *Revelation* (Louisville: John Knox Publishers, 1989), 143.

8. Joseph A. Seiss, *The Apocalypse – Exposition of the Book of Revelation* (Grand Rapids: Kregel Publications, 1987), 236.

9. Robert H. Mounce, *The Book of Revelation,* of *The New International Commentary on the New Testament,* 2nd ed. (Grand Rapids: Eerdmans Publishing Company, 1998), 213.

10. Martin Kiddle, *The Revelation of St. John*, of *The Moffatt New Testament Commentary* (London: Hodder and Stoughton, 1940), 189.
11. J.P.M. Sweet, *Revelation*, of *Westminster Pelican Commentaries* (Philadelphia: Westminster, 1979), 182.
12. Kenneth L. Barker and John R. Kohlenberger III, ed., *Zondervan NIV Bible Commentary*, vol. 2 (Grand Rapids: Zondervan Publishing House, 1994), 1176.
13. Alfred Marshall, *The Interlinear NKJ-NIV Parallel New Testament in Greek and English* (Grand Rapids: Zondervan Publishing House, 1975), 747.
14. Barnes, *Revelation*, 271–273.
15. Mounce, *The Book of Revelation*, 215.
16. Matthew Henry, *Matthew Henry's Commentary on the Whole Bible* (Peabody, Massachusetts: Hendrickson Publishers, 1991), 2476.
17. Mounce, *The Book of Revelation*, 217.
18. Lenski, *The Interpretation of St. John's Revelation*, 334–335.
19. Seiss, *The Apocalypse*, 242–243.
20. James M. Freeman, *The New Manners and Customs of the Bible*, ed. Harold J. Chadwick (North Brunswick, New Jersey: Bridge-Logos Publishers, 1998), 73.
21. Simon J. Kistemaker, *Revelation*, of *New Testament Commentary* (Grand Rapids: Baker Books, 2001), 330.
22. Barton et al., *Life Application Bible Commentary: Revelation*, 121; Mounce, *The Book of Revelation*, 216.
23. Seiss, *The Apocalypse*, 250.
24. Henry, *Commentary on the Whole Bible*, 2476.
25. Barton et al., *Life Application Bible Commentary: Revelation*, 125.
26. Seiss, *The Apocalypse*, 264.
27. George T. Montague, *The Apocalypse: Understanding the Book of Revelation & the End of the World* (Ann Arbor: Servant Publications, 1992), 138.
28. Sweet, *Revelation*, 187.
29. Mounce, *The Book of Revelation*, 226.
30. Barton et al., *Life Application Bible Commentary: Revelation*, 134.

CHAPTER TWELVE

1. Steve Gregg, ed., *Revelation: Four Views, A Parallel Commentary* (Nashville: Thomas Nelson Publishers, 1997), 252–257.
2. William MacDonald, *Believer's Bible Commentary,* ed. Art Farstad (Nashville: Thomas Nelson Publishers, 1995), 2369; Joseph A. Seiss, *The Apocalypse – Exposition of the Book of Revelation* (Grand Rapids: Kregel Publications, 1987), 279–280.
3. Gregg, *Revelation: Four Views,* 254.
4. Walter A. Elwell, ed., *Baker Commentary on the Bible* (Grand Rapids: Bakers Books, 1989), 1216.
5. Seiss, *The Apocalypse,* 289.
6. Bruce B. Barton et al., *Life Application Bible Commentary: Revelation* (Wheaton: Tyndale House Publishers, 2000), 139.
7. Robert H. Mounce, *The Book of Revelation,* of *The New International Commentary on the New Testament,* 2nd ed. (Grand Rapids: Eerdmans Publishing Company, 1998), 235–236.
8. R. C. H. Lenski, *The Interpretation of St. John's Revelation,* of *Commentary on the New Testament* (Columbus: Wartburg Press, 1943), 362–363; Albert Barnes, *Revelation,* of *Barnes' Notes on the New Testament* (1884; reprint, Grand Rapids: Baker Books, 2001), 301.
9. Charles F. Pfeiffer and Everett F. Harrison, *The Wycliffe Bible Commentary* (Chicago: Moody Press, 1962), 1511–1512.
10. Gerhard A. Krodel, *Revelation,* of *The Augsburg Commentary on the New Testament* (Minneapolis: Augsburg Publishing House, 1989), 242.
11. Mounce, *The Book of Revelation,* 235–236.
12. Seiss, *The Apocalypse,* 310.
13. Barnes, *Revelation,* 312; Kenneth L. Barker and John R. Kohlenberger III, ed., *Zondervan NIV Bible Commentary,* vol. 2 (Grand Rapids: Zondervan Publishing House, 1994), 1185; Lenski, *The Interpretation of St. John's Revelation,* 380.
14. Barton et al., *Life Application Bible Commentary: Revelation,* 143; Gregg, *Revelation: Four Views,* 269.
15. Mounce, *The Book of Revelation,* 239.
16. Merrill C. Tenney, *Interpreting Revelation: A Reasonable Guide to Understanding the Last Book in the Bible* (1957; reprint, Peabody, Massachusetts: Hendrickson Publishers, 2001), 77.

17. Warren W. Wiersbe, *Wiersbe's Expository Outlines on the New Testament* (Colorado Springs: Victor Books, 1992) 831.

18. Wayne Grudem, *Systematic Theology* (Grand Rapids: Zondervan Publishing House, 1994), 1104.

19. Barton et al., *Life Application Bible Commentary: Revelation,* 146.

20. Mounce, *The Book of Revelation,* 242; Tenney, *Interpreting Revelation,* 77.

CHAPTER THIRTEEN

1. *New American Standard Bible, New International Version, New Century Version,* and *New Living Translation* are among the major translations that render the subject standing on the seashore as the dragon rather than John.

2. R. C. H. Lenski, *The Interpretation of St. John's Revelation,* of *Commentary on the New Testament* (Columbus: Wartburg Press, 1943), 389–390; Steve Gregg, ed., *Revelation: Four Views, A Parallel Commentary* (Nashville: Thomas Nelson Publishers, 1997), 276.

3. Charles R. Erdman, *The Revelation of John* (Philadelphia: Westminster, 1936), 112.

4. Joseph A. Seiss, *The Apocalypse – Exposition of the Book of Revelation* (Grand Rapids: Kregel Publications, 1987), 323.

5. Robert H. Mounce, *The Book of Revelation,* of *The New International Commentary on the New Testament,* 2nd ed. (Grand Rapids: Eerdmans Publishing Company, 1998), 245.

6. Bruce B. Barton et al., *Life Application Bible Commentary: Revelation* (Wheaton: Tyndale House Publishers, 2000), 153.

7. W. E. Vine, *Vine's Expository Dictionary of Old and New Testament Words* (Nashville: Thomas Nelson Publishers, 1997), 1075, 229.

8. Mounce, *The Book of Revelation,* 245.

9. Merrill C. Tenney, *Interpreting Revelation: A Reasonable Guide to Understanding the Last Book in the Bible* (1957; reprint, Peabody, Massachusetts: Hendrickson Publishers, 2001), 77–78.

10. Simon J. Kistemaker, *Revelation,* of *New Testament Commentary* (Grand Rapids: Baker Books, 2001), 392.

11. Mounce, *The Book of Revelation,* 245.

CHAPTER FOURTEEN

1. Albert Barnes, *Revelation,* of *Barnes' Notes on the New Testament* (1884; reprint, Grand Rapids: Baker Books, 2001), 340–341.
2. Bruce B. Barton et al., *Life Application Bible Commentary: Revelation* (Wheaton: Tyndale House Publishers, 2000), 163–166.
3. Ronald F. Youngblood, gen. ed.; F.F. Bruce and R.K. Harrison, eds., *Nelson's New Illustrated Bible Dictionary* (Nashville: Thomas Nelson Publishers, 1997).
4. Kenneth L. Barker and John R. Kohlenberger III, ed., *Zondervan NIV Bible Commentary,* vol. 2 (Grand Rapids: Zondervan Publishing House, 1994), 1197; Merrill C. Tenney, *Interpreting Revelation: A Reasonable Guide to Understanding the Last Book in the Bible* (1957; reprint, Peabody, Massachusetts: Hendrickson Publishers, 2001), 78.
5. George Eldon Ladd, *A Commentary on the Revelation of John* (Grand Rapids: Eerdmans Publishing Company, 1972), 193.
6. R. C. H. Lenski, *The Interpretation of St. John's Revelation,* of *Commentary on the New Testament* (Columbus: Wartburg Press, 1943), 432.
7. Robert H. Mounce, *The Book of Revelation,* of *The New International Commentary on the New Testament,* 2nd ed. (Grand Rapids: Eerdmans Publishing Company, 1998), 274–275.
8. W. E. Vine, *Vine's Expository Dictionary of Old and New Testament Words* (Nashville: Thomas Nelson Publishers, 1997), 923.
9. Merrill C. Tenney, *Interpreting Revelation: A Reasonable Guide to Understanding the Last Book in the Bible* (1957; reprint, Peabody, Massachusetts: Hendrickson Publishers, 2001), 79; *New Geneva Study Bible,* ed. R.C. Sproul (Nashville: Thomas Nelson Publishers, 1995), 2024.
10. Gleason L. Archer, Jr., Paul D. Feinberg, Douglas J. Moo, Richard R. Reiter, *Three Views on the Rapture: Pre; Mid; or Post-Tribulation?* (Grand Rapids: Zondervan Publishing House, 1996), 200.
11. Walter A. Elwell, ed., *Baker Commentary on the Bible* (Grand Rapids: Bakers Books, 1989), 1219; Matthew Henry, *Matthew Henry's Commentary on the Whole Bible* (Peabody, Massachusetts: Hendrickson Publishers, 1991), 2479.
12. Youngblood, *Nelson's New Illustrated Bible Dictionary.*

CHAPTER FIFTEEN

1. W. E. Vine, *Vine's Expository Dictionary of Old and New Testament Words* (Nashville: Thomas Nelson Publishers, 1997), 503, 717.
2. Robert H. Mounce, *The Book of Revelation*, of *The New International Commentary on the New Testament*, 2nd ed. (Grand Rapids: Eerdmans Publishing Company, 1998), 285.
3. George Ricker Berry, Lexicon of *Greek to English Interlinear New Testament (KJV)* (Grand Rapids: World Publishing, 1981), 105.
4. Joseph A. Seiss, *The Apocalypse – Exposition of the Book of Revelation* (Grand Rapids: Kregel Publications, 1987), 370.

CHAPTER SIXTEEN

1. Robert H. Mounce, *The Book of Revelation*, of *The New International Commentary on the New Testament*, 2nd ed. (Grand Rapids: Eerdmans Publishing Company, 1998), 291–292.
2. George Ricker Berry, Lexicon of *Greek to English Interlinear New Testament (KJV)* (Grand Rapids: World Publishing, 1981), 653.
3. R. C. H. Lenski, *The Interpretation of St. John's Revelation*, of *Commentary on the New Testament* (Columbus: Wartburg Press, 1943), 469.
4. Gregory K. Beale, *The Book of Revelation: A Commentary on the Greek Text*, of *New International Greek Testament Commentary* (Grand Rapids: Eerdmans Publishing Company, 1998), 818.
5. Bruce B. Barton et al., *Life Application Bible Commentary: Revelation* (Wheaton: Tyndale House Publishers, 2000), 186.
6. Fanny Crosby, "Room for the Penintent," in *Welcome Tidings*, comp. Robert Lowry (New York: Biglow and Main, 1877).
7. Lenski, *The Interpretation of St. John's Revelation*, 473.
8. Simon J. Kistemaker, *Revelation*, of *New Testament Commentary* (Grand Rapids: Baker Books, 2001), 446; Mounce, *The Book of Revelation*, 296–297.
9. Walter A. Elwell, ed., *Baker Commentary on the Bible* (Grand Rapids: Bakers Books, 1989), 1221.
10. Kistemaker, *Revelation*, 446.
11. Mounce, *The Book of Revelation*, 299.
12. Excerpt from "While Men Grow Bold in Wicked Ways," words by Isaac Watts, in *The Psalms of David*, 1719. Public Domain.

13. J.B. Jackson, *A Dictionary of Scripture Proper Names* (Neptune, New Jersey: Loizeaux Brothers, 1909), 10.
14. Lenski, *The Interpretation of St. John's Revelation*, 481.
15. Robert L. Thomas, *Revelation 8–22: An Exegetical Commentary* (Chicago: Moody Press, 1995), 207.
16. Kistemaker, *Revelation*, 456.

CHAPTER SEVENTEEN

1. W. E. Vine, *Vine's Expository Dictionary of Old and New Testament Words* (Nashville: Thomas Nelson Publishers, 1997), 455.
2. Warren W. Wiersbe, *Wiersbe's Expository Outlines on the New Testament* (Colorado Springs: Victor Books, 1992) 845; Robert Jamieson, Andrew R. Fausset, and David Brown, *Jamieson, Fausset, and Brown's Commentary* (Grand Rapids: Zondervan Publishing House, 1961), 1540.
3. G. R. Beasley-Murray, *The Book of Revelation*, of *The New Century Bible Commentary* (Grand Rapids: Eerdmans Publishing Company, 1974), 248–249.
4. Robert H. Mounce, *The Book of Revelation*, of *The New International Commentary on the New Testament*, 2nd ed. (Grand Rapids: Eerdmans Publishing Company, 1998), 311; John F. Walvoord and Roy B. Zuck, *Bible Knowledge Commentary* (Colorado Springs: Chariot Victor Publishing, 1983), 970.
5. Vine, *Vine's Expository Dictionary of Old and New Testament Words*, 770.
6. R. C. H. Lenski, *The Interpretation of St. John's Revelation*, of *Commentary on the New Testament* (Columbus: Wartburg Press, 1943), 496.
7. Walvoord and Zuck, *Bible Knowledge Commentary*, 972.
8. J.D. Douglas, ed., *New Bible Dictionary*, 2nd ed. (Wheaton, IL: Tyndale House Publishers, 1962), 113.
9. John Gill, *Exposition of the Old and New Testaments*, vol. 9 (1810; reprint, Paris, Arkansas: The Baptist Standard Bearer, 1989), 820–822.
10. Walter A. Elwell, ed., *Baker Commentary on the Bible* (Grand Rapids: Bakers Books, 1989), 1222–1223; Mounce, *The Book of Revelation*, 306–321;

11. George Eldon Ladd, *A Commentary on the Revelation of John* (Grand Rapids: Eerdmans Publishing Company, 1972), 220–234; Bruce B. Barton et al., *Life Application Bible Commentary: Revelation* (Wheaton: Tyndale House Publishers, 2000), 199–208.
12. Merrill C. Tenney, *Interpreting Revelation: A Reasonable Guide to Understanding the Last Book in the Bible* (1957; reprint, Peabody, Massachusetts: Hendrickson Publishers, 2001), 83.
13. John Knox, *The Second Volume of the Ecclesiastical History: containing the Acts and Monuments of History* (reprint, Columbus, Ohio: Lazarus Ministry Press, 2000), 257–259.
14. Simon J. Kistemaker, *Revelation,* of *New Testament Commentary* (Grand Rapids: Baker Books, 2001), 469–470; Barton et al., *Life Application Bible Commentary: Revelation,* 201; Mounce, *The Book of Revelation,* 314.
15. Tenney, *Interpreting Revelation,* 84; Kistemaker, *Revelation,* 469.
16. Beasley-Murray, *The Book of Revelation,* 256; J.D. Douglas, ed., *New Bible Dictionary,* 1038–1039.
17. John MacArthur, *MacArthur Study Bible* (Nashville: Thomas Nelson Bibles, 1997), 2016; Barton et al., *Life Application Bible Commentary: Revelation,* 202–203; Kistemaker, *Revelation,* 470–471; Walvoord and Zuck, *Bible Knowledge Commentary,* 971.
18. Joseph A. Seiss, *The Apocalypse – Exposition of the Book of Revelation* (Grand Rapids: Kregel Publications, 1987), 391–392; Ladd, *A Commentary on the Revelation of John,* 227; Lenski, *The Interpretation of St. John's Revelation,* 504.
19. Kistemaker, *Revelation,* 471.
20. Charles C. Torrey, *The Apocalypse of John* (New Haven: Yale University Press, 1958), 61; R.C. Sproul, *The Last Days According to Jesus* (Grand Rapids: Baker Books, 1998), 146–147.
21. Mounce, *The Book of Revelation,* 316–317; Kistemaker, *Revelation,* 472.
22. Seiss, *The Apocalypse,* 393–394; Ladd, *A Commentary on the Revelation of John,* 229.
23. Barton et al., *Life Application Bible Commentary: Revelation,* 203.
24. Vern S. Poythress, *The Returning King: A Guide to the Book of Revelation* (Phillipsburg, New Jersey: P & R Publishing, 2000), 166.

25. Walvoord and Zuck, *Bible Knowledge Commentary,* 971–972.
26. Isbon T. Beckwith, *The Apocalypse of John* (New York: Macmillan Publishers, 1942), 700; Mounce, *The Book of Revelation,* 319.
27. Kistemaker, *Revelation,* 477; Mounce, *The Book of Revelation,* 320.

CHAPTER EIGHTEEN
1. G. R. Beasley-Murray, *The Book of Revelation,* of *The New Century Bible Commentary* (Grand Rapids: Eerdmans Publishing Company, 1974), 262.
2. John F. Walvoord and Roy B. Zuck, *Bible Knowledge Commentary* (Colorado Springs: Chariot Victor Publishing, 1983), 972.
3. Robert H. Mounce, *The Book of Revelation,* of *The New International Commentary on the New Testament,* 2nd ed. (Grand Rapids: Eerdmans Publishing Company, 1998), 328.
4. Isbon T. Beckwith, *The Apocalypse of John* (New York: Macmillan Publishers, 1942), 715; R. C. H. Lenski, *The Interpretation of St. John's Revelation,* of *Commentary on the New Testament* (Columbus: Wartburg Press, 1943), 518–519.
5. Vern S. Poythress, *The Returning King: A Guide to the Book of Revelation* (Phillipsburg, New Jersey: P & R Publishing, 2000), 159–160.
6. Poythress, *The Returning King,* 171.
7. Steve Gregg, ed., *Revelation: Four Views, A Parallel Commentary* (Nashville: Thomas Nelson Publishers, 1997), 433.
8. Simon J. Kistemaker, *Revelation,* of *New Testament Commentary* (Grand Rapids: Baker Books, 2001), 496.
9. W. E. Vine, *Vine's Expository Dictionary of Old and New Testament Words* (Nashville: Thomas Nelson Publishers, 1997), 1067.
10. George Eldon Ladd, *A Commentary on the Revelation of John* (Grand Rapids: Eerdmans Publishing Company, 1972), 243.

CHAPTER NINETEEN
1. G. R. Beasley-Murray, *The Book of Revelation,* of *The New Century Bible Commentary* (Grand Rapids: Eerdmans Publishing Company, 1974), 272.

2. Ronald F. Youngblood, gen. ed.; F.F. Bruce and R.K. Harrison, eds., *Nelson's New Illustrated Bible Dictionary* (Nashville: Thomas Nelson Publishers, 1997).
3. Youngblood, *Nelson's New Illustrated Bible Dictionary.*
4. Paraphrased from "Jesus, Thou All Redeeming Lord" by Charles Wesley, *Hymns and Sacred Poems,* 1749.
5. Simon J. Kistemaker, *Revelation,* of *New Testament Commentary* (Grand Rapids: Baker Books, 2001), 517–518.
6. Joseph A. Seiss, *The Apocalypse – Exposition of the Book of Revelation* (Grand Rapids: Kregel Publications, 1987), 436.
7. Robert H. Mounce, *The Book of Revelation,* of *The New International Commentary on the New Testament,* 2nd ed. (Grand Rapids: Eerdmans Publishing Company, 1998), 353.
8. Vern S. Poythress, *The Returning King: A Guide to the Book of Revelation* (Phillipsburg, New Jersey: P & R Publishing, 2000), 174.
9. "Bride of the Lamb, Awake, Awake," words by Edward Denny, in *Hymns for the Poor of the Flock,* 1837. Public Domain.
10. Matthew Henry, *Matthew Henry's Commentary on the Whole Bible* (Peabody, Massachusetts: Hendrickson Publishers, 1991), 1915.
11. Mounce, *The Book of Revelation,* 355.

CHAPTER TWENTY
1. Steve Gregg, ed., *Revelation: Four Views, A Parallel Commentary* (Nashville: Thomas Nelson Publishers, 1997), 458–459.
2. Robert H. Mounce, *The Book of Revelation,* of *The New International Commentary on the New Testament,* 2nd ed. (Grand Rapids: Eerdmans Publishing Company, 1998), 360.
3. Gregg, *Revelation: Four Views,* 460–464.
4. Wayne Grudem, *Systematic Theology* (Grand Rapids: Zondervan Publishing House, 1994), 1127–1129.
5. Kenneth L. Barker and John R. Kohlenberger III, ed., *Zondervan NIV Bible Commentary,* vol. 2 (Grand Rapids: Zondervan Publishing House, 1994), 1220–1221; William MacDonald, *Believer's Bible Commentary,* ed. Art Farstad (Nashville: Thomas Nelson Publishers, 1995), 2377.
6. Warren W. Wiersbe, *Wiersbe's Expository Outlines on the New Testament* (Colorado Springs: Victor Books, 1992) 852–853; John

MacArthur, *MacArthur Study Bible* (Nashville: Thomas Nelson Bibles, 1997), 2021.

7. Mounce, *The Book of Revelation*, 364–366.

8. R. C. H. Lenski, *The Interpretation of St. John's Revelation,* of *Commentary on the New Testament* (Columbus: Wartburg Press, 1943), 584.

9. Bruce B. Barton et al., *Life Application Bible Commentary: Revelation* (Wheaton: Tyndale House Publishers, 2000), 238–239.

10. "Thy Kingdom Come, O God," words by Lewis Hensley, in *Hymns for the Minor Sundays from Advent to Whitsuntide* (London: Bell and Daldy, 1867). Public Domain.

11. John F. Walvoord and Roy B. Zuck, *Bible Knowledge Commentary* (Colorado Springs: Chariot Victor Publishing, 1983), 981; Barton et al., *Life Application Bible Commentary: Revelation,* 244; MacArthur, *MacArthur Study Bible,* 2021.

12. F. F. Bruce, *The Revelation to John,* of *A New Testament Commentary* (London: Pickering & Inglis, 1969), 662; Simon J. Kistemaker, *Revelation,* of *New Testament Commentary* (Grand Rapids: Baker Books, 2001), 543.

13. David L. Edwards and John R. W. Stott, *Essentials: A Liberal-Evangelical Dialogue* (London: Hodder and Stoughton, 1988), 275–276; Philip E. Hughes, *The True Image: The Origin and Destiny of Man in Christ* (Grand Rapids: Eerdmans Publishing, 1989), 405–407.

14. Robert A. Peterson, *Hell on Trial: The Case for Eternal Punishment* (Phillipsburg, New Jersey: P & R Publishing, 1995), 89–90.

15. Ladd, *A Commentary on the Revelation of John,* 271.

16. G. R. Beasley-Murray, *The Book of Revelation,* of *The New Century Bible Commentary* (Grand Rapids: Eerdmans Publishing Company, 1974), 301; Barton et al., *Life Application Bible Commentary: Revelation,* 248–249; Lenski, *The Interpretation of St. John's Revelation,* 604–605.

17. MacArthur, *MacArthur Study Bible,* 2022; MacDonald, *Believer's Bible Commentary,* 2378.

18. Mounce, *The Book of Revelation,* 377; Ladd, *A Commentary on the Revelation of John,* 273.

19. Lenski, *The Interpretation of St. John's Revelation,* 608.

20. Kistemaker, *Revelation*, 548
21. Excerpt from "I Dreamed That the Great Judgment Morning," words by Bert Shadduck, 1894. Public Domain.

CHAPTER TWENTY-ONE
1. Simon J. Kistemaker, *Revelation,* of *New Testament Commentary* (Grand Rapids: Baker Books, 2001), 565.
2. Hanns Lilje, *The Last Book of the Bible,* trans. Olive Wyon (Philadelphia: Muhlenberg Press, 1957), 259; Robert H. Mounce, *The Book of Revelation,* of *The New International Commentary on the New Testament*, 2nd ed. (Grand Rapids: Eerdmans Publishing Company, 1998), 382.
3. John F. Walvoord, *The Revelation of Jesus Christ* (Chicago: Moody Press, 1966), 313; R. C. H. Lenski, *The Interpretation of St. John's Revelation,* of *Commentary on the New Testament* (Columbus: Wartburg Press, 1943), 616–618.
4. Frank S. Mead, ed., *12,000 Religious Quotations* (1965; reprint, Grand Rapids: Baker Book House, 1989), 219.
5. Mead, *12,000 Religious Quotations,* 217.
6. Mead, *12,000 Religious Quotations,* 406.
7. John H. Gerstner, *The Rational Biblical Theology of Jonathan Edwards* (Powhatan, Virginia: Berea Publications, 1992), 343.
8. *New American Standard Bible* and *New Century Version* are among the major translations that render the description in verse fourteen as foundation stones.
9. William Hoste, *The Visions of John the Divine* (Kilmarnock, Scotland: John Ritchie Press, 1932), 178; John F. Walvoord and Roy B. Zuck, *Bible Knowledge Commentary* (Colorado Springs: Chariot Victor Publishing, 1983), 986; Hanns Lilje, *The Last Book of the Bible,* 267.
10. George Eldon Ladd, *A Commentary on the Revelation of John* (Grand Rapids: Eerdmans Publishing Company, 1972), 282; G. R. Beasley-Murray, *The Book of Revelation,* of *The New Century Bible Commentary* (Grand Rapids: Eerdmans Publishing Company, 1974), 322; John MacArthur, *MacArthur Study Bible* (Nashville: Thomas Nelson Bibles, 1997), 2023.

11. Albert Barnes, *Revelation,* of *Barnes' Notes on the New Testament* (1884; reprint, Grand Rapids: Baker Books, 2001), 448; Henry B. Swete, *The Apocalypse of St. John* (New York: Macmillan Publishers, 1906) and Moses Stuart, *A Commentary on the Apocalypse* (Andover, Massachusetts: Allen, 1845) in Steve Gregg, ed., *Revelation: Four Views, A Parallel Commentary* (Nashville: Thomas Nelson Publishers, 1997), 495.
12. *Nelson's Three-in-One Bible Reference Companion* (Nashville: Thomas Nelson, 1982), 161.
13. Bruce B. Barton et al., *Life Application Bible Commentary: Revelation* (Wheaton: Tyndale House Publishers, 2000), 261.
14. Mead, *12,000 Religious Quotations,* 217.
15. W. E. Vine, *Vine's Expository Dictionary of Old and New Testament Words* (Nashville: Thomas Nelson Publishers, 1997), 774.
16. Barton et al., *Life Application Bible Commentary: Revelation,* 264.
17. Henry, *Matthew Henry's Commentary on the Whole Bible,* 2484.
18. Ladd, *A Commentary on the Revelation of John,* 285.
19. Matthew Henry, *Matthew Henry's Commentary on the Whole Bible* (Peabody, Massachusetts: Hendrickson Publishers, 1991), 2484.

CHAPTER TWENTY-TWO

1. Merrill C. Tenney, *Interpreting Revelation: A Reasonable Guide to Understanding the Last Book in the Bible* (1957; reprint, Peabody, Massachusetts: Hendrickson Publishers, 2001), 94.
2. George Eldon Ladd, *A Commentary on the Revelation of John* (Grand Rapids: Eerdmans Publishing Company, 1972), 286.
3. Robert Jamieson, Andrew R. Fausset, and David Brown, *Jamieson, Fausset, and Brown's Commentary* (Grand Rapids: Zondervan Publishing House, 1961), 1589.
4. Isbon T. Beckwith, *The Apocalypse of John* (New York: Macmillan Publishers, 1942), 765; Albert Barnes, *Revelation,* of *Barnes' Notes on the New Testament* (1884; reprint, Grand Rapids: Baker Books, 2001), 453.
5. Robert H. Mounce, *The Book of Revelation,* of *The New International Commentary on the New Testament,* 2nd ed. (Grand Rapids: Eerdmans Publishing Company, 1998), 399.

6. Mounce, *The Book of Revelation*, 399–400.
7. Cleon L. Rogers, Jr. and Cleon L. Rogers III, *The New Linguistic and Exegetical Key to the Greek New Testament* (Grand Rapids: Zondervan Publishing House, 1998), 651.
8. Joseph A. Seiss, *The Apocalypse – Exposition of the Book of Revelation* (Grand Rapids: Kregel Publications, 1987), 512.
9. Mounce, *The Book of Revelation*, 408.
10. G. R. Beasley-Murray, *The Book of Revelation*, of *The New Century Bible Commentary* (Grand Rapids: Eerdmans Publishing Company, 1974), 343–344.
11. Bruce B. Barton et al., *Life Application Bible Commentary: Revelation* (Wheaton: Tyndale House Publishers, 2000), 275–276; Tenney, *Interpreting Revelation*, 97.
12. Excerpt from "Whate'er My God Ordains is Right," words by Samuel Rodigast, 1676, trans. Catherine Winkworth, 1863. Public Domain.

Bibliography

Archer, Gleason L. *Encyclopedia of Bible Difficulties.* Grand Rapids: Zondervan Publishing House, 1982.

Archer, Gleason L., Paul D. Feinberg, Douglas J. Moo, and Richard R. Reiter. *Three Views on the Rapture: Pre; Mid; or Post-Tribulation?* Grand Rapids: Zondervan Publishing House, 1996.

Barker, Kenneth L., and John R. Kohlenberger III, ed. *Zondervan NIV Bible Commentary.* Vol. 2. Grand Rapids: Zondervan Publishing House, 1994.

Barnes, Albert. *Revelation,* of *Barnes' Notes on the New Testament.* 1884. Reprint, Grand Rapids: Baker Books, 2001.

Barton, Bruce B., Linda Taylor, Neil Wilson, and Dave Veerman. *Life Application Bible Commentary: Revelation.* Wheaton: Tyndale House Publishers, 2000.

Beale, Gregory K. *The Book of Revelation: A Commentary on the Greek Text,* of *New International Greek Testament Commentary.* Grand Rapids: Eerdmans Publishing Company, 1998.

Beasley-Murray, G. R. *The Book of Revelation,* of *The New Century Bible Commentary.* Grand Rapids: Eerdmans Publishing Company, 1974.

Beckwith, Isbon T. *The Apocalypse of John*. New York: Macmillan Publishers, 1942.

Berry, George Ricker. *Greek to English Interlinear New Testament (KJV)*. Grand Rapids: World Publishing, 1981.

Boring, M. Eugene. *Revelation*. Louisville: John Knox Publishers, 1989.

Bruce, F. F. *The Revelation to John*, of *A New Testament Commentary*. London: Pickering & Inglis, 1969.

Calvin, John. *Commentaries on the Book of the Prophet Daniel*. Vol. 1 of vol. 12 of *Calvin's Commentaries*. Trans. Thomas Myers. 1843. Reprint, Grand Rapids: Baker Books, 1999.

Charles, R. H. *The Revelation of St. John*. Vol. 1 of *The International Critical Commentary*. Edinburgh: T & T Clark, 1920.

Criswell, W. A. *Expository Sermons on Revelation*. Grand Rapids: Zondervan Publishing House, 1962.

Douglas, J.D., ed. *New Bible Dictionary*. 2nd ed. Wheaton, IL: Tyndale House Publishers, 1962.

Edwards, David L., and John R. W. Stott. *Essentials: A Liberal-Evangelical Dialogue*. London: Hodder and Stoughton, 1988.

Elwell, Walter A., ed. *Baker Commentary on the Bible*. Grand Rapids: Bakers Books, 1989.

Erdman, Charles R. *The Revelation of John*. Philadelphia: Westminster, 1936.

Freeman, James M. *The New Manners and Customs of the Bible*, ed. Harold J. Chadwick. North Brunswick, New Jersey: Bridge-Logos Publishers, 1998.

Gerstner, John H. *The Rational Biblical Theology of Jonathan Edwards*. Powhatan, Virginia: Berea Publications, 1992.

Gill, John. *Exposition of the Old and New Testaments*. Vol. 9. 1810. Reprint, Paris, Arkansas: The Baptist Standard Bearer, 1989.

Gregg, Steve, ed. *Revelation: Four Views, A Parallel Commentary*. Nashville: Thomas Nelson Publishers, 1997.

Grudem, Wayne. *Systematic Theology.* Grand Rapids: Zondervan Publishing House, 1994.

Hendrickson, William. *More Than Conquerors.* Grand Rapids: Baker Books, 1944.

Henry, Matthew. *Matthew Henry's Commentary on the Whole Bible.* Peabody, Massachusetts: Hendrickson Publishers, 1991.

Hoste, William. *The Visions of John the Divine.* Kilmarnock, Scotland: John Ritchie Press, 1932.

Jackson, J.B. *A Dictionary of Scripture Proper Names.* Neptune, New Jersey: Loizeaux Brothers, 1909.

Jamieson, Robert, Andrew R. Fausset, and David Brown. *Jamieson, Fausset, and Brown's Commentary.* Grand Rapids: Zondervan Publishing House, 1961.

Josephus, Flavius. *Antiquities of the Jews,* in *The Complete Works of Flavius Josephus.* Trans. William Whiston. Grand Rapids: Kregel Publications, 1960.

Kempis, Thomas A. *The Imitation of Christ.* Milwaukee, Wisconsin: Bruce Publishing Company, 1940.

Kennedy, D. James. *An Historical Perspective on the End Times.* Ft. Lauderdale, Florida: Coral Ridge Ministries, 1999.

Kiddle, Martin. *The Revelation of St. John,* of *The Moffatt New Testament Commentary.* London: Hodder and Stoughton, 1940.

Kistemaker, Simon J. *Revelation,* of *New Testament Commentary.* Grand Rapids: Baker Books, 2001.

Krodel, Gerhard A. *Revelation,* of *The Augsburg Commentary on the New Testament.* Minneapolis: Augsburg Publishing House, 1989.

Ladd, George Eldon. *A Commentary on the Revelation of John.* Grand Rapids: Eerdmans Publishing Company, 1972.

Lenski, R. C. H. *The Interpretation of St. John's Revelation,* of *Commentary on the New Testament.* Columbus: Wartburg Press, 1943.

Lilje, Hanns. *The Last Book of the Bible.* Trans. Olive Wyon. Philadelphia: Muhlenberg Press, 1957.

MacArthur, John. *MacArthur Study Bible.* Nashville: Thomas Nelson Bibles, 1997.

MacDonald, William. *Believer's Bible Commentary.* Art Farstad, ed. Nashville: Thomas Nelson Publishers, 1995.

Marshall, Alfred. *The Interlinear NKJ-NIV Parallel New Testament in Greek and English.* Grand Rapids: Zondervan Publishing House, 1975.

McGee, J. Vernon. *Thru the Bible.* Vol. 5. Nashville: Thomas Nelson Publishers, 1982.

Miller, Stephen R. *The New American Commentary.* E. Ray Clendenen, ed. Nashville: Broadman and Holman Publishers, 1994.

Moffatt, James. *The Revelation of St. John the Divine.* Vol. 5 of *The Expositor's Greek Testament.* Grand Rapids: Eerdmans Publishing Company, 1951.

Montague, George T. *The Apocalypse: Understanding the Book of Revelation & the End of the World.* Ann Arbor: Servant Publications, 1992.

Mounce, Robert H. *The Book of Revelation,* of *The New International Commentary on the New Testament.* Grand Rapids: Eerdmans Publishing Company, 1977.

Nelson's Three-in-One Bible Reference Companion. Nashville: Thomas Nelson, 1982.

New Geneva Study Bible, R.C. Sproul, ed. Nashville: Thomas Nelson Publishers, 1995.

Peterson, Robert A. *Hell on Trial: The Case for Eternal Punishment.* Phillipsburg, New Jersey: P & R Publishing, 1995.

Pfeiffer, Charles F., and Everett F. Harrison. *The Wycliffe Bible Commentary.* Chicago: Moody Press, 1962.

Poythress, Vern S. *The Returning King: A Guide to the Book of Revelation.* Phillipsburg, New Jersey: P & R Publishing, 2000.

Practical Christianity Foundation. *Daniel: In God I Trust.* Holiday, Florida: Green Key Books, 2001.

Richardson, Donald W. *The Revelation of Jesus Christ.* Louisville: John Knox Publishers, 1964.

Rogers, Cleon L. Jr., and Cleon L. Rogers III. *The New Linguistic and Exegetical Key to the Greek New Testament.* Grand Rapids: Zondervan Publishing House, 1998.

Rosenthal, Marvin. *The Pre-Wrath Rapture of the Church.* Nashville: Thomas Nelson Publishers, 1990.

Seiss, Joseph A. *The Apocalypse – Exposition of the Book of Revelation.* Grand Rapids: Kregel Publications, 1987.

Sproul, R.C. *The Last Days According to Jesus.* Grand Rapids: Baker Books, 1998.

Stott, John R. W. *What Christ Thinks of the Church, Expository Addresses on the First Three Chapters of the Book of Revelation.* Grand Rapids: Eerdmans Publishing Company, 1958.

Strong, James. *Strong's Exhaustive Concordance of the Bible.* Iowa Falls: World Bible Publishers, 1986.

Stuart, Moses. *A Commentary on the Apocalypse.* Andover, Massachusetts: Allen, 1845.

Sweet, J.P.M. *Revelation,* of *Westminster Pelican Commentaries.* Philadelphia: Westminster, 1979.

Swete, Henry B. *The Apocalypse of St. John.* New York: Macmillan Publishers, 1906.

Tenney, Merrill C. *Interpreting Revelation: A Reasonable Guide to Understanding the Last Book in the Bible.* 1957. Reprint, Peabody, Massachusetts: Hendrickson Publishers, 2001.

Torrey, Charles C. *The Apocalypse of John.* New Haven: Yale University Press, 1958.

Vine, W. E. *Vine's Expository Dictionary of Old and Testament Words.* Nashville: Thomas Nelson Publishers, 1997.

Wall, Robert W. *Revelation,* of *New International Biblical Commentary.* Peabody, Massachusetts: Hendrickson Publishers, 1991.

Walvoord, John F., and Roy B. Zuck. *Bible Knowledge Commentary.* Colorado Springs: Chariot Victor Publishing, 1983.

Walvoord, John F. *The Revelation of Jesus Christ.* Chicago: Moody Press, 1966.

Wiersbe, Warren W. *Wiersbe's Expository Outlines on the New Testament.* Colorado Springs: Victor Books, 1992.

Wilcock, Michael. *The Message of Revelation.* Downers Grove: Inter-Varsity Press, 1975.

Youngblood, Ronald F., gen. ed.; F.F. Bruce and R.K. Harrison, eds. *Nelson's New Illustrated Bible Dictionary.* Nashville: Thomas Nelson Publishers, 1997.

Also available from the

PRACTICAL CHRISTIANITY FOUNDATION
Devotional Commentary Series

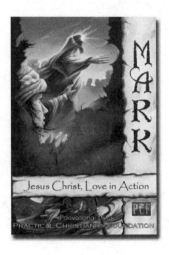 

Mark: Jesus Christ, Love in Action
450 pages, ISBN No. 0970599641, $12.97

Daniel: In God I Trust
258 pages, ISBN No. 0970599609, $12.97

Available at your local Christian bookstore

Coming Winter 2003–2004
The General Epistles